PROSE CURRENT

PROSE
CURRENT

Edited by

EDGAR WHAN
Ohio University

D. C. Heath and Company
Boston

COVER PHOTOGRAPH:

"WATER PLANT" — KINETIC SCULPTURE BY GEORGE RICKEY.

(COLLECTION ADDISON GALLERY OF AMERICAN ART;

GIVEN BY AN ANONYMOUS DONOR THROUGH

THE AMERICAN FEDERATION OF ARTS.)

A FOREWORD
TO THE TEACHER

Prose Current is an anthology of contemporary prose readings designed for use in composition courses. Selected from recent issues of American and British periodicals, this collection provides examples of contemporary rhetorical patterns and illustrates currently accepted levels of style and usage.

In subject matter these essays approximate as nearly as possible the range of the student's interests and experience; in style and organization they represent levels of accomplishment which he can comprehend and imitate. To encourage the student to read each selection as he would read a magazine article, rhetorical and thematic labels have been omitted. The arrangement of the essays is based on recurring degrees of thematic and rhetorical complexity rather than on a strict progression of difficulty.

The extent to which the textbook editor should participate with teacher and student in the classroom is always difficult to determine. Here the intention has been to minimize the editor's role. A short, general comment on organization and style follows each essay; specific questions are left to the instructor. The "Suggestions for Writing," on the other hand, have been made as specific as possible.

Miss Nancy Stevenson and Miss Patricia Grlicky have helped in the preparation of the manuscript. I am indebted here as elsewhere to the Greans, Goedickes, Goldbergs, Summerses, Roes, and Purdums.

E. W.

Athens, Ohio

CONTENTS

PROSE CURRENT

THE TOWN DUMP

WALLACE STEGNER

THE TOWN DUMP of Whitemud, Saskatchewan, could only have been a few years old when I knew it, for the village was born in 1913 and I left there in 1919. But I remember the dump better than I remember most things in that town, better than I remember most of the people. I spent more time with it, for one thing; it had more poetry and excitement in it than people did.

It lay in the southeast corner of town, in a section that was always full of adventure for me. Just there the Whitemud River left the hills, bent a little south, and started its long traverse across the prairie and international boundary to join the Milk. For all I knew, it might have been on its way to join the Alph: simply, before my eyes, it disappeared into strangeness and wonder.

Also, where it passed below the dumpground, it ran through willowed bottoms that were a favorite campsite for passing teamsters, gypsies, sometimes Indians. The very straw scattered around those camps, the ashes of those strangers' campfires, the manure of their teams and saddle horses, were hot with adventurous possibilities.

It was as an extension, a living suburb, as it were, of the dumpground that we most valued those camps. We scoured them for artifacts of their migrant tenants as if they had been archaeological sites full of the secrets of ancient civilizations. I remember toting around for weeks the broken cheek strap of a bridle. Somehow or other its buckle looked as if it had been fashioned in a far place, a place where they were accustomed to flatten the tongues of buckles for reasons that could only be exciting, and where they made a habit of plating the metal with some valuable alloy, probably silver. In places where the silver was worn away the buckle underneath shone dull yellow: probably gold.

It seemed that excitement liked that end of town better than our end. Once old Mrs. Gustafson, deeply religious and a little raddled in the head, went over there with a buckboard full of trash, and as she was driving home along the river she looked and saw a spent catfish, washed in from Cypress Lake or some other part of the watershed, floating on the yellow water. He was two feet long, his whiskers hung down, his fins and tail were limp. He was a kind of fish that no one had seen in the Whitemud in the three or four years of the town's life, and a kind that none of us children had ever seen anywhere. Mrs. Gustafson had never seen one like him either; she perceived at once that he was the devil, and she whipped up the team and reported him at Hoffman's elevator.

We could hear her screeching as we legged it for the river to see for ourselves. Sure enough, there he was. He looked very tired, and he made no great effort to get away as we pushed out a half-sunken rowboat from below the flume, submerged it under him, and brought him ashore. When he died three days later we experimentally fed him to two half-wild cats, but they seemed to suffer no ill effects.

At that same end of town the irrigation flume crossed the river. It always seemed to me giddily high when I hung my chin over its plank edge and looked down, but it probably walked no more than twenty feet above the water on its spidery legs. Ordinarily in summer it carried about six or eight inches of smooth water, and under the glassy hurrying of the little boxed stream the planks were coated with deep sun-warmed moss as slick as frogs' eggs. A boy could sit in the flume with the water walling up against his back, and grab a cross brace above him, and pull, shooting himself sledlike ahead until he could reach the next brace for another pull and another slide, and so on across the river in four scoots.

After ten minutes in the flume he would come out wearing a dozen or more limber black leeches, and could sit in the green shade where darning needles flashed blue, and dragonflies hummed and darted and stopped, and skaters dimpled slack and eddy with their delicate transitory footprints, and there stretch the leeches out one by one while their sucking ends clung and clung, until at last, stretched far out, they let go with a tiny wet *puk* and snapped together like rubber bands. The smell of the river and the flume and the clay cutbanks and the bars of that part of the river was the smell of wolf willow.

But nothing in that end of town was as good as the dumpground that scattered along a little runoff coulee dipping down toward the river from the south bench. Through a historical process that went back, probably, to the roots of community sanitation and distaste for eyesores, but that in law dated from the Unincorporated Towns Ordinance of the territorial government, passed in 1888, the dump was one of the very first community enterprises, almost our town's first institution.

More than that, it contained relics of every individual who had ever lived there, and of every phase of the town's history.

The bedsprings on which the town's first child was begotten might be there; the skeleton of a boy's pet colt; two or three volumes of Shakespeare bought in haste and error from a peddler, later loaned in carelessness, soaked with water and chemicals in a house fire, and finally thrown out to flap their stained eloquence in the prairie wind.

Broken dishes, rusty tinware, spoons that had been used to mix paint; once a box of percussion caps, sign and symbol of the carelessness that most of those people felt about all matters of personal or public safety. We put them on the railroad tracks and were anonymously denounced in the *Enterprise*. There were also old iron, old brass, for which we hunted assiduously, by night conning junkmen's catalogues and the pages of the *Enterprise* to find how much wartime value there might be in the geared insides of clocks or in a pound of tea lead carefully wrapped in a ball whose weight astonished and delighted us. Sometimes the unimaginable outside world reached in and laid a finger on us. I recall that, aged no more than seven, I wrote a St. Louis junk house asking if they preferred their tea lead and tinfoil wrapped in balls, or whether they would rather have it pressed flat in sheets, and I got back a typewritten letter in a window envelope instructing me that they would be happy to have it in any way that was convenient for me. They added that they valued my business and were mine very truly. Dazed, I carried that windowed grandeur around in my pocket until I wore it out, and for months I saved the letter as a souvenir of the wondering time when something strange and distinguished had singled me out.

We hunted old bottles in the dump, bottles caked with dirt and filth, half buried, full of cobwebs, and we washed them out at the horse trough by the elevator, putting in a handful of shot along with the water to knock the dirt loose; and when we had shaken them until our arms were tired, we hauled them off in somebody's coaster wagon and turned them in at Bill Anderson's pool hall, where the smell of lemon pop was so sweet on the dark pool-hall air that I am sometimes awakened by it in the night, even yet.

Smashed wheels of wagons and buggies, tangles of rusty barbed wire, the collapsed perambulator that the French wife of one of the town's doctors had once pushed proudly up the planked sidewalks and along the ditchbank paths. A welter of foul-smelling feathers and coyote-scattered carrion which was all that remained of somebody's dream of a chicken ranch. The chickens had all got some mysterious pip at the same time, and died as one, and the dream lay out there with the rest of the town's history to rustle to the empty sky on the border of the hills.

There was melted glass in curious forms, and the half-melted office safe left from the burning of Bill Day's Hotel. On very lucky days we might find a piece of the lead casing that had enclosed the wires of the town's first telephone system. The casing was just the right size for rings, and so soft that it could be whittled with a jackknife. It was a material that might have made artists of us. If we had been Indians of fifty years before, that bright soft metal would have enlisted our maximum patience and craft and come out as ring and metal and amulet inscribed with the symbols of our observed world. Perhaps there were too many ready-made alternatives in the local drug, hardware, and general stores; perhaps our feeble artistic response was a measure of the insufficiency of the challenge we felt. In any case I do not remember that we did any more with the metal than to shape it into crude seal rings with our initials or pierced hearts carved in them; and these, though they served a purpose in juvenile courtship, stopped something short of art.

The dump held very little wood, for in that country anything burnable got burned. But it had plenty of old iron, furniture, papers, mattresses that were the delight of field mice, and jugs and demijohns that were sometimes their bane, for they crawled into the necks and drowned in the rain water or redeye that was inside.

If the history of our town was not exactly written, it was at least hinted, in the dump. I think I had a pretty sound notion even at eight or nine of how significant was that first institution of our forming Canadian civilization. For rummaging through its foul purlieus I had several times been surprised and shocked to find relics of my own life tossed out there to rot or blow away.

The volumes of Shakespeare belonged to a set that my father had bought before I was born. It had been carried through successive moves from town to town in the Dakotas, and from Dakota to Seattle, and from Seattle to Bellingham, and Bellingham to Redmond, and from Redmond back to Iowa, and from there to Saskatchewan. Then, stained in a stranger's house fire, these volumes had suffered from a house-cleaning impulse and been thrown away for me to stumble upon in the dump. One of the Cratchet girls had borrowed them, a hatchet-faced, thin, eager, transplanted Cockney girl with a frenzy, almost a hysteria, for reading. And yet somehow, through her hands, they found the dump, to become a symbol of how much was lost, how much thrown aside, how much carelessly or of necessity given up, in the making of a new country. We had so few books that I was familiar with them all, had handled them, looked at their pictures, perhaps even read them. They were the lares and penates, part of the skimpy impedimenta of household gods we had brought with us into Latium. Finding those three thrown away was a little like finding my own name on a gravestone.

And yet not the blow that something else was, something that impressed me even more with the dump's close reflection of the town's intimate life. The colt whose picked skeleton lay out there was mine. He had been incurably crippled when dogs chased our mare, Daisy, the morning after she foaled. I had labored for months to make him well; had fed him by hand, curried him, exercised him, adjusted the iron braces that I had talked my father into having made. And I had not known that he would have to be destroyed. One weekend I turned him over to the foreman of one of the ranches, presumably so that he could be cared for. A few days later I found his skinned body, with the braces still on his crippled front legs, lying on the dump.

Not even that, I think, cured me of going there, though our parents all forbade us on pain of cholera or worse to do so. The place fascinated us, as it should have. For this was the kitchen midden of all the civilization we knew; it gave us the most tantalizing glimpses into our lives as well as into those of the neighbors. It gave us an aesthetic distance from which to know ourselves.

The dump was our poetry and our history. We took it home with us by the wagonload, bringing back into town the things the town had used and thrown away. Some little part of what we gathered, mainly bottles, we managed to bring back to usefulness, but most of our gleanings we left lying around barn or attic or cellar until in some renewed fury of spring cleanup our families carted them off to the dump again, to be rescued and briefly treasured by some other boy with schemes for making them useful. Occasionally something we really valued with a passion was snatched from us in horror and returned at once. That happened to the mounted head of a white mountain goat, somebody's trophy from old times and the far Rocky Mountains, that I brought home one day in transports of delight. My mother took one look and discovered that his beard was full of moths.

I remember that goat; I regret him yet. Poetry is seldom useful, but always memorable. I think I learned more from the town dump than I learned from school: more about people, more about how life is lived, not elsewhere but here, not in other times but now. If I were a sociologist anxious to study in detail the life of any community, I would go very early to its refuse piles. For a community may be as well judged by what it throws away—what it has to throw away and what it chooses to—as by any other evidence. For whole civilizations we have sometimes no more of the poetry and little more of the history than this.

COMMENT

Two words, *excitement* and *poetry,* near the end of the first paragraph establish the theme and suggest the organization of this essay without breaking its informal rhythm. Mr. Stegner first accumulates sensuous and narrative details to create the excitement of his childhood experiences; he then picks up the reference to the discarded Shakespeare volumes and moves into a discussion of poetry and civilization. This kind of organization, effective as it is difficult, is more often used in poetry and fiction than in exposition.

SUGGESTIONS FOR WRITING

1. Try to follow Mr. Stegner's technique as you describe in detail some experience (your first date, your first job, the death of a pet animal). Arrange your details in such a way that you can conclude your essay by hinting at some deeper meaning of your experience.
2. Write a short "archeological" paper based on the markings in a used textbook, on fraternity walls, in a family Bible, or on the contents of a wastepaper basket or an attic trunk. Your success here will depend on how well you can maintain a single theme or tone.

VULTURE
COUNTRY

John D. Stewart

SPAIN IS THE STRONGHOLD of the vultures. There are four listed species in Europe, two common and two rare; if they are anywhere, they are in Spain. The bearded vulture and the black survive there, the Egyptian flourishes, and the great griffon swarms. The further south you go the more numerous they become, until you reach the hot grazing plains of Andalusia. There, summer and winter through, they hang in hordes in the roofless sky, for Andalusia is the vulture country.

There are three essential qualities for vulture country: a rich supply of unburied corpses, high mountains, a strong sun. Spain has the first of these, for in this sparsely populated and stony land it is not customary, or necessary, to bury dead animals. Where there are vultures in action such burial would be a self-evident waste of labor, with inferior sanitary results. Spain has mountains, too, in no part far to seek; and the summer sun is hot throughout the country. But it is hottest in Andalusia, and that is the decisive factor.

The sun, to the vulture, is not just something which makes life easier and pleasanter, a mere matter of preference. His mode of life is impossible without it. Here in Andalusia the summer sun dries up every pond and lake and almost every river. It drives the desperate frogs deep into the mud cracks and forces the storks to feed on locusts. It kills the food plants and wilts the fig trees over the heads of the panting flocks. Andalusia becomes like that part of ancient Greece, "a land where men fight for the shade of an ass."

All animals, both tame and wild, weaken in these circumstances, and the weakest go to the wall and die. The unpitying sun glares down on the corpses and speeds their putrefaction, rotting the hide and softening the sinews and the meat, to the vulture's advantage. But the sun plays a still greater part in his life. Its main and vital function, for him, is the creation of thermal currents in the atmosphere, for without these he would be helpless.

Reprinted from *The Atlantic Monthly*, by permission of Jacques Chambrun, Inc.

The vulture must fly high—high enough to command a wide territory, for, except at times of catastrophe, dead animals are never thick on the ground. His task is to soar to ten thousand feet, more or less, two or three times in a day, and to hang there and keep constant survey. A male griffon weighs up to sixteen pounds, so that to hoist himself up to that necessary viewpoint would call for fifty-three thousand calories, the equivalent of fifty pounds of meat. To find and eat three times his own weight in a day is clearly impossible; a short cut must be made. In the dawn of any day, in Andalusia, you may see the vulture discovering that short cut.

The eagles, buzzards, kites, and falcons are already on the wing, quartering the plain fast and low, seeking reptiles and small game. But the vulture sits on a crag and waits. He sees the sun bound up out of the sierra, and still he waits. He waits until the sun-struck rocks and the hard earth heat up and the thermal currents begin to rise. When the upstream is strong enough, he leaps out from the cliff, twists into it, and without one laborious wingbeat, spirals and soars.

By the time the vulture reaches his station, a half hour later and maybe more, the sun is blazing down on the plain and betraying every detail to his telescopic eye, and the updraft is strengthening as the day approaches its zenith. His ceiling for this day is fixed by two factors. One is the strength and buoyancy of his chosen thermal, which will vary with the strength of the sun and the behavior of the upper winds. But the more important factor, for it fixes his horizontal bearings as well, is the distribution of neighboring vultures in the sky, his colleagues and competitors.

He cocks his head from side to side and checks their various positions. There they hang, dotted across the clear sky at intervals of a mile or so— at the corners of one-mile squares. Height and lateral distances all adjusted, the vulture settles, circling slowly on his invisible support, and begins his long and lonely vigil.

This griffon vulture, which I select from the four species as being by far the most prevalent and typical, is almost sure to be a male. The female rarely leaves her nest from early March, when she lays her rough white egg, until August, when her huge poult is fledged and flying. The father has to feed and carry for all three.

At first glance, from below, he appears as one great wing, ten feet from tip to tip and two feet broad. His tail is square and very short, which is all it needs to be, for there are no sharp or sudden quirks in his flight that would call for a strong rudder. His movements are premeditated, stressless, and leisurely, for his energy must be conserved at all costs and never wasted on aerobatics.

The vulture's head and neck, too, protrude very little in front of his wing plane, and this distinguishes his flight silhouette from the eagle's. His neck is, in fact, some two feet long, but since it is bare—and must be bare—he folds it back into his collar to keep it warm. His head, apart from its nakedness, is like an eagle's; his yellow claws, which never kill and rarely carry, are shorter and not so strong. His plumage is a uniform sandy color, faded and tattered by work and waiting and, perhaps, by old age. It is relieved only by his coffee-colored ruff and the broad black primary wing feathers fingering the air.

The vulture sails in silence, for no vocal signals could serve him at such a distance from his fellows. He croaks, growls, and whistles only in his family circle, and at his feasts. He circles by almost imperceptible adjustments of his wing planes, aided by slight twists of his tail. But his head is in constant and active movement. He swivels it from one side to the other, bringing each eye in turn to bear on the earth. Then he bends his neck to right or left to check on one of his neighbors to north, south, east or west.

The whole vulture network is interdependent. Each vulture can give and receive two signals or, as the scientists call them, "visual stimuli." Circling means "Nothing doing"; dropping, or its resultant hole in the sky, calls "Come here!" Like all other vultures, he rests reassured by the first and is rapidly and relentlessly drawn by the second.

It is demonstrable how, with a special density of nerve endings on his retina, the vulture can see a small animal from a great height. Many other birds—gannets, for example—have the same propensity. Their eyesight is surprising only when we compare it with the poor standards of our own. But a mystery remains: how does the bird know that the animal is dead? The sense of smell is to be ruled out straightway. It is impossible that it would operate at such a distance, even allowing for the upward current of air. Birds are not, generally, well endowed in this respect, and in the vulture's case this may be especially fortunate.

No book, no expert, could answer this question for me, and I carried it through the vulture country for years, the one tantalizing imponderable, the broken link. Then, one hot afternoon, I lay down beside an old swineherd in the shade of a cork oak on the foothills overlooking the great plain of La Janda. For fifty years, he told me, he had watched pigs on that plain—the pigs, yes, and the vultures. I put my problem to him.

The swineherd's theory is not to be proved, but it is a wise one and I shall hold it until I find a better. No, he said, it is not the white belly skin that distinguishes the dead animals. White fur may fix the vulture's eye, but it does not offer him evidence of death. All herds and flocks, said the old man, lie down together and at one time. They have their place and their hour of rest. When a vulture sees an animal lying alone and apart, he is bound to notice it. The next time he crosses, the same image strikes his eye and startles him again. Over and over again he marks it and waits and watches; but now, alerted, he watches it more closely.

The next day the animal is still there; his attention is fixed upon it now, so he circles a little lower, his eye riveted, seeking the slightest movement of limb or lung. He sees none, but he continues to wait, said the old man. It takes him two days, at least, to confirm death. He goes on circling, but lower. He becomes more engrossed, and more sure. The other vultures note his behavior and move over a little in the sky. Every time he falls, they move closer. Now he is very low. He seeks the heaving of the flanks or eye movements; he sees neither. At some point, perhaps, he receives a visual stimulus in some death sign—the protruding tongue or the wide and whitened eye. Then he falls quickly, landing heavily at a little distance from the corpse.

The swineherd and I watched the first vulture land. We watched him sidling and circling the dead goat, standing erect to see better, wing tips trailing, naked neck stretched to the full, head swiveling rapidly to bring alternate eyes to bear. He hopped closer and paused, peering intently. If he could smell, even as well as we, his doubts would have been over. But he stood there, irresolute, famished yet fearful, with his bill open and his wings ready for use.

Then a big shadow swept across the brown grass, and the vulture glanced upwards. His involuntary signal had been answered, and a tall column of vultures wheeled overhead. He hopped to close quarters, stretched forward, pecked the corpse, and leapt back. He watched it for a second more; no movement. Then he croaked once, as though to bless himself, and threw himself on the body. He struck his heavy beak into the flank, flapped for balance, and thrust backwards with feet and wings to strip the hide from the ribs and belly.

Almost immediately there were eight more vultures at the corpse, and we saw that all of them sought and fought for the same place. Their aim was to penetrate, their object the viscera. Watching them thrusting their long necks deep into the belly cavity and withdrawing them befouled and bloodstained, I saw why those necks must be bare. Yes, said the swineherd, and that is the one part the vulture cannot reach to clean. His mate may clean it for him later, for pure greed, but if he had feathers there he would have maggots in them.

Now sixteen more vultures swept down, landing heavily in their haste and flap-hopping to the feast—the second square from the sky pattern. The corpse was covered, submerged in a heaving, struggling mass of broad brown wings. A new column wheeled above us, circling lower. There should be twenty-four up there, I reckoned. There were twenty-three.

The latecomers landed on nearby trees, including ours, and their weight bent thick limbs to the ground. From points four miles distant, we could expect thirty-four more, and at the height of the carnival I counted just short of one hundred birds.

A mule lasts two hours, said the old man, and an ox, three. This goat became bones in the sun in half an hour.

As the hundred fed, or hoped and waited, many more vultures circled high above, assessing the situation and the prospects and treasuring their altitude. Toward the end, when the feasters scattered and exposed the small skeleton, the watchers flapped and drifted wearily away to resume their distant stations. But they had fulfilled their function. They had marked the spot and drawn the Egyptian vultures and the kites.

Now the little Egyptian vultures landed daintily and dodged nimbly through the throng of giants. They are bare on the face and throat only, with well-feathered head and neck, and so, perforce, they are cleaner feeders. The dirty work has been done; now the long and delicate beak comes into play. The Egyptian vultures attack the skull, the large joints, and the crevices of the pelvic girdle—all parts inaccessible to the griffon's heavy beak. They extract brains, membranes, and the spinal cord, and clip out tendons and ligaments. They dodge out through the encircling griffons with their spoils, gobble them swiftly, and dance back for more. The griffons, gorged with meat and panting in the sun, pay them scant attention.

Finally, when all but the whistling kites have left the scene, comes the great solitary bearded vulture, the fierce lammergeier. His whole head is feathered, so he despises carrion. He lives aloof from all the rest of the vulture tribe, but they serve his interests, so he keeps them within sight. The old swineherd calls him *Quebrantahuesos*—the bone smasher—and Aeschylus noted him, long ago, for the same behavior. The lammergeier seizes the largest bones, carries them high, in his claws, and drops them on the rocks. Then he swoops down and rakes out the marrow.

Like an eagle, he can kill as well as carry with his claws, and he has not the true vulture's patient, soaring habit. He attacks flocks and herds and carries off the lambs and kids and piglets. After his work has been done nothing will remain except an empty skull and some small bones, which the ants and carrion beetles pick and polish.

Our griffon, first on the scene, will not be the first to leave it. He is sure to have gorged himself with his advantage. Crop, throat, and neck distended, he squats back on his tail, with his wings spread to steady him and his beak hanging open. From time to time he chokes and belches and gags, and it is an hour, maybe, before the meat subsides in him.

When he is ready, the griffon runs and leaps across the plain, thrashing heavily with his big wings, and labors into the air. He finds a thermal, circles in it to his altitude, then slips sideways and sweeps gently across the sierra to his distant nest.

The griffon vultures are gregarious in nesting, with colonies throughout the mountains at fairly regular intervals of thirty miles. They are said to pair for life. Certainly they return every year to the same nest. In January they begin to repair the nest, a broad and battered saucer of strong branches, topped with twigs and grass. They are careless builders, and many nests have bare rock protruding in them. No attempt is made to cover it. The egg is laid in late February and incubated for forty days. The new chick is bare and blue-skinned and looks as though he might become a dragon, but soon he sprouts white down and begins to assert the characteristics of his race. In a month he is voracious, and by the end of April he will demand four pounds of meat every day. Before he is fledged he will need eight pounds. Providentially, his demands coincide with the heyday of death.

When the male vulture arrives at the nest he settles on a nearby ledge, vomits, and sorts out the result with his beak. The female helps with this assessment, feeding herself hungrily on the larger relics. Then she offers her gape and crop to her cowering, whistling infant. The chick gobbles madly. With vultures it can never be "little and often," for animals die irregularly, as they must, so the birds, young and old, must gorge to the neck when opportunity offers. That is their instinct and their nature.

A male vulture with family responsibilities cannot rest for long. Now that his load is delivered and eaten, he is likely to be the hungriest of the family. This, too, is as it should be, for the hunger sends him out and up again, however little daylight may remain, to circle in the sky until the sunset reddens the sierra.

Time was when the summer drought killed thousands of beasts every year and the floods of winter hundreds more. Nowadays there are fewer casualties, but the vultures still have a fairly constant food supply in the charnel gorges, which lie below most mountain villages.

Grazalema, Arcos, Casares, and a hundred more were built, for protection from the raiding Moors, on the edge of the precipice. All dead and dying animals, as well as all the garbage of the town, are simply pushed over the cliff and left to the birds. There is a bird in Andalusia for every class and size of refuse. From the escarpment you can watch all the scavengers of the air, soaring below you or fighting on the feast. The great black vulture may be here, the griffon and Egyptian for sure, and two kinds of kites. The cunning ravens and carrion crows wait on the outskirts, dashing in to snatch their choice. Clouds of choughs and jackdaws wheel and cry above them.

There is a new feeding ground in the unfenced highways of Andalusia. As motor traffic increases, these offer more and more dead dogs, cats, kids, pigs, and rabbits. If you are abroad at dawn, it is a common thing to run down a vulture intent on scraping a dead dog off the asphalt. Even so, with an apparently limitless population of these great birds, each looking for some thirty pounds of meat every day, one wonders how they flourish.

Their wonderful feeding system has, it seems to me, one fatal flaw. They can signal "Food here," but not how much. At the feast which I have described only some succeeded in feeding at all, and only two or three ate their fill. A majority came the distance and lost their height for little or for nothing.

In Africa, also vulture country, there is no such difficulty, for there all the game is big game, and every funeral is worth attending. It may be that some of our Andalusian vultures go there in the winter. Certainly our vulture population increases here, but that is because the vultures from further north crowd in as the heat decreases and the air currents weaken in their homelands. Fortunately, there is a seasonal food supply ready for them all, for it is the time of birth, with all its failures and fatalities. After the winter storms, too, the torrents offer up their toll of corpses. And in winter, each bird has only himself to feed. But you would not doubt, if you knew the constant panic for food which dominates him summer and winter alike, that the vulture leads a competitive and anxious life. He has strong forces for survival. It is held—and we know it to be true of eagles—that the vulture has a very long life. If this longevity is a fact, then the solitary chick each year may add up to a good replacement rate.

The nest is inaccessible, and the hen guards it constantly against the only possible natural enemy—other vultures or raptors. So the survival rate must be high, as is proved by the evident increase toward saturation point.

At times, lying on my back on the plain with binoculars trained on the sky, I have seen vultures circling in two or three layers, each one high above the other. What can this mean? A hungry duplication, or triplication, hopelessly covering the same feeding ground and using the only available thermals? Or the opposite—idle and well-fed reserves standing by for surplus?

No one can tell me. But here in the vulture country there are no birds more spectacular, more fascinating to watch and to study. In time we may find out the last of their secrets. I lie on the plains and keep on watching them. And they, I know, keep on watching me.

COMMENT

"Vulture Country" follows the pattern often employed in the reports of the amateur observer. Beginning with a general summary of the vulture's behavior in his natural habitat, the essay introduces a particular problem, advances a solution based on personal observation, returns to a general discussion, and concludes with an application of the nature study to human life ("And they, I know, keep on watching me"). From a study of this article the beginning writer can learn much about the use of specific detail and how to create the tone of authority appropriate to the amateur.

SUGGESTIONS FOR WRITING

Collect your observations on one of the following (or on a similar subject suggested by the following). Write an essay in which you begin with a generalized statement, proceed to a specific problem, offer your observations, and conclude by offering a theory which solves your problem.

Feeding Habits of Rock Bass in Square Lake

Feeding Habits of the American Coed (or College Boy)

Mating Practices I Have Known

The High School Party

JAMES
AGEE
in 1936

WALKER EVANS

AT THE TIME, Agee was a youthful-looking twenty-seven. I think he felt
he was elaborately masked, but what you saw right away—alas for con-
spiracy—was a faint rubbing of Harvard and Exeter, a hint of family
gentility, and a trace of romantic idealism. He could be taken for a lik-
able American young man, an above-average product of the Great Democracy from any part of the country. He didn't look much a poet, an intellectual, an artist, or a Christian, each of which he was. Nor was there
outward sign of his paralyzing, self-lacerating anger. His voice was pro-
nouncedly quiet and low-pitched, though not of cultivated tone. It gave
the impression of diffidence but never of weakness. His accent was more
or less unplaceable, and it was somewhat variable. For instance, in Alabama it veered toward country-Southern, and I may say he got away with
this with the farm families and himself.

His clothes were deliberately cheap, not only because he was poor but
because he wanted to be able to forget them. He would work a suit into
fitting him perfectly by the simple method of keeping it on most of the
time. Eventually the cloth would mold itself to his frame. Cleaning and
pressing would have undone this beautiful process. I exaggerate, but it
did seem sometimes that wind, rain, work, and mockery were his tailors.
On another score, he felt that wearing good, expensive clothes involved
him in some sort of claim to superiority of the social kind. Here he occasionally confused his purpose and fell over into a knowingly comical
inverted dandyism. He got more delight out of factory-seconds sneakers
and a sleazy cap than a straight dandy does from waxed calf Peal shoes
and a brushed Lock & Co. bowler.

Physically, Agee was quite powerful, in the deceptive way of uninsistent
large men. In movement he was rather graceless. His hands were large,
long, bony, light, and uncared for. His gestures were one of the memo-

Reprinted from *The Atlantic Monthly* by permission of the author.

rable things about him. He seemed to model, fight, and stroke his phrases as he talked. The talk, in the end, was his great distinguishing feature. He talked his prose, Agee prose. It was hardly a twentieth-century style; it had Elizabethan colors. Yet it had extraordinarily knowledgeable contemporary content. It rolled just as it reads; but he made it sound natural—something just there in the air like any other part of the world. How he did this, no one knows. You would have blinked, gaped, and very likely run from this same talk delivered without his mysterious ability. It wasn't a matter of show, and it wasn't necessarily bottle inspired. Sheer energy of imagination was what lay behind it. This he matched with physical energy. Many a man or woman has fallen, exhausted, to sleep at four in the morning, bang in the middle of a remarkable Agee performance, and later learned that the man had continued it somewhere else until six. Like many born writers who are floating in the illusory amplitude of their youth, Agee did a great deal of writing in the air. Often you had the impulse to gag him and tie a pen to his hand. That wasn't necessary; he was an exception among talking writers. He wrote, devotedly and incessantly.

Night was his time. In Alabama he worked I don't know how late. Some parts of *Let Us Now Praise Famous Men* read as though they were written on the spot at night. Later, in a small house in Frenchtown, New Jersey, the work, I think, was largely night written. Literally, the result shows this; some of the sections read best at night, far in the night. The first passage of *A Country Letter* is particularly night permeated.

Agee worked in what looked like a rush and a rage. In Alabama he was possessed with the business of finding out everything he could about the lives he intended to describe. He must not have slept. He was driven to see all he could of the families' day, starting, of course, at dawn. In one way, conditions there were ideal. He could live inside the subject, with no distractions. Back-country poor life wasn't very far from him, actually. He had some of it in his blood, through relatives in Tennessee. Anyway, he was in flight from New York magazine editorial offices, from Greenwich Village social-intellectual evenings, and especially from the whole world of high-minded, well-bred, money-hued culture, whether authoritarian or libertarian. In Alabama he sweated and scratched with submerged glee. The families understood what he was down there to do. He'd explained it, in such a way that they were interested in *his* work. He wasn't playing. That is why in the end he left out of *Let Us Now Praise Famous Men* certain completed passages that were entertaining, in an acid way. One of these was a long, gradually hilarious aside on the subject of hens. It was a virtuoso piece heightened with allegory and bemused with the pathetic fallacy.

He won almost everybody in those families—possibly too much—even though some of the individuals were hard-bitten, sore, and shrewd. Probably it was his diffidence that made them accept him. That nonassurance was, I think, a hostage to his very Anglican childhood training. His Christianity—if an outsider may try to speak of it—was a punctured and residual remnant, but it was still a naked, root emotion. It was an ex-Church, or non-Church matter, and it was hardly in evidence. All you saw of it was an ingrained courtesy, an uncourtly courtesy that emanated from him toward anyone, perhaps excepting the smugly rich, the pretentiously genteel, and the police. After a while, in a roundabout way, you discovered that, to him, human beings were at least possibly immortal and literally sacred souls.

The days with the families came abruptly to an end. Their real content and meaning has all been shown. The writing they induced is, among other things, the reflection of one resolute, private rebellion. Agee's rebellion was unquenchable, self-damaging, deeply principled, infinitely costly, and ultimately priceless.

COMMENT

As its title indicates, this essay is a character sketch of an interesting personality at a particular point in his development and as he was observed under specific conditions. A character sketch so well defined and limited has a sharper if smaller cutting edge than a generalized portrait. Notice too that the order of the paragraphs in an informal sketch need not be so rigorously controlled; the shaping force can be emotional rather than logical.

SUGGESTIONS FOR WRITING

Write a character sketch in which you restrict your observations to a specific time and place. Describe a member of your family on the day you left for school, at a moment of crisis, or in some habitual activity. Observe your roommate cleaning your room. Analyze a friend's behavior at a football game, at a dance. Try to discover *significant* actions, those that actually reveal character.

Arthur T. Hadley

COMPLEX QUERY:

WHAT MAKES A GOOD SPY?

THE WORLD OF THE SECRET AGENT is a solitary world. His is the aloneness of the infantryman proceeding up a deserted enemy street. The hostile world stretches out infinitely in all directions around him with the tension of a high note held too long. Within this world he has no friend. He and his fear exist alone.

Just so was Francis Gary Powers alone on his U-2 spy-plane mission when he was brought down 1,200 miles within the Soviet borders.

I remember sitting in a quiet Georgetown garden with an old friend. It was a soft, mint-julep afternoon in the spring of one of those fat, contented years shortly after the Korean war's end. My friend and I maintain the fiction that I don't know what he does. It's easier. That afternoon he was obviously on the rack. So much so, and this was so unusual, that I broke our rule and said, gesturing at the soft green peace of the garden to indicate the apparent peace of the world, "It must be even rougher, now."

"It is," he answered. And then, after an instant: "I blew a nasty one last week. Killed a few people. Must have set the cold war back months."

He should not have come out of his world apart and said that to me. But in his own world of secret intelligence there was no one he could talk to. His superiors would have regarded his depression as a dangerous sign of weakness. Intelligence security is so rigid his colleagues couldn't know what he was doing. So he sat alone in his separate world, while the peaceful world of the garden went on happily, not understanding.

The official bureaucratic designation for a man who takes on this demanding work is "agent, intelligence, covert." In the argot of his trade he is "opps black"—a "black operator." "White operators," or "agents, intelligence, overt," are those who analyze foreign technical journals, listen to Russian broadcasts, interview refugees. Their work may be secret, but they do not pretend to be something they are not. Theirs is not the ex-

First appeared in *The New York Times Magazine*. Reprinted by permission of the author.

18

treme isolation and danger. They are not "in black." Agents like Powers, who both pretend to be something they are not and penetrate the Curtain, Bamboo or Iron, are "in deep black."

What mental and psychological qualities make up the ideal black agent? Different nations set different standards. Nevertheless, intelligence agents themselves are in general agreement about the necessary attributes. The man they describe is a far remove from the all-American boy or the pip-pip-and-all-that British colonel of spy fiction. These agents outline their ideal with such observations as:

"Lonely, complicated jobs take lonely, complicated guys."

"The quiet, bookish type, without bravado, sticks longest."

"Team players who don't need the coach or the team."

"The thinking fanatic."

Obviously, the ideal black agent on either side of the cold war must have extreme technical competence. The Soviet Union is a well-guarded, closed society. Those who snoop in or around it cannot be amateurs. The West, while not so secretive, has effective counter-espionage, too. There is a legendary story in intelligence about a British colonel in World War II who, at great hazard, broke into a supersecret German torpedo factory and blew up the coffee urn. Being a tea drinker, he didn't recognize that piece of equipment. Those days, one hopes, are past.

Many black agents now are electronics specialists. Parabolic microphones and transistorized radio transmitters the size of a book of matches have changed agents' methods of operation. So has the aqualung, the inflatable airplane, high-speed aerial photography, infra-red and radar detection devices, and the electronic processing of data.

Beneath the armor of technical competence lie the essential basic traits. Intelligence is an absolute must—not quiz-show glibness, but the ability to sit down with a sheet of paper and solve complex, original problems.

Much of the time, the agent has no "book" to go by. The situation he confronts is unique. There is no one to turn to for guidance, no committee to render a considered opinion, no staff to brief him on the big picture. On his decision rests not merely the future of some company, but that awesome entity, the national security.

His intelligence should be imaginative. He must outthink, not outfight, the enemy. Then, there are certain tough basic questions to which the ideal agent has worked out his answers. For example: "Since almost all men talk under torture in time (and women, too, though their psychology enables them to hold out longer), how long should I hold out? And why?" Or: "Since the enemy will stoop as low as necessary to gain his ends, how far should we stoop?"

The ideal agent must have faced up to the possible necessity of suicide.

Actually, the dividing line between suicide and other hazards does not appear so great to those inside the black area. There is a macabre joke well-known in intelligence circles about a secret agent going off alone on a particularly dangerous job inside an enemy country. The last words of his chief are: "Hold out, and keep reporting to the last man."

The agent has one overriding security rule: if he knows certain types of information he is to kill himself rather than fall into enemy hands, and he is issued the necessary equipment to do so. Other situations are left to his judgment.

The ideal agent must be a psychologically well-balanced individual— not ordinary, but so well-balanced as to appear normal. He needs the same deep, introspective knowledge of himself that the ideal psychiatrist needs. He should have looked perceptively at himself and the world around him and come up with his own philosophy.

His balance must be self-sustaining, an internal gyroscope. The man who needs praise, fellowship, coaching or even understanding cannot maintain the pace. Nor will the shibboleths of conventional wisdom sustain the agent in his dark hour. Conventional wisdom does not recognize the occasional necessity of murder or suicide.

The introspective intelligence necessary in the ideal agent shows up in the postwar published writings of British black operators about their work. A mystic quality permeates "Hugh Dormar's Diaries." Both W. Stanley Moss' "Ill Met by Moonlight" and Fitzroy Maclean's "Eastern Approaches" are ripe with scholarship.

French resistance leaders had the same intellectual quality. Albert Camus is remembered as a philosopher, not as an agent. The man who called himself Colonel Remy wrote in "How a Resistance Dies"—perhaps the most agonizing tale ever told of an agent's work—an excellent antidote for anyone bemused by the glamour of working in black.

Ideal agents are hard to come by. Defectors from the Soviet Union indicate that even Russia has trouble finding them. The West must not only find them, but persuade them to volunteer. Inevitably, many of any country's agents are foreign nationals.

Since good agents are so hard to find, their superiors are likely to condone eccentricities in their off-duty behavior—which, to be frank, is often very odd. Two highly successful American black agents spring to mind. One used to borrow suits of armor from a museum and ride through the countryside looking for someone to joust with. (He found people who would, too.) The other would put on a ragged suit of clothes about once every two months and, going to the toughest part of a rather tough town, start a barroom brawl. He didn't always win, but he claimed it kept him in shape and worked off his tensions.

The tensions are constant. The presence of danger not only creates its own anxiety, but heightens the anxiety-producing factors in the agent's other problems.

One is schizophrenia—never letting on in one life what is being done in the other. Several Soviet agents have defected to the West because their "Western" personalities finally became dominant. One American, whose job is recruiting new agents, greets his friends with the mocking question: "Met any well-balanced schizophrenics lately?"

The secrecy of the work produces tensions in another way. An agent knows only his small portion of the job, not where he fits into the whole. He must be able to accept the necessity of performing morally despicable actions in situations of extreme danger over prolonged periods of time without knowing why.

The moral horror of certain actions he must take contributes to his psychological malaise. For example: You are a secret agent who has been leading a twenty-man resistance group in a hostile country for two years. You have shared desperate and intimate hardships with your men and have their complete trust. You are now ordered to betray your resistance group into ambush and to make certain none of them survives.

The example is not farfetched. In the middle of July, 1944, when it became obvious to the Russians that the war in Europe was won, secret orders went out to Communist agents working with resistance groups in France, Yugoslavia, Poland and Greece to liquidate non-Communist resistance groups. From the French Alps to Mount Olympus, Red agents betrayed their closest comrades to the Germans. In liberated France, it was easier to murder, and explain to the Americans that the murdered were really collaborators.

The black operator does not face decisions every day as tough as the example. But even in the easiest, difficult moral choices are there. For some agents, after a time, the decisions become impossible. They break down. Every government in the business maintains special hospital rooms, plus doctors and nurses with security clearances, to handle the emotional problems of agents whom the work has pushed too far.

A more subtle form of breakdown that faces the Western agent in particular comes when the decisions all begin to seem easy. The agent has become either brutalized or so fanatical about his cause that his human values have disappeared. As Arthur Koestler has pointed out (and Koestler and George Orwell will be found among the black agents' most quoted authors) the yogi and the commissar, in the end, show the same image to the mirror.

Quite a few years ago, I talked to one of America's most famous intelligence agents—famous, that is, within the small circle where such fame is possible. I had sought him out because I had heard that he had accurately forecast what the enemy was going to do before one of America's bitterest military disasters. His warning had been rejected and, after the débâcle, his reports had been destroyed and he had been relieved for having been right.

I asked him about the incident. He answered that his superiors were absolutely right to destroy his reports and relieve him. Faith in the national leadership was essential for the war effort and he and his reports jeopardized that faith.

I was younger then, and I looked at the man closely for signs of irony or bitterness as he made that statement. I saw none. I concluded that the poor man had been beaten down by the magnitude of his job. I felt, as many reading this may feel, that he needed a good psychiatrist or a tonic to buck him up and help him regain his lost confidence.

I now realize the man had that final ingredient of the ideal intelligence agent: a fanatical devotion to duty. He had been absolutely right. His warnings had not been misunderstood or disregarded, but deliberately set aside. The result had been a major American disaster. For the country's future, his retirement had become a necessity. It is not always wise to prove the boss wrong in industry, either.

However, when a man has been removed for such reasons, we in America and throughout the West feel he has been treated badly. The ideal agent must feel he has been treated in the only way possible. In Koestler's novel, "Darkness at Noon," the hero, Rubishov, confesses to things he has not done rather than embarrass the regime. He knows his voluntary confession will mean his death.

This necessity for fanaticism makes the role of the Westerner-turned-agent particularly difficult. The agent himself, like the criteria by which he is selected, is in large part the product of his environment. We in the West consider many of the actions an agent must take morally reprehensible. People who do such things, or order them done, or even those who write about the agent's problem with sympathy, are considered ogres or worse. Yet for national survival our agents are ordered to—and do—perform such actions.

But, and the but is crucial, the Western agent cannot just perform the action and forget it. He must, in his "worst" moments, retain his respect for life and human dignity. He is under orders not to become the mirror image of the enemy.

The rack on which the Western agent is stretched is well-described in Shakespeare's "Henry V." King Henry wanders in disguise among his soldiers, conversing with them, just before the battle of Agincourt. The soldiers are debating how they will fight on the morrow. One of them wonders what will happen to his soul if the cause for which he dies "be not good."

"If the King's cause be wrong," replies another soldier, "our obedience to the King wipes the crime of it out of us."

Not so, answers Henry. "Every subject's duty is the King's. But every subject's soul is his own."

Our Western philosophy of freedom and moral responsibility splits the Western-reared agent in two. In societies where the subject's duty and soul both belong to the King, agents don't have the same problems—nor citizens the same freedoms.

The lack of complete fanaticism, the holding to moral values, puts an agent brought up in a free society under a much greater strain than his opposite number elsewhere. As a result, the West will lose rounds in the cold war. The strains and the losses are unavoidable.

To combine the West's humanistic heritage of the individual's responsibility and freedom with the need for obedience and service to the state is not easy in 1960. Deciding the proper mix of freedom and responsibility is a problem we all face. The secret agent, the black operator, merely faces the problem in its most acute form. He is our frontiersman in more ways than we realize.

COMMENT

Any writer attempting to define the characteristics of a particular group or occupation in the space of a short paper faces difficulties. Without presenting masses of evidence, he must correct or modify the stereotyped image which already exists in the minds of his readers and persuade them that he is correct in his reading of the character under discussion. He must, therefore, select his evidence carefully and write with an air of authority. Study and evaluate the success with which Mr. Hadley solves these difficulties in his analysis of the modern spy.

SUGGESTIONS FOR WRITING

1. Describe an occupation with which you are familiar. Begin with a sketch of the commonly accepted picture of your subject and proceed to show in what particulars it is wrong.

2. List the traits you consider essential to the successful athlete, honor student, or roommate. Compress the most obvious qualities into your first paragraph so that you may hold your reader's interest by concentrating upon some trait he might not have thought of for himself.

3. Mr. Hadley plays his analysis of the new spy against the conception of the spy we have derived from television, movies, and spy novels. One of his most effective methods is the terse, melodramatic style he uses in

the opening paragraphs. Try writing such an analysis yourself. You might compare the real father, mother, girl friend, professor, policeman, or priest with his or her stereotype in popular fiction. If you can manage to parody the style of the latter at the same time, do so. Parody requires very real skill, however.

J. IRWIN MILLER

THE DILEMMA

OF THE CORPORATION MAN

THERE IS MUCH TALK today that the organization is the enemy of the individual, and that while all organizations are enemies of sorts, the arch-enemy is undoubtedly the Business Organization. It produces "the man in the gray flannel suit"—this fellow who is a registered Republican and a member of the Chamber of Commerce, who believes in lower taxes and stronger defenses, opposes "giveaway" foreign aid, and is the husband of the Corporation Wife. The charge is that the Organization Man has lost his individuality and has become no more than a cog, indistinguishable from other cogs, in a machine composed not of metal parts but of linked and intermeshed human beings.

There is a great deal of truth to the charge. We know that it is not the whole truth, and that even within the fearfully demanding, complex, high-speed large business organization, many men find attraction and challenge. But I choose to ignore the blessings of the organization and instead to concentrate upon its genuine threat to the individual, trying to describe some of the manifestations of this threat, and finally to make a few suggestions as to how the threat may be successfully opposed.

Let me make a side comment on smaller businesses and the professions before looking at the lot of people in the big organization. How do individuals who are free of the big organization flourish outside of this powerful, compressive force? It is quite true that they may not dress or act like the Organization Man, or share his peculiar ambitions. But they do dress and look all too much like each other, and their houses are indistinguishable from one another, all being compounded out of *House Beautiful* and the *Ladies' Home Journal*. They are to be found every Monday noon dozing through a Rotary Club program that warns about the threat to the American way of life. They are all vigorous free enterprisers, who sponsor, if they are realtors, bills to fix real-estate commissions; if they are bankers, bills to set ceilings on savings interest; if they are dairymen, bills

Reprinted from the August 1959 issue of *Fortune Magazine*, by permission of the author and the publisher; © 1959 Time Inc.

to prevent selling milk below a liberally calculated "cost." While the Organization Men are alike in fearing their boss and in conforming in order to achieve the same promotion, the entrepreneurs are also conformed by a common fear that someone is going to take something away from them. All this is true of the labor leader, who is not able to indulge in any public criticism of his own organization. It may be true even of the college professor, who also has his uniform pattern of dress, of liberal politics, and of standardized nonconformity.

Is this a special sickness of our own day that other ages of men have successfully resisted? I think not. The problem of the individual versus the organization is a very old problem that man has had little luck in solving. The problem is new today only in its manifestations.

Man apparently feels he has to organize. We have all had in our elementary courses in economics the story that the last independent man was the early New England farmer, who grew or made everything he needed; and we were told that to achieve better standards man had to organize into larger and more complex groups, all of which is truly described in the economics textbooks. Man does have to organize, and in so doing he has to expose himself to the demands of the organization.

Perhaps for the greater number of human beings this conforming to the organization is no great worry, for the organization has its comforts for the mind and the spirit, just as it has for the body. Because of the organization we are no longer compelled to walk if we don't want to. The organization transports us. And for our minds the organization supplies acceptable opinions on politics, on business, on labor, on marriage, on religion. We do not have to think for ourselves if we do not wish, and most of the time this is a comfort. And while it is fashionable to view this situation with alarm, the truth is most of the time we love it.

There appear to me to be several reasons why we alternate between love and hate of the organization. First of all, I seriously doubt that there is any one of us who is really ever entirely sure that he belongs. The intense desire to be accepted by the group is so strong in all of us that it generates doubt that we are wholly accepted and wholly approved. It makes us uncritically eager to conform to the society with which we desire to identify ourselves, and it makes us violently critical of the "offbeat" member; by driving him out, we hope to thrust ourselves more surely into the center of the group.

This desire is expressed within the business organization in the standard forms of griping around the Coke machine and the standard forms of bootlicking in the boss's office and around the conference table. It is a sort of tyranny imposed by ourselves on ourselves, and it arises basically out of fear. This fear also has another manifestation. If we are a boss or a supervisor, it causes us to demand in the area within our control an excessive and unreasonable amount of agreement, and I think it is against this particular type of conformity and pressure that we find the most obvious resistance and complaint. It is true, more often than the business manager likes to think, that the more doubtful he is about the wisdom of a course of action, the more insistent he is that his associates openly and repeatedly agree that the policy is the absolutely correct one. Out of his fear the subordinate is overeager to conform to the group. Out of his fear the boss is overeager that the group conform to him.

My point so far is not that business organizations are generally composed of spineless and contemptible human beings; it is another kind of point—namely, that each one of us in different times fits this picture and shares these same sharp fears concerning himself and the opinions of men, and exhibits in varying degrees these same essentially cowardly responses. When we do, we are quite ashamed of ourselves, and we proceed then to damn the very organization whose favor and approval we desire above everything else. And so in our anger we now identify the organization, not as our god, but as our enemy. Someone has said that there is no such thing as sand, there are only grains of sand. The organization, in addition to the many other good, bad, useful, and dangerous things it may be, is also a collection of internally isolated human beings, each, from time to time, consciously or unconsciously fearful that he doesn't belong to the collection in some important sense.

Let us for the moment turn from the individual as he reacts to the organization and examine the monster, to see whether we can identify any representative types of problems that exist within the organization itself rather than within the individual. In my opinion most of these problems in business today may quite probably arise because the most important new situation is the interdependence of very large numbers of persons who are at the same time far removed from each other by organization structure. Because of this fact many a businessman's problems sometimes seem to him to be simply past his solving.

To illustrate, let us suppose we can see inside the head of the president of a large manufacturing organization. His company employs 20,000 persons and operates half a dozen plants. It distributes its products in every state and in many foreign countries, and—most frightening of all—it has competitors.

Now let us suppose that these competitors are extremely vigorous, and that our president knows that to maintain his share of the market and to make earnings which will please his directors, he must accomplish the following very quickly: design and perfect a brand-new and more advanced line of products: tool up these products in such a way as to permit higher quality and lower costs than his competitors; purchase new machinery; arrange major additional long-term financing. At the same time his corporation's labor contract is up for negotiation, and this must be rewritten in such a way as to obtain good employee response and yet make no more concessions than do his competitors. Sales coverage of all customers has to be intensified, and sales costs reduced. Every one of these objectives must be accomplished simultaneously, and ahead of similar efforts on the part of his competitors—or the future of the company is in great danger. Every head of a corporation lives every day with the awareness that it is quite possible to go broke. At the same time he lives with the awareness that he cannot personally accomplish a single one of these vital objectives. The actual work will have to be accomplished by numerous individuals, some actually unknown to him, most of them many layers removed from his direct influence in the organization. It is because of this that a president becomes frantic.

Feeling that every one of these goals must be accomplished in the way he conceives them, and at the same time feeling that other people down the line do not fully share either his understanding of the company's need or his own sense of urgency, realizing that he cannot personally supervise all whose work is necessary to the achievement of the program, he becomes dogmatic. He issues orders. He says things are jolly well going to be done this way and no other. He says the company's negotiators are not to give in on the union's demand for premium pay or the union shop. He says every salesman must make so many calls each day. He says you can't add a single person to this office, which has already got too many people in it. And he pounds the table every time he says these things. For he feels that this great, vast, and ponderous organization is his enemy and that inside its faceless exterior all his plans, his programs, his timetables will be diluted, slowed down, and ultimately defeated. Successes seem to him to have come only in rare instances, and to have been of a temporary and ephemeral nature. He thinks of himself as being in a race that has no finish line. And his real antagonist is neither the customer, nor his bankers, nor the union. His real antagonist is the organization.

Let us turn our attention to another fellow in this act—an executive from the ranks known as "middle management." He is several positions removed from our unhappy president. In fact he may never have seen him, being in charge of one of the distant plants that the president has not yet got around to visiting. But we must not make the mistake of supposing our man is a man with little responsibility. As a matter of fact, he is running a plant employing a thousand persons, which is bigger than the founder of the company ever ran throughout his whole business career. This plant, in addition, is the major employer in its small community. Now let us assume that our middle-management executive is bargaining for his first labor contract.

And let us suppose that every other plant in town has for years had a union-shop contract. Our middle-management executive knows that if he grants a union-shop contract, the rest of his negotiations may not be too difficult, but that refusal to grant such a contract may not only involve him in a strike, it may earn him the lasting hostility of the community. From the head office he receives a wire that says, "No union shop. Period. All our other plants have successfully negotiated contracts without it, and you are not going to negotiate one with it." When, therefore, he obediently refuses the union shop, the bargaining committee says, "How come? Are you antilabor? If you were to conduct an election, you would have an almost unanimous vote in favor of it. Are you afraid to ask the men how they feel about it?" If our middle-management executive replies, "Boys, I know you're right, but the big speckled bird up in the head office says, 'No,' " the committee can have only one reply, and that is, "Then what is the use bargaining with you? You aren't allowed to do any negotiating. The only way we'll get anywhere with this company is to strike," which they do. The head of the corporation, when he learns of this and sees that no success is made in settling the strike, begins to wonder whether Bill, the manager in the plant, is really executive material or not.

Or Bill may be required to tool up a product that has been designed at the company's research center. One part in the product may be so designed that an extraordinary amount of scrap results. Bill's crew finds out that a small change in the design would eliminate this problem, but the word from on high is, "You fellows have got to stop making changes. Get this model into production before we lose all our business to our competitors." So if Bill tells his people, "You make it like it is because the big shot says so," his boys know that Bill is not really running the plant. If, on the other hand, he accepts full responsibility himself for the head-office decision, then his boys put him down as stupid. And when his costs soar, the head office wonders for the second time if Bill is management material. By this time Bill, who is now on a milk diet, is beginning to wonder the same thing.

The special problem of the middle-management man is this: On the one hand, he is required to discharge what in the past have been considered very great responsibilities. On the other hand, the need to conform to the broad programs of the whole organization, which are established without the possibility of his direct participation, deprives him of the power of determination and decision that his own people expect him to have and forces him at times to carry out policies and programs he may passionately believe to be wrong, at least in their local application. So the organization also becomes his special enemy, and appears always to be able to deprive him of genuine accomplishment. This arouses his fears and induces in him a conformity which at times he despises and yet from which there is no escape, at least on terms he is willing to contemplate.

How shall we advise him to go about handling his problems? Since we have shown that at least some of our examples are probably natural characteristics of the large organization, a man is going to have better luck modifying his own approach to the organization than he is trying to remake the monster itself. My first suggestion is a fairly obvious one. The man in the business organization who is determined to master the special problems of the organization must neither embrace the organization uncritically nor despise it categorically. Instead, he must try to understand it, which of course is easier said than done. How do you go about understanding such a thing? You begin, as in most things, by using your mind, and you determine early in your organization life not to listen to the cynical advice: "Give the boss what he wants. Never mind what *you* think." The Corporation Man has got to have the courage to reject this basically adolescent notion, and the good sense, as well, to reject that other attitude: "We'll take care of our own department; let the damn engineers solve their own problems." The wise man will try to understand the part that his department or group is playing, and the requirements laid on him individually, if his actions are to be consistent with the main purpose of the institution. Those who are in positions of business management realize how rare is the member of the organization deep in the ranks who succeeds in keeping the purpose and aim of the institution uppermost in his mind.

Of course, even if he does succeed, all his problems are not yet ended, for, while his actions and his plans and his decisions may be of an astonishing quality, this very quality, this habit of appearing to aim at goals beyond those of his associates, may earn him the active dislike and resentment of those around him, including his own boss—unless he knows and understands how these people with whom he associates feel and operate.

We have pictured two broad kinds of problems: the first arising from an individual's consuming desire to "belong" and his surrender of individuality to the organization in the hope of gaining his desires; the second arising from the way the organization manages to defeat both the individual who runs it and the individual who works within it.

If I stop here without some qualifications, I will be guilty both of oversimplification and of exaggeration. These are not the only problems that can be said to face the individual in the business organization, but I do feel that they are examples of the kinds of problems which are encountered, and that useful solutions to these problems have some valid, general application. And while I admit that the aspect presented by the organization to the individual is not nearly so uniformly dismal as I have implied, nevertheless the problems are like the theme in a symphony, which sometimes dominates the music, at other times goes unnoticed in a minor part, later appears in altered aspect, and never quite disappears. Our Organization Man may be more conscious of these conditions and problems at some times than at others, but for him they can never be wholly absent from his mind and spirit. He has to learn how to handle them, rather than resent them, or indulge in the vain hope that he may somehow, someday, be rid of them. The spectacle of the businessman who chooses the world of tension, frustration, confusion, compromise, and crisis for his life's work and then complains because he has to grapple with tension, frustration, confusion, compromise, and crisis is more pathetic than tragic.

Men don't cry. This may be a silly-sounding statement, but bear with me while I try to make it more respectable. We are born as persons who are capable of tears, of anger, of great joy, of passionate love, of rending sorrow, but the Anglo-Saxon tradition in which we and our fellows are raised compresses these feelings and squeezes out their power. It is beaten deep into every boy: men don't cry; gentlemen don't get angry; be civilized about love; excessive enthusiasm is unsophisticated; uncritical admiration is childlike. All of this is summed up in the phrase of our day, "Don't get shook up."

Men who are true to the type will probably have read their last poem when they leave college. There will be no creation of art that will move them to tears. There will be no shocking condition in the world of tragic event that can cause consuming anger in them or raise genuine righteous indignation. Their marriages will be mild and convenient. Their capacity to feel will be slowly extinguished, and only the appetites will remain. How, then, will they understand those with whom they live and work? If they have no feelings left of their own, how can they enter into and share and comprehend those of others? And, if they do not, how can they hope to walk through life without giving grievous offense?

Somewhat more important to the man in the organization than a knowledge of double-entry bookkeeping, or of the ins and outs of corporate politics, is the cultivation of a capacity to feel. Does it seem odd that painting and poetry and music and suffering and great causes and dedication to religion are essential to the making of an effective Organization Man? Well, they are, for without them he is a half-man, half happy, half bored, half effective, killing the time of which at the end he learns there was so very little.

Finally, in dealing with the corporation he must cultivate courage. I mean the courage to take a right stand and to draw a right line, and, what is more important, to accept the consequences of so doing. It may mean the willingness to change a job or to lose a job. It means the kind of courage to speak the truth as you see it, to your customer if you are a salesman, to your boss, to your union if you are a negotiator. And it means the courage to do all this when you have families to support, children to educate, debts to pay, pension reserves to lose—and at a time when you have reached the age at which prospective employers consider you no longer young. These may sound like very prosaic remedies—to think, to feel, to be brave. They are in all the copybooks. But they are perhaps man's only weapons, and the persons who employed them well are also in all the history books. Those of us who take up these weapons and grow strong and skilled in their use may find the organization altering surprisingly before our eyes. The organization will no longer appear as the enemy of the individual but, instead, a most effective means to the individual's fulfillment.

COMMENT

Because "The Dilemma of the Corporation Man" was originally delivered as a speech (at Dartmouth College), its organization stands out in bolder relief than essays written for private reading. Each of the three main blocks of development is carefully noted: How does the individual react to the organization? How does the organization inhibit the expression of individuality? What can a man do to maintain his identity in the organization? Observe the way in which the first sentence in each paragraph links with the preceding paragraph and leads into the new.

SUGGESTIONS FOR WRITING

1. Mr. Miller writes of the business organization. Take one of his judgments and apply it to an organization with which you are familiar. In what ways, for instance, does the college or high school as an institution work to frustrate the development of the individual? Describe and analyze a specific situation in which group pressure has affected your conduct.

2. The author dramatizes his point by discussing various problems which his fictional character "Bill" must solve. Write an essay in which you introduce the reader to a dilemma, demonstrate how this dilemma manifests itself in the life of a fictional individual, and conclude with a well-developed judgment. Take a precise problem so that you do not oversimplify the issues. The following topics may be helpful: How can a student be honest in an atmosphere of moral cynicism? How can a young person maintain his integrity against the pressures of the complicated code governing relationships between the sexes?

3. Man can assert his manhood against the forces of the group only if he has the will "to think, to feel, and to be brave." Give careful consideration to this thought. What forces in your life seem to work against the expression of your beliefs in beauty, justice, or love? Write a paper on a narrowed aspect of this problem.

STEPHEN K. BAILEY

Ethics and the Politician

INSOFAR as I refer specifically to experiences in Middletown, Connecticut, during the years when I was mayor of that city, I hope that friends there will show me the same charity that Huckleberry Finn showed Mark Twain. Referring to *The Adventures of Tom Sawyer,* Huck commented, "That book was made by Mr. Mark Twain, and he told the truth, mainly. There was things which he stretched, but mainly, he told the truth. That is nothing. I never seen anybody but lied one time or another, without it was Aunt Polly. . . ." And Huck Finn was perceptive in spotting the moral flaw in Aunt Polly and in her old maid sister, Miss Watson: a flaw of self-righteousness so hideous that when Huck learned that Miss Watson was living "so as to go to the good place," Huck could "see no advantage in going where she was going," so he made up his mind he wouldn't try for it.

I have worried far more about the ethical consequences of my decisions as mayor since leaving office than I ever did as an incumbent. And perhaps this is the first point to be made. Most elected executives find that there is an ethics of *action* which is normally far more compelling than the urge to balance with precision the ethical niceties of pressing public issues. There are times when the good of the community demands firmness and decision at the expense of marginal injustice. Those who would make justice the sole criterion of the good society are not only, in my judgment, myopic in their ethical vision; they establish an impossible operating norm for administrators.

When the nicest people have rationalized their selfishness with a tactical deference to the public interest, elected political executives are often grateful that they are too preoccupied to be ethically astute. Even where venality seems clearest, as in the rare case of an attempt at straight brib-

Abbreviated for *The New Republic* from "The Ethical Problems of an Elected Political Executive," prepared for *Challenges to Traditional Ethics: Government, Politics, and Administration,* Sixteenth Conference on Science, Philosophy and Religion in Their Relation to the Democratic Way of Life, sessions held at the Jewish Theological Seminary of America in New York City, August 29 through September 1, 1960; to be published by the Conference, which holds copyright.

ery ("Mayor, here's $1,000 in $5 bills if you get that easement through
the council"—the political version of "payola"), the ethical issues may
not be self-evident. Let us make some assumptions: suppose that the
mayor knows that the easement will go through "on its merits" (begging
what *that* slippery phrase means). Suppose further that the mayor knows
that the party needs money not only to run the forthcoming election but
to pay debts on a past election. Suppose the mayor knows further that
the voting public has not responded favorably and positively to the appeal
of the American Heritage Foundation for everyone to give to the party
of his choice. Suppose finally that the mayor believes that a working two-
party system is the nation's and the community's greatest safeguard of democracy and freedom. If it could be proved to the mayor's satisfaction that
the lack of $1,000 at the moment could do irreparable damage to the
two-party system in the area, would it be a higher principle in a naughty
world for the mayor to accept the money on behalf of the party, or to refuse the money?

Stated this way, the issue is still not very complex for most people.
"They've known what's right and wrong since they've been 10." You do
not accept bribes, period; and you most certainly do not compound evil
by cheating the briber. This is all very clear. But is it, really? There are
ways of playing slight variations on this theme which would remove from
the sternest Presbyterian moralist any burden of guilt. The briber has
made a number of contributions to the party over the years. The latest
thousand is simply another indication of his belief in the great principles
of the party. On the easement question, every party member on the council, including the mayor, attempts to examine the issue on its merits.
But a "will to believe" has set in—a subtle coloration of the problem.
Good old Joe is a friend who provided all the favors for the party picnic.
Isn't it fortunate the merits of the easement case are on his side?

And bribery can take so many forms: money, favors, flattery, help in
time of trouble, influence in building status. To pretend that bribery is a
simple and easily spotted phenomenon is naïve. To pretend it takes place
only in politics is silly. I have seen the egos of older university professors
successfully bribed by astute and ambitious instructors; I have seen great
institutions bribe men into conformity with promises of promotions or
demotions. I have seen them kill, spiritually, those who resisted. I have
received threats that unless such-and-such happened, I'd be voted out at
the next election. Is this not attempted bribery? Is money any more a thing
of value than power or status or re-election?

I was never asked to fix a traffic or parking ticket in Middletown; but
I cannot swear that tickets were not occasionally fixed while I was mayor.
And I am not sure that under certain circumstances (*e.g.,* a hectic
woman delayed in buying her six children school clothes) I would not

have paid the dollar fine myself rather than penalize her for something beyond her effective control. Nothing is more unjust than unexceptional law except law that is all exceptions. Surely, one of the most difficult ethical problems in all governance is the drawing of lines between rules and exceptions. That the lines, to be moral, must be drawn near the rules end of the spectrum I do not question. But that exceptions are never warranted seems to me the most callous of all moral judgments.

George Bernard Shaw once wrote what many politicians must at times have felt. Shaw learned that a Labour candidate named Joseph Burgess had refused to compromise on some issue and had thereby lost his seat in Parliament. Shaw commented bitterly: "When I think of my own unfortunate character, smirched with compromise, rotted with opportunism, mildewed by expediency—dragged through the mud of borough council and Battersea elections, stretched out of shape with wire-pulling, putrefied by permeation, worn out by 25 years pushing to gain an inch here, or straining to stem a backrush, I do think Joe might have put up with just a speck or two on those white robes of his for the sake of the millions of poor devils who cannot afford any character at all because they have no friend in Parliament. Oh, these moral dandies, these spiritual toffs. . . . Who is Joe, anyhow, that he should not risk his soul occasionally like the rest of us?"

I was once confronted with a possible kickback on a fire truck purchase. The party representative reminded me that it costs money to run elections: that generosity from fire truck manufacturers to those who had the insight to see the need for public safety in their communities was rather standard, and that no one would really suffer. The gift would come as a preordained slice of the salesman's commission; he would give of his own income because "he believed in the principles of the Democratic Party." I drew myself up to my maximum height, stared at my good friend, and said in what I am sure must have been the most patronizing of tones, "If the party needs four or five hundred dollars, I shall be happy to try to raise the money personally; but I shall not do it that way." I then went a step further. I called the poor fire truck salesman into the office and made him add about $400 worth of extra equipment to the fire truck at the bid price he had quoted. In a swift double blow I had proved my moral worth and defended the taxpayers' interests. I had proved that at least in one American community "public office is a public trust."

I had also proved that it is easy to be moral when the pressure is not really on. Suppose the party coffers *had* been empty? Suppose my confident bluff to raise "four or five hundred dollars" for the party had been called? Suppose the alternative to a Democratic re-election was the election of a rather disreputable Republican gang who would have practiced "boodle" with more frequency and with infinitely less flair than the Democrats? What then? And why should we refuse to accept money for the imperative cause of political party machinery, almost regardless of source, when the so-called "good" people of the community would not be caught dead giving to their political party—to the system of options which does far more than the Constitution to guarantee freedom and democracy?

The only serious ethical struggle I had with party leaders in Middletown dealt with a request for a zoning exception. Here I was firm, morally aroused, and dogmatic, and would be to this day. A contractor, who had contributed liberally to both political parties locally, hired a leading Democratic lawyer to plead for a commercial spot zone in a strictly residential area. The people of the area were almost solidly opposed to the change. Even if they had not been, nothing can ruin the orderly and esthetic development of a growing city like politically-inspired spot zoning in contravention of a general plan. The members of the zoning committee, to their credit, said to me, "Mayor, there's a lot we'll do for the party, but we won't do this." The final showdown on this case took place in the lawyer's office with all major party leaders present. I walked in swinging. I made it quite clear that if the plumbing broke down in city hall, I would hire a licensed Democratic plumber over a licensed Republican plumber any day of the week; that if the law did not force us to go to bid, I would buy insurance from a Democratic rather than a Republican insurance agent; but that when it came to what Edmund Burke once called "the permanent forces" in the community, I was ready to do battle. I suggested that although there was much in politics that one rendered to Caesar, almost without qualms, city planning was rendered only to God. A few party leaders were upset; but most of them were understanding; and the lawyer in question, who over the years had been one of the most brilliant as well as constructive forces in the community and state, had the grace to accept my position without rancor.

But contrary to what many people seem to believe, the hard ethical issues of public life rarely concern party politics. Party decisions tend to roll according to pre-set patterns. Every elected executive works out a few obvious benchmarks for relationships with political leaders (for example, "consult party leaders on all appointments, but solicit their help in trading little appointments to the party for big appointments to you"). In any case, to suggest that most party officials are frequently ethical "problems" is to distort their normal role beyond recognition. For every occasion when a party leader asked me for a favor that disturbed my conscience, I can think of a dozen times when the same party leader helped me defend the public interest against the importunities of non-party pressure groups.

Upon reflection, it is my firm belief that insofar as party politics interferes with the pursuit of the public interest, it is largely a result of the necessities of campaign finance. Most venality in public life could be abolished or reduced to insignificance if the public would assume responsibility for broadly-based campaign financing and would insist upon the public auditing and disclosure of all campaign gifts and expenditures. This would not eliminate corruption entirely, for wherever power and money converge some venality will be found. But our present method of financing political campaigns is, in my estimation, the single most corrupting factor in our political life—local, national, and, especially, state.

Take 10 problems which faced me as mayor, and which are typical of perhaps 100 I faced in two years as an elected executive.

1. A peacock farm on the edge of town kept neighbors awake for a month or so a year during the peacock mating season. The city government was asked by the neighbors to see to it that the birds were quieted. Ethical question: is a temporary irritation—including loss of sleep—for 10 families worth the destruction of a hobby and a partial livelihood for one person?

2. The best detective on the chronically underpaid police force is suspected of taking protection money from some local two-bit gamblers. The evidence is too vague and unsubstantial to stand in court. Ethical question: is the *possibility* of the evidence being correct important enough to warrant a substantial investigation, with a consequent probable loss in efficiency and morale in the police department during and long after the investigation, a certain loss in public confidence in the whole force, and the ever-present possibility that the rumor was planted by a crank? And out of the many pressing issues coming across the mayor's desk, how much time and effort does such an investigation warrant from the mayor himself?

3. The whole scheme of volunteer fire departments is looked upon by the chief of the city's only paid department as wasteful, inefficient and dangerous to the public safety. The volunteers claim that their fire-fighting record is topnotch, that they save the taxpayers money. Ethical question: if neither side can be proved incorrect, how does one weigh the values of volunteer community endeavors against marginal inefficiencies in operation of a vital service?

4. Many years ago, one department store was farsighted enough to have bought up some land for off-street parking. This off-street parking gave the store quite a competitive advantage. The city, in a new municipal parking program, needed a portion of the private parking lot assembled by the department store years before. When established, the municipal lot might destroy the store's competitive advantage. Ethical question: at

what point does the public interest demand that private farsightedness be penalized?

5. Two mayors in four years happened to have lived on Wyllys Avenue. Wyllys Avenue desperately needed repaving. But so did some other streets in the city. Ethical question: should Wyllys Avenue be paved, granted a heavy presumption that many citizens would claim that the mayor had "taken care of himself"?

6. A federal grant-in-aid cut in half the city's welfare load, making a sinecure out of one of the two city welfare positions. The holder of the sinecure was a Negro appointed by the opposition party. Ethical question: should work somehow be "made" for the Negro, or should he be dropped? (For anyone who knows the problems of status, morale and upward mobility among Negroes in a largely white community, the political questions posed by this case are easy compared to the long-range ethical questions.)

7. The virulent opposition of a local printer-publicist might be tamed on a few key issues with the proper placing of a few city printing contracts. Ethical question: obvious.

8. Buying of tires in wholesale lots would save the taxpayers $300 a year—about one cent per citizen per annum. A score of little Middletown tire merchants would lose $10 or more in income. Ethical question: how does one balance one cent each for 30,000 people *versus* $10 each for 20 merchants?

9. Parents concerned with the safety of their children on the way to and from school are constantly demanding increased police protection and more sidewalks. A more legitimate demand would be hard to imagine. But there are limits. Ethical question: granted that *total* safety never can be assured, what grounds beyond obvious necessity and "the squeaky wheel gets the grease" can be found for awarding or denying protection?

10. There is a likelihood that one of the major industries in town will have to close down a sizable slice of its operations. This may mean 2,000 unemployed. A steel company is looking for a New England site for a steel mill. It finds an "ideal" location in Middletown. That "ideal" location is a stretch of the Connecticut River which is unspoiled and is deeply treasured by small-boat owners and by nature lovers. Ethical question: is the provision of employment for 2,000 people worth the destruction forever of natural beauty?

If I should be asked today how I resolved, in my own mind, the ethical dilemmas posed in the previous paragraphs, I should not know how to answer. Most of the dilemmas were not mine to resolve alone. Other people shared official power with me, and many citizens without official power assumed substantial unofficial responsibility for community decisions. But insofar as I had to make up my mind by myself, or felt that my judgment might be determining in the minds of others, I did repair to two or three very general propositions for ethical guidance. In practice, the propositions were never articulated, but in retrospect I know that they were there. All of them had been woven into my life by parental, religious, and academic influences—in most cases by all three. My father, although never a minister, was a Professor of Religion and a firm believer in the Social Gospel. My studies at Oxford had brought me close to Immanuel Kant and Jean Jacques Rousseau. Ideas like "the categorical imperative" and "the general will" were connected in my mind with such Biblical injunctions as "Let justice roll down as waters; and righteousness as a mighty stream."

The most helpful single question I could ask myself seemed to be, "What do you want Middletown to be like 10 years from now?" Against this, many things fell into place. I wanted more beauty, fewer slums, less bigotry, more recreation, more community spirit, a more sustained sense of public responsibility, a more dynamic and prosperous economy, better education, a stronger and more truly competitive two-party system, and a heightened sense of personal dignity for all. These were some of the benchmarks against which specific ethical issues were measured or rationalized. They were not my marks. They were the marks of the civilization of which I was a minuscule reflection.

There are, perhaps, two other matters which ought to be touched upon. The first has to do with the effect of power upon personality. I remember one evening when I was returning with political friends from a television performance. For a half hour they told me what a brilliant performance mine had been. By the end of the half hour I was aware only that a new political star had been born on the horizon: namely, myself, and that I could not long deny the people of the State of Connecticut the chance to vote for me either for Governor or at the very least for United States Senator. It was not until I got home that my wife—with that wonderful sixth sense of a level-headed and thoughtful woman—reminded me that my performance had, in fact, been a little on the mediocre side—but that she was sure I had just had an off night. The most devastating traps of public office are the ones set to catch the ego. It is so easy to forget that the tribute is to the office, not to the person. Even a mayor stands out a little; fathers bring up their daughters to "shake the mayor's hand"; the mayor sits at head tables; he officiates; he is often the central figure in ceremony. All this inflates the sense of personal worth and waters the thirsty garden of vanity. The consequences are often pathetic, often silly, sometimes dangerous.

But Acton was wrong in suggesting that the only flowers in the garden of vanity are the weeds of corruption. Power may corrupt, but it also can ennoble. The sense that you, and the office you hold, are widely valued often creates a heightened sense of responsibility, a desire to live close to the public expectation, a wish to become a kind of community example. I have seen men utterly transformed by a judgeship. A politician—an old pro in western Connecticut—once confided to me that he hated all judges. "What are they but some hack lawyers who happened to know a politician?" And he went on, "After you've made 'em, what do they do? They turn around and kick you in the teeth! They draw their robes around them as though they were Solon or something! You can't touch them! Who the hell do they think they are?" The fact is that they think they *are* Solon; they suddenly realize that instead of petty politicians they are an essential part of the fabric of civilization—a fabric which can last only so long as there is a widespread public belief that judges in courts of law will try to be just. And what is true of judges is equally true of elected executives.

This brings me to my final point. All ethical questions ultimately revert to propositions about the nature of man. Perched precariously on a whirling planet, blind to his origins, blind to his reasons for being, beset by the terrors of nature and of his own creation, man wobbles drunkenly between a certainty that he is nothing and an occasional, blinding revelation that he has a transcendent dignity and perhaps destiny. When man feels alienated from his universe, he may huddle in fear with his fellow men; but he cannot reach them with that fullness of feeling, that intenseness of identity, which is suggested by the Christian concept of love, or by the civil concept of community. I am not a mystical person, but I sense strongly that my best moments as mayor came when I felt—in an almost religious way—that what we were attempting to do in Middletown had meaning beyond itself. I remember Fred Smith, the editor of the local paper, once writing me an intimate note when I was particularly discouraged about the public response to some issue. "Never," he wrote, "lose faith in your neighbors." And he went on to explain, not that they were perfect, but that he had known them for a long time, and that they would ultimately respond to the good if they could be shown the good.

Surely this is the ultimate ethical postulate in a democracy: not that man is good, but that he is capable of good; not that he is free from corruption, but that he is desperately sick of it; not that he has fashioned the good society, but that he has caught an unforgettable glimpse of it.

COMMENT

The raw material of this essay consists of a series of personal experiences illustrating the complexities of "ethics of action." These various experiences are controlled by the author's philosophical commentary as he examines each one, moves to another, and reaches his concluding remarks about the effects of power and the nature of man. This essay illustrates two important principles of effective writing: (1) that the use of detailed and concrete examples prevents clichés and platitudes; (2) that honesty in the essay is as refreshing as it is elsewhere.

SUGGESTIONS FOR WRITING

1. The author cites Lord Acton's famous statement, "Power corrupts." Write an essay demonstrating the truth of this statement. You might do well to show how power has corrupted *you*, not Fidel Castro. Ask yourself honestly how your behavior changes when you are babysitting, or driving a powerful car, or serving as an officer in a club, or when you have been asked to do an important favor for someone.

2. Conduct an investigation of bribery as it is practiced in your circle of acquaintances. Compile a list of examples, study them, arrange them into appropriate sequence, reach a conclusion, and then write your paper. The most difficult questions will be the most rewarding: Is it bribery to do more than your instructor requires? Is a date a bribe? Are good manners bribes for status?

3. Mr. Bailey tells us that all ethical questions ultimately revert to propositions about the nature of man. Take an ethical question (almost any question beginning with "Is it right . . .") and show how various answers grow out of differing estimates of the nature of the human being. Don't choose this topic unless you are prepared to give it considerable thought.

WHO'S AFRAID
OF A LITTLE GAME?

Stephen Birmingham

AS AN ALL-ROUND NONATHLETE, one of the questions I am frequently asked is: Why are you invited to take part in so many sporting contests? It is a good question. Tennis weekends at Southampton, polo matches at Meadowbrook, golf at St. Andrews—invitations to bucket along on such snazzy athletic jaunts are always coming my way with no effort on my part.

And these are only three of perhaps 114 sports at which I display no proficiency whatsoever. Just the other day, over cold expense-account lobster and baby peas at the Plaza, I was urged to play on a field hockey team that was meeting the following Saturday at Greenwich, Conn. As usual, I accepted. I do not, of course, have the slightest notion of how to play field hockey. I cannot recall that I have ever seen the game played. Certainly this was no time for me to learn.

In the car going up, I said casually that I played field hockey the way the British did—I hoped they didn't mind. This caused appropriate consternation and uneasiness among the team members. The day was drizzly and damp, which put the weather decidedly in my favor. When we arrived at Greenwich I made a few rapid-fire calculations. The field looked soggy, and I said so, but added cheerfully, "Well, who's afraid of a little mud?"

There were, on the faces of some members of the team, looks which seemed to reflect grim resignation. Possibly there were those to whom the prospect of playing in the rain was less than merry. However, since the only ones who had showed up on our side were the 11 players, plus one spindly and unusable-looking manager, I knew that if I used a technique which took me out of the game personally, but left the team short-handed, I would be marked unmistakably as a rat. So whatever I did would have to be in the direction of getting the game called off altogether. In a loud

First published in *Sports Illustrated*; © 1960 Time Inc. Reprinted by permission of Brandt & Brandt.

voice I said, "You know, I've played this game so much lately that frankly I'm a little sick of it. Darn near threw my stick away. Anybody here get as bored with it as I do?"

Nobody answered, and a few minutes later, as we were lacing ourselves into our uniforms and the rain was coming down with increased velocity, I was wondering desperately if I would be forced to demolish a shin guard with a spiked shoe. "Say," I said suddenly, "we can play hockey any time. But look—here we are, with 12 men on our side, and 12 men on their side. How often do you get a perfect setup like that for six tables of bridge?'"

As we sat down at the table, I said, "Of course, I only play the South African transfer." Thus I made the Greenwich trip, had a wonderful time, returned to New York with my friendships unbroken as my shins, and no one guessed that I did not know how to play field hockey—or bridge.

How do I manage to get so much fun of sport with none of the effort it ordinarily requires? Simple. I have taught myself to talk a good game. Field hockey, I tell everyone, is a wonderful game. I like it almost as much as Belgian pigeon flying. I find the trips to faroff places that you get when you play field hockey are every bit as exciting as the annual Toulouse-to-Brussels pigeon race. Of course, talking a good game has its own variety of thrills, spills and rewards to the victor. At the last moment, when all else seems to have failed, and you are about to pile out onto the field and disgrace yourself, great resourcefulness is needed if you are to extricate yourself from the situation. To avoid playing field hockey in Greenwich, I used a variety of techniques to create the illusion of playing without actually doing so. This is not so difficult as the bruised noninitiate might think.

Suppose, for example, that like many of us (more than will admit it) you are not a skier. Well, you are still fond of weekends in the country, aren't you? If a friendly voice booms over long distance, "Come up to Vermont for a little skiing!" the invitation will be summarily withdrawn if you mutter lamely, "Yeah, but I can't ski."

What you must do is go, and create the impression of skiing without actually skiing. Of course, in talking a good game, some care is necessary. Certainly there is no sorrier *gaffe* than a sports *gaffe*. I am thinking of the North Shore debutante who, during a discussion of the Patterson-Johansson fight, inquired, "Let's see—is that Sugar Ray Johansson?" Or the fellow who said, in reference to Bob Feller's 1940 no-run, no-hit game: "I've never followed football too closely." My mother put down the newspaper a few afternoons ago and said, "They're talking about the World Series. I thought they had that last year." It is hard to say which is the more disgraceful—admitting total ignorance of a sport, admitting one can't play it, or using incorrect terms while pretending one *can* play it.

But if you know how to talk a good game you need face none of these distasteful alternatives. To show how simple it all is, I have set down a few easily-remembered rules:

I. SHOUT. Nothing creates a firmer impression of athletic ability and knowledge than a confident, even strident, tone. Explosiveness throws your questioner off, makes him think he has accidentally stumbled on the one sport at which you really excel, and causes him to wonder if you aren't a good deal better at it than he is.

II. SMILE. If asked if you would like to do a little trapshooting, smile as you shout, "Trapshooting! By God! Yes." Or laugh cheerily as you come back with a sharp, quick "When?" Chuckle, as if over some private joke.

III. CRY. Well, not really cry—but it is sometimes advantageous, when the name of a sport comes into the conversation, to act sad. Or act insulted. This has the effect of implying that something rather unpleasant once happened to you, long ago, perhaps in a ringtoss game—possibly the loss of a dear friend, or a front tooth. Since the sport stirs up harsh memories for you, it was really very tactless of anybody to mention it in your presence.

IV. USE SPORTING TERMS. This is vitally important—no matter which of the three previous reactions you select. Pepper your speech with all-purpose athletic jargon, such as team spirit, the rulebook, locker room, gear, AAU, trick shoulder, Fanny Blankers-Koen, trick knee, fracture, body English, fans, jock strap, pulled tendon, Peter Dawkins, pulled ligament. Terms such as these, larded into your conversation, will mark you unmistakably as an all-round sports expert. Note that I have mentioned the name of one woman athlete and one man. When the talk turns to women in sport you can put in with: "What about Fanny Blankers-Koen?"

If the sports talk is general you can interject with perfect safety: "How do you suppose Dawkins would have handled it?" (If Peter Dawkins' nickname were Spike—which it isn't—it would be effective to use this. In sports parlance, however, the use of the last name only is common, which means you will appear more knowledgeable if you refer to Peter Dawkins simply as Dawkins.) The word gear is even more useful. It is handy when referring to sports cars and motorboats and Italian bicycles, all of which have gears, and can also be used in this context: "I'd love to play, but darn it, I left all my gear in Chicago!" (Of course, if you are already in Chicago, this must be modified by using the name of some other place.)

These examples are for beginners. For the specialist, or advanced good-game talker, there are key words and authoritative terms to fit specific sports that should be learned. The novice should exercise a bit of caution here. It is important that the key word relating to each sport be carefully selected before it is permanently placed in the vocabulary. The key word should not, to begin with, be an obvious one. Everyone knows that the word umpire relates to baseball. The person who selects umpire as his key to talking a good baseball game is getting nowhere. A more effective baseball term would be "2 o'clock hitter."

In addition, it is wise for the advanced talker to have the name of one important but obscure celebrity for each sport. To continue with our example of baseball, the name of Babe Ruth would obviously be wrong for the important but obscure celebrity of that game. Better would be a name like W. H. Van Cott, who was the first president of the National Association of Baseball Players when it was organized in 1858.

V. DRESS RIGHT. Always have the right clothes for the game—or some of them. Arrive with an expensive, fitted golf bag, but no clubs (they must have been stolen from the trunk of the car). At that weekend of skiing in Vermont, arrive with a handsome pair of ski pants and the left member of a pair of imported ski boots. The right one, by a stupid oversight, was left out of your suitcase by the maid (or wife) who packed for you. Show up for tennis with a white cable stitch sweater, a splendid pair of tennis shoes and no shorts. Or show up with everything but the shoes. Display a broken ski or tennis racket or polo mallet, a cracked lacrosse stick, a bent fencing foil, a leaky regulator for your Aqualung. You leave the impression, this way, that you are not only an enthusiastic and strenuous player of the sport in question, but that, alas, for the time being anyway, you are out of commission.

VI. REFUSE TO BORROW. Always "feel funny" about using someone else's things. Others will almost certainly try to lend you what you need. Do not let them. You must never feel right about accepting borrowed goods. The reason you don't feel right about using someone else's squash racket is that you know how fiercely you guard your own squash racket. You would feel pretty badly if something happened to that borrowed racket while you were playing with it. What if you broke it? Of course, if the person offering you the racket continues adamant, break it is what you must do, by putting your foot through it on the way to the courts.

VII. ACQUIRE BAD HABITS. Bad habits are the mark of the true athlete, and if you are trying to pose as an athlete you must confess to having picked up some. They will stand you in good stead when it comes to avoiding the contest. In golf, for example, the commonest bad habit is the slice. "I've got to work on this slice of mine—gosh knows where I've picked it up," you say. "You fellows play around, and I'll go out and slam a few pails on the driving range." (Note how golfy the poseur's language sounds with the adroit sprinkling of such expressions as "play around" and "slam out" and "pails.") Your companions, of course, will have no way of knowing whether you are working on your slice on the driving range or on a gin and tonic at the clubhouse.

With tennis, the bad habit can be a faulty serve, and with almost any sport it can be: "This funny thing I've been doing with my foot lately. I don't want to play a serious game until I've spent a little time on it—by myself. I think, frankly, I've been using a little too much body English, but I may be wrong."

VIII. FOLLOW BRITISH STANDARDS. As I did in the field hockey and bridge crises, say you "play it the way the British play it." This is a sneaky one. It always helps to build up an atmosphere of discouragement, and it may serve at the last moment when all else has failed, and you are about to have to go out and face calamity. This remark will be received with open mouths and unbelieving stares. Talk loudly, smile and say something about Oxford and Cambridge and Eton and Harrow, and then add, "So suppose I sit here and watch you fellows slug it out for a while, until I get the hang of your rulebook."

IX. HAVE AN OLD INJURY. Mention a sports-connected disability. Obvi-ously, ordinary injuries (stubbed toes, sprained ankles, smashed thumbs) or everyday ailments (colds, viruses, stomach-aches) do not carry the weight in the sports world of those directly the result of sport (cracked ribs, separated shoulders, the bends). And if you have been asked to play something, the injury with the most prestige is the one that clearly came about from playing that particular game, and not some other.

X. LOOK FOR ALLIES. Learn to spot other nonathletes. They are your friends. They are on your side, and when the time comes for choosing up sides, this means that you are on the side that's against choosing up sides. When the subject comes up—"Let's all go out and knock the old ball around for a couple of hours before dinner"—you can spot your fellow nonathletes by the way their faces light up too brightly. You will recognize their frozen smiles, their furtive looks at their watches and the way their eyes travel quickly around the room to see how everybody is taking the suggestion. You should sidle over and say, "Gosh, there's nothing I'd like better than a good game of touch football right now, but with this trick knee of mine. . . ." A nonsporting type will give you a quick grateful look, and you can proceed with, "So what do you say you and I have a gin and tonic on the terrace?"

XI. KNOW EVERYTHING. You will have a much better time at sports gatherings and house parties if, in the conversation, you can establish yourself as an expert in one sport and keep steering the conversation back to it. You will have for all sports significant names and phrases, but for this one sport—preferably an esoteric one—you will be invincible in your knowledge. Falconers being in short supply these days (scarcer than chicken hawks' teeth), you will not find many people who will pick you up on your falconry or want to join you in the field with your tercel to go after a little quarry.

XII. BE EXHAUSTED. Say you've played too much lately. This is a tricky one to bring off. If your host wants a brisk workout with the beanbags, it isn't so easy to squash his plan by sighing that you've tossed so many beanbags lately you're a little sick of it. If a young lady asks you to join her on the trampoline, it is hard to say that where trampolines are concerned you are all bounced out. Invited to explore the *Andrea Doria,* you can't very well imply that you've been down there too often. Some sports, in other words, simply do not lend themselves to this rule. The fed-up-with-it-all routine, however, can be combined with missing or damaged equipment. The phrase "I just threw it away" is a useful one here. A young New Yorker friend of mine was asked to the Harvard Club for lunch and a little squash, and because he was fond of lunch, but not squash, he said, "Thank you, but I got so fed up with squash the other day that I threw away my racket!" His squash-playing friend was immediately sympathetic. "I know just how you feel," he said. "So come over and have lunch anyway."

XIII. HAVE WIDE INTERESTS. Suggest another game. There is on record an occasion where—with a single, last-minute suggestion—a whole roomful of croquet players, beady-eyed with desire for some roughhouse over the wickets, was diverted to an afternoon of dominoes. Clearly, not all the rules are applicable to all cases. And often it is not one rule, but a winning combination of several rules that will save the day. Talking a good game, you see, is really a sport in itself. To play it well, the player must choose his own rules as he goes along—playing it, from time to time, entirely by ear. He must size up his opponent, reckon his strength. When I got out of playing field hockey that afternoon in Greenwich, I really used a combination of Rules XII and XIII—both professing to be fed up with field hockey and, at the last moment, suggesting another game.

A great deal depends, of course, on timing, and a great deal more depends on luck. After all, if you are a pure good-game talker, all your efforts should be bent toward forestalling any game, or at least your part of it. Still, there will be times when you will appear to be outnumbered. With the force of a great tide, the handball players will be dragging you onto the court, the softball players will be forcing a mitt onto your hand or the skin-divers will be strapping you into a tank. You must come up with a suggestion, fast, that strikes everyone as a better thing to do than the thing at hand. Only good-game talking of championship caliber will save you here, for the suggestion must be one appropriate to the circumstances as well as one that extricates you from your dilemma. It would be folly at the top of a ski jump to cry out, "Let's all go bowling!"

You should never have permitted things to go that far.

COMMENT

Generally speaking, humor should not be analyzed, but "Who's Afraid of a Little Game?" can be studied to show the ways in which close observation of speech rhythms and special vocabulary profits the writer. Not every writer can sustain irony as successfully as Mr. Birmingham does here, but the basic technique of saying one thing when you mean something else is familiar to all and should be in every writer's repertoire.

SUGGESTIONS FOR WRITING

Write an essay on "Three Ways to Avoid a Blind Date," "How to Play the Field and Go Steady at the Same Time," "How to Go to a Dance without Dancing," "Four Simple Ways to Avoid Paying the Check." Other subjects of this kind will recommend themselves to you upon consideration. Don't underestimate your audience; humor requires no comment or explanation.

Head, Heart and Hand Outstretched

KENNETH EBLE

TO RIGHT-THINKING MEN everywhere, college football is and has been from its inception a beastly sport. Its players are snake-hipped and ox-headed; its coaches have the guile of foxes and the hides of elephants; its supporters roar like the lion and bray like the ass. Yet the beast survives. Over almost every college campus its banner flies: head in helmet, heart on a chalk-striped field, hand outstretched.

The alchemy which unites pigskin and egghead is as mysterious as the reasons why some college presidents become positive boobies when they contemplate the glories of their athletic programs. Every year, college professors damn big-time athletics. Every two or three years, a committee meets to investigate. Every decade, writers summarize athletics' sorry record. Seldom has so thoroughly discredited an activity maintained such vigorous life and in such high-principled company.

What is new, if anything, about this old sordid story is that college athletics today have won full acceptance as legitimate university activities, and with acceptance, tacit approval of practices which even a backward school, much less a major university, might have frowned upon twenty-five years ago. College athletics thrive today chiefly because of corrupt practices which have been incorporated into codes of legitimate conduct.

Initially, intercollegiate athletics gained a place in the universities, insofar as academic men had anything to do with it, as a result of idealism, wistfulness, and expediency. *Mens sana in corpore sano* was the classical ideal which obscured the dubious relationship. The wistfulness which men who spend their lives chasing abstractions often feel toward violent physical contact lent attractiveness to the ideal. For university presidents facing the necessity of distilling raw animal spirits into purer forms, football seemed a likely expedient. That it could add to a college's fame and increase its income made its expediency certain.

Reprinted by permission of the author and of *The Columbia University Forum*.

49

Once established, college athletics drew heavily upon ambition, pride, and sentimentality. In the Midwest, where football frenzy was passed on from the East, personal sentiments were mixed with the universities' ambitions and the states' pride. Schools without traditions manufactured them. In Iowa, a pig became one of the spoils of victory. He was called Floyd of Rosedale and was probably the only resident of the state who didn't much care whether Iowa beat Minnesota. All over the land, the newspapers ground out stories about heart and grit and playing the game.

Today, these simpler impulses of the past have been largely replaced by the philosophy of mercenary idealism: the outstretched hand and the question, "How much?" An army of recruiters sells the full free ride like pardoners peddling indulgences. An eternity of losing seasons yawns for the coach who fails to exact his tithes. "At Iowa State," said the young coach who was leaving for Texas A. & M., "I had very little money to develop my athletic dreams. There was little money in the budget, little money for recruiting athletes and not much in the way of facilities to attract the athletes we could contact. There is no comparison between our facilities now at College Station and at Iowa State. For example, we have seven new cars assigned to the athletic department, and I can't wait to get home to see our new athletic dormitory. We have spaces for 92 student-athletes in this new building and the entire building is air-conditioned and we have wall-to-wall carpeting."

Recruiting is at the center of the corruption which marks big-time college sports. In 1929, the Carnegie investigation called subsidizing and recruiting "the most disgraceful phase" of intercollegiate athletics. Today, recruiting flourishes, sanctioned by a code which is not so much a guide to conduct as a measure of earning power. Under the NCAA regulations, when financial aid to an athlete "exceeds commonly accepted educational expenses (tuition and fees, room and board, books, and not to exceed $15 per month for laundry) . . . it shall be considered to be 'pay' for participation." The principles regulating recruiting activities are equally delicate. Coaches cannot offer more financial inducement than the free ride; each college gets to pay for the prospect's visit to the campus one time "and one time only"; the prospect cannot bring along relatives or girl friends except at his own expense; entertainments are restricted to two days and two nights and must not be "excessive." It is as if banks condoned embezzlement as long as the embezzlers followed the regulations set forth by the National Board of Peculation.

How far athletics have developed in thirty years can be roughly measured by comparing present legitimate practices with the practices criticized in the Carnegie Foundation report. Henry S. Pritchett summarized the findings:

The paid coach, the special training tables, the costly sweaters and extensive journeys in special Pullman cars, the recruiting from the high school, the demoralizing publicity showered on the players, the devotion of an undue proportion of time to training, the devices for putting a desirable athlete, but a weak scholar, across the hurdles of the examinations—these ought to stop and the intercollege and intramural sports be brought back to a stage in which they can be enjoyed by a large number of students and where they do not involve an expenditure of time and money wholly at variance with any ideal of honest study.

None of these practices have stopped. The NCAA, which shared the feeling for reform in the 1920's, has brought most of these activities in under the code. That those involved in athletics still find ways to violate the rules proves that intercollegiate athletics does, indeed, sharpen the wits. The recurring scandals—basketball fixing, cheating, tampering with academic records, condoned brutality, contract-jumping, slush funds—suggest that weakening the code is no way to strengthen the character.

For the athletic mess, the universities have themselves to blame. The NCAA, though topheavy in its administration with coaches and athletic directors, is a college and university body. As long ago as 1922, it adopted a resolution urging "absolute faculty control" of athletics. And though faculty members of football universities know how far from "absolute" even absolute faculty control is, they probably have more control than they have ever exercised. The reasons they haven't exercised it are not hard to find.

In the first place, American colleges and universities have never been much concerned with the intellectual life. The colleges and universities that do honor the intellectual life are those like Reed, Antioch, Chicago, Johns Hopkins, which do not maintain big-time athletics, or those, like the Ivy League schools, which have achieved in recent years a measure of de-emphasis. It is well to remember that the level of intellectual life in the Ivy League schools when football grew to power was probably not much higher than it is in the state universities today.

In the state universities, now the chief supporters of inflated athletic programs, the intellectual life is the concern of a small group at best. The liberal arts college within the state university is often the most keen in its criticism of the university's athletic practices, but even within this college, faculty members hold widely differing views. Some genuinely enjoy the game. Others tolerate it as one among many human follies. Many are creatures of habit, and being in the stadium on Saturday afternoons is not much different from being in the super market on Saturday mornings.

When Phi Beta Kappa refused to grant new chapters to institutions whose aid to athletes was out of proportion to aid granted other students, faculty members from some liberal arts colleges objected to such a firm stand. They pointed out, with some justice, that the regulations were not being applied to existing Phi Beta Kappa chapters. With less justice and a shrinking sense of responsibility, they also argued that the liberal arts college was too small to control university policy and that the liberal arts college breathed a purer air than that of the fieldhouse. Phi Beta Kappa has stood by its principles, but it is virtually the only organization within or related to the academic cosmos that has.

In the second place, college and university faculties are singularly inept at doing anything about their problems. Academic protests against low salaries have been as numerous, and as futile, as those against athletics. Members of faculty senates, fierce exponents of democracy, inveigh against the fraternity and sorority system and then approve the appointment of one more assistant dean of student life to assist in inter-fraternity affairs. Cheating in the classroom, autocracy in the administration building, and an entangling bureaucracy throughout the campus are other problems which were long ago placed on the committee agenda and which have never been taken off.

Third, the athletic departments have flummoxed the academicians by playing their kind of game. They have become research departments, amassing books and monographs, acquiring equipment, and graduating M.A.'s and Ph.D.'s. An academic department of any kind is as hard to dislodge as an ape from a tree. When it has stored up the fruits of research, it is invulnerable. On the playing field, coaches operate within a complex of scouts, spies, and spotters equipped with binoculars, field phones, and wrist radios. Off the field, they read monographs like "Two and Three Dimensional Slide Images Used with Tachistoscopic Training Techniques in Instructing Football Players in Defenses," or articles beginning, "Bat selection is a profoundly important task." Such absurdities of title and profundities of thought are, of course, not uncommon to other academic periodicals, but no other journals are so solemn and pious. Only in *The Athletic Journal,* "America's First Coaching Magazine," is one likely to find the "Huddle Prayer," specially written for the Pop Warner Conference for Kiddie Football by Father Cavanaugh of Notre Dame, Rabbi Max Klein, and Norman Vincent Peale:

> Grant us the strength, Dear Lord, to play
>   This game with all our might;
> And while we're doing it we pray
>   You'll keep us in your sight;
> That we may never say or do
> A thing that gives offense to you.

Finally, the vast momentum the game has picked up over the years rolls over the most strenuous efforts at reform. Today's players become the I-men and the coaches for the next generation, and in many states, the high school principals and superintendents. College publicity departments grind out the copy upon which the daily newspapers feed. To the sports fraternity, as they call themselves, the existence of big-time athletics in the universities is proof enough that they are desirable and relevant activities. "While there will be a segment of the egghead species in educational circles," the sports editor of my daily paper wrote recently, "that abhors even the hint of physical exertion aside from the pursuit and capture of academic degrees, the average professor looks upon athletic activity in a true light."

If any substantial changes take place in the conduct of college athletics, they will not come about because of the actions of conscience-stricken men. Rather they will be the result of athletic practices themselves and of changing conditions in higher education. There is some evidence that athletic handouts are already causing indigestion. Bud Wilkinson recently warned his fellow coaches that students weren't going out for football. "Part of it," he said, "is probably due to the fact that we all contact athletes. If a boy doesn't get a scholarship then he apparently feels unwanted." Ten years ago at Oklahoma, the freshman squad consisted of 110 athletes. Last year, only 37 turned out, 27 of whom were on athletic scholarships. The glory of varsity sports, always a dubious reward for the hamburger squads, is today pretty much proportional to the cash received, and the price of hamburger is going up. The cost of athletic programs is as hard to find out as an office-mate's salary, but certainly the majority of big athletic programs lose money, some a great deal of money. Partly because of the expense, the number of colleges playing football dropped from 709 in 1940, to 690 in 1947, and 623 in 1959. As costs increase, even more will give up the sport.

The recruiting of players has had another consequence. In football, players are bought by the pound; in basketball, by the yard. High school athletes of ordinary dimensions, however impressive their records, are not prime prospects for athletic scholarships. The catering to exceptional physical specimens has separated college athletics from the spectators and from the undergraduates whose duty it is to whip up frenzy for the game. Gigantism, specialization of function, and intensive coaching have not made the team sports better spectacles. Despite tinkering with the rules, basketball threatens to score itself out of public interest and football to expire from interminable delays.

The changing character of higher education also seems to be having an impact upon big-time athletics. Columbia's president was reported in my local paper as telling his alumni, "I hope you may feel that some of the prestige Columbia has lost in football in these years has been offset by the award of four Nobel Prizes to Columbia men in the last three years

and of another Nobel Prize this year to another Columbia College graduate." The chancellor of the University of Denver, Chester Alter, flatly
predicted that the days of big-time football were numbered. California, a
West Coast reporter wrote, is going Ivy League. And James L. Morrill,
retiring president of Minnesota, defended a losing coach: "Athletic entertainment is not the primary purpose of the University of Minnesota or
the justification for its existence."

This last remark from the Midwest, a region passionately attached to
football, basketball, and funny papers, is a significant one. There is a
logic in thinking that the Big Ten schools may before long de-emphasize.
Universities like Minnesota, Michigan, Wisconsin, and others have the
physical facilities, the faculties, and can select the students which would
make them primarily intellectual institutions. States are already seeing
the wisdom and the economy of using the smaller public and private colleges as the general undergraduate college and of reserving the state university for a *higher* higher education. The subordination of sports to intellect in the Big Ten would do much to restore sanity to college athletics.

I have the feeling that even now, big-time sports are maintaining themselves largely on the accumulated glories of the past. This would explain
why, on college faculties, the support for football comes from aging professors of the classics as well as from young professors of athletic administration. Those faculty members nearing retirement age now were undergraduates in the golden days of the sport. They had Knute Rockne in the
flesh. The young professors had to settle for Pat O'Brien. Those now in
the graduate school lack even so much. Students, it seems to me, are less
"gung ho" than before the war. Band directors tell me it's hard to get the
band out on Saturday afternoons, and at pep rallies on our campus, the
players frequently outnumber the boosters.

If athletics do subside, it will not be because of moral indignation, and
its decline will be attended by wailing and weeping and gnashing of
teeth. Recognition of a changing attitude toward sports, if such an attitude comes about, will come slowly to the booster clubs, the athletic departments, and the newspapers. These groups have never been disturbed
by the disparity between the shoddiness of athleticism and the high purposes of a university. They have preserved the myths of sport long after
such myths have lost what small part of truth they may once have possessed.

The melancholy truth is that reached by Plato long ago. Man's glory
is his reason, but it exists at the small end of the triangle. He carries with
him "the heavy bear," and in the end as in the beginning, the beast will
have him. Civilization is still a clearing in the jungle, and if apes gambol
in the public square, one may be dismayed but should not be surprised.

COMMENT

This essay is about intercollegiate football, but its basic organization may be adapted to many other uses: What is the present condition? How did it come about? Who is at fault? What are the prospects for improvement? Notice how skillfully the transitional elements (Initially . . . Once established . . . Today . . .) work to keep the reader informed about his progress through the argument. The beginning writer will do well to observe that Mr. Eble does not attempt to discuss the broad subject of intercollegiate football in 500 words.

SUGGESTIONS FOR WRITING

1. Select some activity or enterprise which you feel has grown out of proportion or is becoming unhealthy. Organize your thinking around the four subdivisions Mr. Eble uses in his essay. Write your paper on one of these subdivisions.

2. Write an essay on school spirit in which you dispose of all such matters as dances, games, and parades in the first paragraph.

3. Conduct your own investigation into the subject of intercollegiate football. Who are the most enthusiastic fans? Freshmen? Seniors? Graduate students? Alumni? Townspeople? Discriminate between the subclasses of the groups and write an essay evaluating intercollegiate football on the basis of the audience to whom it most strongly appeals.

Kingsley Amis

The Delights
of Literary Lecturing

PUBLIC LECTURING IN AMERICA is the perfect vehicle for that rich compound of vanity and greed which makes up the literary character. I say
"in America" not because Americans are particularly devoted to the two
qualities mentioned, but because in Britain, at least, neither of them will
get much of an outing at this form of sport: "I'm sorry so few people
have turned up," one is likely to be told, "but our Mr. Snodgrass is also
lecturing tonight—on French cathedrals—with lantern slides," and again,
"I'm sorry the fee is so tiny, but we find if we charge admission nobody
turns up at all."

In America, under I know not what system of inducement or threat,
enough people will turn up to tickle even a writer's vanity, and greed is
abundantly satisfied. Instead of having to wait a couple of months for
five pounds, the common fate in England, one will probably be given the
check before the audience has finished assembling, and if by any chance
payment should be deferred until afterwards a good reason will be forthcoming: in Washington, I seemed to gather, a compatriot of mine got
his little envelope after the preludial dinner and was never seen again.

Conscious of having had either one martini too few or one too many
(a finer literary judgment is needed here than most of us possess), the
lecturer makes his way to the podium and does his stuff, imperturbable
and trying to sound improvisatory with his dog-eared script, uneasily
alert for any face in the audience that even slightly recalls anybody who
may have heard him deliver the identical talk last week in a different part
of the town. This phobia is perhaps an integral part of the academic
neurosis, likely to afflict all who have had to go through the motions,
year after year, of sounding sprightly about *The Mill on the Floss* or
Martin Chuzzlewit in front of undergraduate audiences; this year's lot
look and behave so much like last year's lot that you can never quite convince yourself they are not the same lot. You need all your reasoning
power for the reflection that nobody who has had to take two runs at
the Freshman Novel Program (as it might be called in this country) is

Reprinted from *Harper's Magazine* by permission of the author.

in danger of recognizing a supposed epigram however often it might be repeated.

But to abandon thoughts of home: our literary lecturer in America will meet, if he has been at all conscientious in preparing his remarks, a polite and attentive reception. The only man who ever made faces at me while I was holding forth turned out to be an official of Her Majesty's Government, which I was mildly denouncing at the time; they were mild faces too. Even that potentially dreadful aftermath, the question period, will generally slip harmlessly by without intervention from the aggressively well-informed or even the plain madman. Those well-tested life belts —asking for a 250-word question to be repeated, answering it with a monosyllable, breaking into uncontrollable laughter, etc.—can be left unused.

My one major error (the only one I know of, anyway) was committed when I gave an address at a well-known university in Philadelphia. Exhausted by the ceaseless search for wit, I had decided to abandon trying to tell jokes and deliver instead what was conceived as a hideously sophisticated joke in action: a long, humorless, pseudo-academic diatribe on the comic spirit recited absolutely deadpan by a supposed comic writer. As I recall—and one does not recall these things well, being concerned only to maintain continuity and aplomb, for all the world like somebody who has had too much to drink—as I recall it went down rather badly, except for a reference to vomiting which laid a single undergraduate in the aisle. But retribution was swift: during the postludial party at the fraternity house somebody stole my script, which naturally, having a living to earn, I had been intending to run off elsewhere a few weeks later. I see now, of course, that the right way to interpret the felony was as (a) a blow against authority, to be welcomed as such, and (b) a second joke in action, a good deal more pointed and economical than my own. But I thought differently then.

It must have been vanity rather than greed which induced me to appear on a kind of public panel in a playhouse in New York: the topic, *Is There a Beat Generation?* My colleagues were Mr. James Wechsler, the editor of the New York *Post,* Mr. Ashley Montagu, the anthropologist, and Mr. Jack Kerouac, who as they say needs no introduction. At the preludial dinner it was explained that Mr. Kerouac was very nice, perfectly charming in fact, provided he was convinced that those present were on his side, felt sympathetic to him, in short *liked him.* I said I saw what was meant. Over in the theater we encountered Mr. Kerouac, conservatively attired in giant's-chessboard shirt, black jeans, and pigskin ankle boots. With hand on hip he piped to me, "Hallo, my dear" (I did need a haircut at the time, admittedly) and said to Mr. Montagu, "I saw you on the Jack Paar show. You didn't have anything new to say."

Having thus variously put the pair of us at our ease, he crossed to the backstage piano without giving us the chance to tell him how much we liked him. Then, seating himself at the instrument, he began a version of the dear old "Warsaw Concerto," but broke off every now and then to appear before the photographers. When he did this he weaved and bobbed rather as if about to start what we squares used to call jitterbugging. The "Warsaw Concerto" gave place at one stage to a boogie-woogie left hand, but was resumed after an interval when no boogie-woogie right hand was forthcoming.

Though Mr. Wechsler had still not arrived, some sort of gesture toward getting started was obviously called for. We trooped onto the stage and huge high-pitched enthusiasm arose from certain sections of the audience, a salute intended not for Mr. Montagu or me, I recognized sadly, but for Mr. Kerouac, who responded with more weaves, bobs, and a chimpanzee-shuffle or two. After some determinedly sedate remarks from the chair, Mr. Kerouac arose for what we all thought was understood to be a ten-minute stint. During it, a stocky figure with overcoat thrown open entered at the back of the hall and made its way onto the stage; no beatnik an-arch, as I had begun to fear, but Mr. Wechsler, in pretty good shape after a three-day editorial crisis and soon disabused of the idea that I was Mr. Montagu. Mr. Kerouac was talking about a swinging group of new American boys intent on life, forecasting the appointment of a beat Secretary of State, and saluting Humphrey Bogart, Laurel and Hardy, and Popeye as ancestral beats. Half an hour or so later he said he would read his poem on Harpo Marx. The texture of his discourse did not change. Throughout it seemed to illustrate the theme of the symposium rather than actually expound it.

Next there was me. Then there was Mr. Wechsler, who performed the considerable feat of advocating political commitment in terms that were both rational and free of cliché. Right at the start of it Mr. Kerouac muttered, "I can't stand this activist crap," and, wearing Mr. Wechsler's hat, began a somnambulistic pacing of the stage, occasionally breaking off to wave balletically at the photographers in the wings. He went on doing this while Mr. Montagu's ironies flew above the beat sections of the audience.

Finally there was "discussion." Mr. Kerouac accused Mr. Wechsler, very inaccurately, of having said a lot about what he didn't believe in and nothing about what he did believe in. Mr. Wechsler gamely responded with a capsule version of positive views. Mr. Kerouac leaned on the podium and said, "Admit it, Wechsler, you came here tonight determined to hate me." It was clear that none of us had managed to convince him that we liked him.

Disengaging myself from a 250-pound brunette who had leaped onto the stage to assure me that, contrary to my apparent belief, there was a beat generation, I followed the others out, reflecting that Mr. Kerouac's performance had acted as a useful supplement to his novels in demonstrating how little spontaneity has to do with talking off the top of the head. I also wondered, and still do, just what it is that people anywhere in the world get out of attending discussions or lectures by literary persons. For the majority, I imagine, one might as well speak in Choctaw; the visual appeal is what counts. For all his evident casualness, Mr. Kerouac was shrewd enough to have grasped that.

COMMENT

When the reader finishes reading this essay, he discovers that Mr. Amis has expressed both his disenchantment with literary lecturing in general and his distaste for Mr. Kerouac in particular without ever expressing any direct judgment on either. This technique of attack by indirection is worth study. Notice that one of the chief requirements for the satirical writer is a respect for the intelligence of his audience.

SUGGESTIONS FOR WRITING

1. Try using one of the time-honored methods of satire. Pretend you are a foreigner writing a letter home. Describe some custom which we accept without much question but which seems ridiculous when seen by an outsider.

2. Take some attitude or action of which you thoroughly disapprove. Pretend that you think it so fine that it should be extended; describe its extension to a ridiculous conclusion without suggesting that you think it ridiculous. Look at Jonathan Swift's "A Modest Proposal" for an example of this technique.

The American's
ENGLAND

ALISTAIR COOKE

BETWEEN the *Edinburgh Review*'s sneering, "Who reads an American book?" and Frank Sinatra's singing, "A Foggy Day in London Town" stands almost a century and a half of archetypes, or pattern-books, of Anglo-American compliments and insults. In all this time there has been an increasing exchange of trade, bric-a-brac, scholarship, technical skill, literature, fashion fads, and tourism. In the last few years, industrial know-how has been at the back of an overnight transatlantic flight either way. And now we are embedded in a shotgun marriage forced on us by the rise of the new Russian Empire at a time when lethal missiles can span a continent in minutes.

Yet the impressions that most travellers carry away from each other's country, or very likely bring with them to reinforce at first hand, do not vary much down the decades. They reflect certain permanent preconceptions picked up, generation after generation, in childhood, sometimes suppressed or modified by education but rarely plucked out. "Is it true that American women rule the country?" asks an eager young Englishman cocking an eye at the Statue of Liberty. "The trouble with England is, it's an old country," says an old American stirring his martini on the rocks. The themes are simple, often easily refutable, but they are held to by Prime Ministers and chorus girls alike. They receive their undying expression in the tabloids of both countries, which are, after all, what most people read.

The Englishman's America, as I assemble it from random pieces in the papers and from conversations provoked in places as far apart as Blackpool and Land's End, is still Dickens's America, with a few streamlined touches. The American people, I am told, are slick in the cities, oafish in the hinterland; their politicians are aggressive and sentimental, save for charming exceptions with English names (e.g., Stevenson, and now Kennedy). They are inventive, volatile, and humorous, but solemn about sports, gregarious and yet somehow full of loneliness. They lack discipline

Reprinted from *The Manchester Guardian* by permission of the author.

in general and spoil children in particular. Nowadays they are obsessed with sex, the Russians, gadgets, money-making, and cars. (It is useless to begin to return these boomerangs to their owners; the examples shriek aloud. Few communities outside a Cornish village or a German country town could be so humourless as American small towns. And it would be hard to discover anywhere such a daily obsession with sex as one finds in the London popular press.)

What is the corresponding American picture of Britain? From a galloping poll of students, bankers, textile men, economists, housewives, newsprint salesmen, glamour girls, and airline hostesses, I am offered the following picture. Of a quaint old land pierced by cathedral spires and roofed with thatch. Of soldiers in musical comedy costumes expressing in rhythm the universal obeisance to the Queen and (we presume) to the "aristocracy." Of adorable Regency crescents, slope-front desks, Queen Anne lowboys, all the charming ornaments of the past. Of a people at once prim and formal but exceedingly polite. Of quaint taxi-cabs that turn on one wheel. Of good Scotch and dull food. Of something vague but admirable called "tradition." Of incongruous and slightly hilarious novelties like Lady Docker, Angry Young Men, and "the telly." Of a green, green countryside and Churchill. Churchill, indeed, is a priceless symbol, and when he goes the American image of Britain will lose some of its splendour; for he represents the sort of courage they admire, the downright alternatives (Russia v. Civilisation) they yearn to believe in, the pawky humour and rolling eloquence their Senators would like to possess: all the tough qualities on a gigantic scale, dressed out with a native grandeur of manner that seems right for the country of Shakespeare and Coronations.

It may be said that one picture is that of Britons who dislike America, and the other of Americans who like England. One trouble about finding the fair equation is that Americans who are Anglophobes make a point of staying away from England and going instead to France, Italy, Spain, Greece, or Istanbul. And since nothing like a comparable proportion of Britons ever gets to the United States at all, it may well be that the analogy is false because one picture is drawn from the movies, magazines, and foreign dispatches, while the other is fashioned at first hand. But however lopsided the comparison may be, it is the one we make. And I'm afraid that if we could isolate a representative statistical sample on each side of the Atlantic, England would come out with a strong prejudice in her favour. For every Englishman who, at the mention of America, thinks of Marilyn Monroe, jazz, and racketeering there must be a corresponding American to whom England instantly suggests Churchill and cathedrals.

At first sight this is a comforting advantage. And certainly it is one that the travel agents enjoy and exploit. Most of the British tourist ad-

vertising in American magazines is uncompromisingly "picturesque" and
may be responsible for impressing on the young the stereotypes we have
mentioned: the soaring spires over Cotswold cottages, the montages of
Beefeaters, rolled-umbrella-types, hunters carrying shiny guns, the Tower
of London, and the rest. In the last few years Americans have come to
equate the choice of a particular tonic water with Rolls-Royces pulled
up to private pools, Lucullan picnics served by flunkies to mink-lined
girls in devastatingly upper-class poses.

This composite picture, so firmly printed on the brain of even the most
intelligent Americans, may well condition the choice of British news
stories featured in America. When you return here you notice that the
Queen plays a more conspicuous part in the life of Britain than even the
society slicks allow her. The row over the *Times* leader "proves" once
more that "the ruling class" has its own paper. The Watney brewery hul-
labaloo recalls the sanctity, to the little Englander, of the pub, the pint,
and the game of darts.

The total effect is of a twentieth-century museum, which, since the war,
has brushed up its pride in the works of Wren and Nash happily un-
bombed, stressed the magnificence of its landed gentry by throwing open
its great houses, and now presents for American tourists what the news-
reel commentators call "a pageant of history." It will swell the coffers
that contain the tourist dollars. But in the meantime England in 1959 is
an unknown isle living behind a grand façade. Only motorists off to the
Lake District or Scotland see much of the Midlands or the North; and
these are the Americans who make a note of "smoky, dirty cities, and
dreadful railway stations" to mar their memory of the South Country as
a perpetual golf-course. The life that John Braine writes about, Kingsley
Amis's university scamps, the normal seething life of the middle and working classes, the flesh and the devil at Blackpool, the world of Midlands
business men on expense accounts in London; the annuity wastrels; the
red-brick universities; the austere life and surroundings of the English
public-school boy compared with the American "prep school" boy; the
whole force and weight of the Labour party: these are only a few of the
essential pigments obliterated by the high colour of the stereotypes.

I doubt if one American in a hundred makes a point of getting into the
House of Commons for question-time. Thirteen years ago, the late Senator
Vandenberg was taken there by a British correspondent. He sat in the
gallery for an hour and when he came out he was visibly sweating. Asked
if he thought the institution might be adopted by the Senate, he shud-
dered: "Not in my time, I hope. My God, these boys are tough!" It was
a momentary insight that most Americans are not looking for. They know
Emerson's dictum that the British are best in adversity. But thanks to
the ancient preconceptions, and the working-over they are getting at the

hands of the travel boys, Britain suffers more than ever to-day from a decorative, dandyish, upper-class reputation that makes no allowance for the political stalemate, for the genuine life of 90 per cent of the natives, or for that "toughness" which flourishes, too, in prosperity.

COMMENT

This essay is an interesting variation on a common type: instead of comparing two countries, Mr. Cooke compares the ideas two countries have of each other. Because he is writing for an English audience, he places more emphasis on the American's idea of England. Notice that the legitimate evidence here is not what *is* but what *seems*.

SUGGESTIONS FOR WRITING

1. Write an essay on "The Town's Gown" in which you discuss the view of college held by the people of a college town. You might reverse the procedure and write on "How the Gown Sees the Town." Study Mr. Cooke's essay for methods to use.

2. Describe the image of tourists held by those who live in resort areas, or you might write "A Tourist's View of the Natives."

3. What aspects of college life do you most often have to explain to folks at home? Arrange them in a pattern which will display the mistaken ideas some people have about college life.

Why Today's Teen-Agers Seem So Different

Eugene Gilbert

IF YOU BELIEVE your teen-age son and daughter are causing you a good deal more trouble than you ever gave your parents, you are probably right. On the other hand, if you are under twenty, there may be good reason for you to regard your elders as a peculiarly insensitive, outmoded, and irrational tribe.

The rift between the generations, in our time, is puzzling because the age gap between them is relatively small. Many of the parents of today's high-school set were teen-agers themselves when they married during the war and have, in effect, "grown up with their children."

Perhaps this is part of the trouble. There are other elements—a few of which I have tried to sort out in the hope that this might help the generations to put up with each other more happily.

I am not a teacher or a sociologist; I am not even the parent of a teen-ager. (I am bracing myself for this event—my son, Howard, has just passed Gesell's "golden age" of ten.) But for some fifteen years I have been carrying on an intensive study of the adolescent in a role where he is most distinctly himself—as a consumer. In 1945, when I was a college student myself, I was struck with the notion that stores and manufacturers were losing a lot of money because they were largely blind to my contemporaries' real tastes and habits. I started then to become a market researcher in a virtually unexplored field. I have been at it ever since. Today the company I head is regularly called on to probe, describe, and analyze the ways of teen-age consumers and has completed more than six million interviews with them. What kind of name, we are asked, will attract the young to a new ice-cream bar? What newspapers, magazines, TV and radio programs do they prefer and why? What makes them like or dislike a particular watch, soft drink, candy, comic book, typewriter, or jacket?

In our hunt for practical, dollars-and-cents answers to such questions we inevitably find out a good deal more. For our information, we not only

Reprinted from *Harper's Magazine* by permission of the author.

interview young people—we also use them to ask the questions. We have a nationwide network of some five thousand young poll-takers. They represent all social strata—children of business and professional men, farmers, white collar and manual workers. They are sharp observers and we use the techniques of opinion and market research to interpret their findings.

Our salient discovery is that within the past decade the teen-agers have become a separate and distinct group in our society. Psychologists and social scientists underline their separateness. Advertisers and merchants cater to their whims. Newspapers devote special sections to the interests of the teen-age reader, who is accepted as a special kind of customer along with the housewife and the adult sports fan. And the response of the teen-ager has been, characteristically, to match the image. I am not speaking here—or elsewhere—of the youngsters who get into trouble. Despite newspaper headlines and our well-founded concern with their problems, delinquents represent only a minute percentage of our teen-age population. I am concerned here not with why a handful of boys and girls behave badly, but with exploring why the great majority seem to their elders so odd. How different are they really?

Adolescents, ever since anyone has observed them, have been rebelling —openly or secretly—against their elders. At the same time they have always been desperately eager to keep in step with their crowd—known to the social scientists today as the peer group. Never before, however, have these phases of human development been given so much public and formal recognition. And never before has quite so young a group exercised the same kind of power—for good or ill. Today's teen-ager is a remarkably independent character. The fact is, he can afford to be.

The high-school boys and girls of 1959 are likely to have about four times as much money to spend as their counterparts in 1945—the individual average is $10 a week compared with $2.50 fifteen years ago. Two-thirds of this is a parental dole—the allowance. But the balance is earned income. Today's teen-agers—despite contrary views from some of their teachers—are an industrious lot.

Within a decade, the number of teen-agers holding steady year-round jobs has doubled—reaching a total of 800,000 in 1956. Some of these youngsters have left school to go to work, but many manage to hold down lucrative jobs after school hours as delivery boys, newspaper route boys, baby-sitters, soda jerks. About four million spend their vacations working and some 4.5 million do part-time work or odd jobs throughout the year.

Typical of most American youngsters today are the students and graduates of the Pearl River High School in Rockland County, New York. Their guidance director circulated a questionnaire last August and found that 90 per cent of the 1959 graduates had found summer jobs in fields which they hoped to pursue in college. Thirty out of seventy-five boys and girls earned more than $400 during the summer at such jobs as clerk, camp counselor, kitchen worker, stock boy, photo-offset press loader, caddie, carpenter, car-pool attendant, church organist, laboratory assistant, salesgirl, and road-maintenance worker. Sixty-five out of seventy-five of the junior class also found summer jobs and earned an average of $250 apiece.

A good slice of such earnings is saved for college expenses. But a considerable part is also spent. Last year teen-agers had purchasing power amounting to an estimated $9.5 billion—enough to cause some major merchandising and fashion upheavals.

The high-school set makes its own decisions about what to buy and where to buy it, often dragging their parents along in their wake. Thus teen-age boys have created the vogue for button-down collars, Bermuda shorts, cashmere sweaters, sport shirts, "Ivy League" jackets and loafers. And the junior miss (who has her own sanctuary in any up-and-coming specialty shop known as the "Young Sophisticates," "Telephone Set Shop," etc.) leads the way in endorsing "separates," "man-tailored" shirts, ballet slippers, and skintight "stem" skirts or ballooning layers of petticoats. She has, over the past few years, built seamless leotard tights (not long ago known merely as a professional dancer's uniform) into a multi-million-dollar industry. One manufacturer of girls' clothing who started out eighteen years ago with a $4,000 investment has, by concentrating on teen-age preferences, blossomed into a $30 million business with six factories around the country and a listing on the American Stock Exchange. This company's brochure—a kind of capsule course in teen-age psychology for retailers—indicates that the junior miss is a shrewd—if impulsive—buyer: she prefers a well-turned seam and preshrunk color-fast fabrics.

For her style ideas, she may lean on one of the half-dozen fashion and service magazines which cater exclusively to the teen-age girl or her married sister (known in the trade as a young adult). But by and large it is some mysterious form of communication within their own age group which dictates high-school and college vogues. Parents, in any event, have little to say about what is bought and where. This is not entirely because the youngster has his own money in his jeans. Indeed, in other times and other societies, earning power did not spell independence. Working children were expected to contribute to the family budget—the need for strong backs on the family farm has, for instance, been a classic pretext of the Irish matriarch for preventing her sons from marrying.

But today's young mother—who probably buys her own clothes in the college shop—is no matriarch. Neither she nor Daddy has ever wielded much authority over the youngsters, and both parents tend to be uncertain in matters of taste, confused about values, and all too ready to abdi-

cate decisions—whether about cereals, car colors, furniture, or clothing—
to sons and daughters who have definite preferences, shared with large
numbers of their contemporaries. In similar fashion, immigrant parents
used to lean on their children as arbiters of taste and interpreters of the
American way.

Today's teen-agers play a dominant role in the making of family decisions at a remarkably early age. The process of growing up, it seems,
has been telescoped. In this precocity, TV and radio have certainly played
a part. Today's teen-agers may suffer from overexposure to Westerns and
gangster movies. But many have also kept the set turned on for newscasts
and during childhood have achieved at least a nodding acquaintance with
the wide adult world. The thirteen-year-old boy now does (or expects to
do) what was reserved for the fifteen-year-old of the recent past. (Learning to drive a car, for instance.) A thirteen-year-old girl wants "sophisticated" party dresses, high-heeled shoes, and make-up. (Eye shadow rather
than lipstick is today's badge of womanhood.) Fifteen years ago less than
half of one per cent of thirteen- and fourteen-year-old girls were "going
steady" with one boy. Today this number has increased twenty-fold. And,
as a not surprising corollary, the peak year for marriage of women is now
eighteen.

The prospect of early marriage does not, however, necessarily mean a
full severing of the useful bonds of home. Seventy per cent of the boys
and girls between thirteen and seventeen whom we questioned on the
subject said they would not object if their parents supported them for a
while after marriage.

"It is the obligation of the older generation," said one boy, "to provide
for the younger until they are able to provide for themselves." Many
parents might agree but find it something of a shock to have their duties
spelled out so bluntly—particularly if they disapproved of the marriage
in the first place.

Brash as their behavior may seem at times, the youngsters themselves
are not too comfortable in simultaneously defying and exploiting their
elders. Their mixed—or perhaps suppressed—guilt feelings about their
parents are revealed in teen-age humor. Much of it seems to express a
burgeoning disrespect for the adult world and for at least one aspect of
the character of Mommy and Daddy. The currently popular "sick jokes"
may be a significant case in point:

> "Daddy, why can't I go out and play like the other kids?"
> "Shut up, son, and drink your beer."

> "But Mommy, I don't want to go to Europe."
> "Shut up, darling, and keep on swimming."

> "I don't care who you are, fat man, get those reindeer off my roof."

For most teen-agers quips like these have the same charm as their own jargon. Said one, "I think we like those jokes because they make us feel like important individuals. Those jokes are our own, and adults can't really understand them or laugh about them. We feel superior when adults can't understand something we are doing."

Another youngster said, "We are a new generation, and we want to make our mark as an individual generation. These jokes are one way of doing it."

Few teen-agers can bring themselves to criticize their parents directly. Most of them—though their conduct may belie their words—say they think Mother and Dad are just as smart as they are. And hardly any dare suggest that their own parents are a bad thing—this came out in a survey which asked young people to list the "worst influence" in their lives. Ninety-one per cent cited bad companions or the evil example of adults outside their families. On the other hand, teen-agers blame the parents (of others) for most juvenile delinquency. Parental love, interest, and understanding are the best antidotes, they say. (Authority is not mentioned.) However, the boys and girls don't hand their parents much on the positive side. They were listed as "best influences" by only 20 per cent of the group questioned. Good companions and inspiring non-relative adults were the choice of the majority.

When pressed to list negative traits of their parents, one boy said of his father, "He's neurotic." The vast majority, however, said in various ways that Mother and Dad are old-fashioned—particularly in matters of courtship and sex.

Paradoxically, many parents find their children too conventional. They wish their daughters would have a few romantic flings before settling down with the boys they were going steady with in junior high. And they would like—or think they would like—to see their sons dreaming of adventuresome careers rather than steady jobs with dependable pension plans.

There are signs that some of the young people themselves are beginning to doubt the wisdom of teen-age marriages—including their own which show an alarming fragility.

On the other hand, conservatism and conformity are clearly on the increase, at least in the more tangible aspects of life. For example, in 1946 a large group of thirteen- to nineteen-year-olds were queried about whether they would like to wear something different from their contemporaries. A third said they would. But in the past year, in response to the same question, 95 per cent chose a leveling sameness.

This is, of course, no different from the imitative drive which sent earlier generations into yellow slickers and raccoon coats. It is just that the odd balls are becoming so scarce. Surprising too were the results of a survey for the Armed Forces which have traditionally attracted the restless youngster who wanted to "join the Navy and see the world." He is, it was found, a vanishing species. So the Army adopted a brand new slogan: "Retire at thirty-seven." It was highly effective.

Today's teen-ager is a very practical youth. For example, the problem of getting good marks places higher on the list of most youngsters' conscious worries than dating, money, or parent-child problems. This is not because mother nags about homework, but because the teen-ager knows he must meet stiff competition from his peers and needs a college degree if he is to get on in the world, which he fully intends to do.

That world, however, is very different from the one in which his parents lived as children and young adults. And herein may lie an important clue to the gap between the generations. For people in their late thirties, forties, and fifties today, the two overwhelming experiences of life were the Depression and World War II. Far more than they realize, the impressions and standards formed in those days have shaped their present attitudes and thinking. But to the teen-ager these are dim, irrelevant periods.

"My, I'm tired of hearing about all those noble causes my mother worked for when she was in college," said one high-school girl. "I don't believe they were all that noble. And who cares now, anyhow?"

The difficulty, it would seem, is global.

"Today's young people don't speak the same language as we do," a middle-aged Yugoslav Communist complained the other day. "They don't feel as we do about things."

Parents from Chattanooga to China would probably agree. Possibly, however, it is the "things" as much as the "feelings" that have changed. And it may be that today's teen-agers are adapting, in their own way, to a situation very different from what any prior generation of adolescents has experienced.

Is there not, for example, a certain crude logic in hastening the growing up process in the shadow of the atom and hydrogen bomb? What meaning have "patriotism," "peace," and the other slogans of the bygone idealism when the dilemma that faces us is not a matter of winning a war but survival? To lose one's identity within the pattern of one's contemporaries, to seek the haven of a steady job rather than personal achievement, to prize material possessions above abstract principles—these may be the best available safety rafts in an insecure world.

The wiser of our politicians are learning gradually that one cannot use the old stock-in-trade of the past twenty years to appeal to young voters. Many of them have scarcely heard of the New Deal. They are not veterans of any war and don't hope to be. New issues must be defined though just what they are no one has yet figured out.

Possibly it is time that parents, too, started shifting their sights. Instead of bemoaning the queer ways of their young, it might be more useful to take a hard look at the society in which they are growing up. After all, we made it for them.

COMMENT

Mr. Gilbert follows standard procedure in this essay as he presents in succession a statement of the problem upon which the paper is based, a summary of his qualifications to discuss it, and a number of facts and opinions each developed with reference to the opening thesis. Notice how the author uses his evidence. He cites enough general statistics early in his article to suggest the scope of his study and enough to lend authority to the quotations and specific examples which follow. He does not, in other words, do much theorizing until he has first made his readers feel that his opinions are based upon knowledge.

SUGGESTIONS FOR WRITING

1. Take issue with some specific item in Mr. Gilbert's study of the teen-ager. Write a paper in which you conduct an orderly refutation of his opinion.
2. Select an issue of a magazine which directs its appeal to a specific group (teen-agers, young women, married women, college boys, sportsmen, movie fans). Write an essay in which you analyze the publisher's conception of his audience.

Teen-Age Heroes:
Mirrors of Muddled Youth

Thomas B. Morgan

EIGHTEEN MILLION AMERICAN TEEN-AGERS growing older in a world they didn't make—a world overpopulated and underfed, overorganized and yet disorganized, impersonal and self-indulgent, machine-tooled, purposeless, yet filled with unrealized possibility and in danger of coming to an apocalyptic end—have settled a new world of their own. They have established a colony Out There in Teen-Land, a kind of pseudo-adult world. It is not a young world, if youth means daring and imagination, idealism and individualism, skepticism and iconoclasm. But it does have such a definite identity and appearance that one can visit it as a tourist, with camera, dictionary, and sick pills. (A nice place to visit, yes; but no place to live.) Because they have to live at home, go to school, belong to clubs, shop for supplies, and appear in court, the teen-agers' colony is attached to the American mainland and carries on foreign relations with it. The hearts and minds of teen-agers, though, are usually in Teen-Land: they are totally aware of themselves as Teen-Agers, something their parents never were when they were younger. They feel and are made to feel (no doubt by articles such as this) that they are a race apart, a minority in an alien land. Thus, they cling with fierce pride to a private set of folkways that seem mysterious and confounding in the extreme to outsiders. These folkways create pressures to conform and inhibit the individual as insistently as those in the adult world, but they give the teen-ager an illusion of choice. Paralleling the adult world, Teen-Land is built on insecurity and its greatest concern is for safety. The cost of safety is uniqueness of personality and the measure of it is membership in the herd.

To understand this complex, young world, one should get to know the heroes of teen-agers. Here is what prompted this inquiry: the assumption that heroes directly and indirectly reveal much about the hero-worshipers' values and that the heroes of teen-agers would contribute some understanding of those who idolize them in an era in which communication between generations has all but broken down.

Reprinted from *Esquire*, March, 1960. © 1960 by Esquire, Inc.

This assumption isn't made because all teen-age heroes have special knowledge. Today, a young man is elected to heroship by teen-age girls who buy phonograph records without regard for his insights. The hero, after a short wait, is then accepted by teen-age boys, who buy him uncritically, perhaps to please the girls. The boys don't have feminine heroines of their own. There are girl singers who are popular with teen-agers, but none receive the adulation that the girls lavish on the males. It seems that teen-age girls, maturing faster than boys, have no interest in worshiping a member of their own sex. They are prepared to accept a male symbol long before the boys have extricated themselves from Mother. It has even been suggested that boys do not care for girl singers because the female voice reminds them of Mom and, worse, Discipline. As it works out, then, both sexes accept the choice of heroes made by one sex, and the weaker sex at that.

What makes the heroes themselves, in the flesh, a potential source of information about teen-agers is that they are, of course, more than mere show-business characters. Most of them are teen-agers and only one is out of his twenties. They not only perform; they also reflect those whom they are performing for and are approved by. They are part of Teen-Land as well as symbols of it. Some are virtually overnight sensations and none are so far from a time when they were nobodies that they cannot remember their own experiences as members of the teen world on the far side of the footlights.

Recently, some of these heroes were tarnished by the payola scandals. But in the outcry over payola, the essential nature of the idols themselves was ignored. The superficial crookedness of individuals in the record business was excoriated, leaving untouched something deeper—the irresponsibility of many who profoundly affect teen-age life.

One recent night, a nineteen-year-old boy named Frankie Avalon, a rock-and-roll ballad singer physically reminiscent of Frank Sinatra, was seen doing his turn at the Steel Pier Music Hall on the boardwalk at Atlantic City. When he stepped on the stage, about two hundred well-fed, well-enough-dressed girls in the first six rows and in the side balconies shrieked in the typically violent and mechanical way we have all come to know and love. The sound was a cross between an explosive high-school cheer and the mating call of the red squirrel. A number of the screamers were not looking at their hero, but at each other, to make sure that they were being seen screaming—i.e., belonging. In general, the Frankie Avalon fans were seated screamers, not the old dance-in-the-aisle kind of the naïve Sinatra days, which had merely been a kind of premonition of things to come. A few, however, left their seats to run up the aisle and take flashbulb pictures of Avalon, screaming a little as they went. Back of the forward wall of noise, row upon row of teen-agers applauded conventionally. This may have been because they were less enthusiastic, but more than likely they did not scream because they were outside the bright glow of the footlights. If the management had turned up the house lights, they might have achieved a more perfect pandemonium.

But perfect or not, by enabling post-pubescent girls to express themselves within the damp warmth and safety of the crowd, a modern teenage hero, such as Avalon, fulfills his function and collects his money. The expression takes many forms. In New Haven, Connecticut, girls in summer frocks pulled the shoes off Avalon's feet in an attempt to drag him from the stage, into the audience. In Buffalo, New York, a wild herd of little women trampled him and sprained his back, while in Milwaukee twenty-one girls fainted during one show. When Avalon sang *Boy Without a Girl* on a television show, the camera panned on girls sobbing in the audience. After that, wherever he appeared in person, girls who had seen him on TV sobbed while he sang this song. Avalon's merchandising business keeps the idolatry percolating at long distance: among his wares for young women are Avalon shirts, sweaters, bracelets, buttons and authentic locks of hair. The latter are collected when Avalon goes to the barbershop —which reminds one of that old boast of the hog business: "We use everything but the squeal."

Now the stimulus for all this is 5 feet 7 inches tall and weighs less than 135 pounds. On stage at the Steel Pier Music Hall, his hair was wavy, his face sweet-to-babyish, eyes sad, skin sallow under make-up, and mouth uncertain. His clothes were a careful combination of show-biz elegance and Pat Boone purity: silk suits and white buck shoes. By nature or design, his manner was gentle, a little frightened, and awesomely humble.

This humility, which is characteristic of many teen-age heroes (Fabian, Ricky Nelson, and the like), was a response to the felt need of the audience to identify with one who was celestial and yet not far out of reach. Since the aspirations of many teen-agers seem to be at the lowest level in the history of America, too much self was taboo and anyone too far away (or out) would be ignored. The cardinal principle of the successful hero would be that humbleness creates an indispensable aura of accessibility.

Avalon first sang *Pretty-eyed Baby,* the words of which were totally unintelligible, followed by *De De Dinah,* his first recorded hit song, which was also unintelligible. He sang with a microphone, but his voice was almost inaudible. He did a little soft shoe, which must have been intended to tell those who couldn't hear that the music was playing. Avalon was drowned out not only by the repeated squealings of the audience down front, but also by the orchestra itself, which played loud and hard, driving the backbeat. The trumpet was loud, in part deliberately and in part due to the fact that the trumpet player had cotton stuffed in his ears against the waves of sound from the teen-agers. The drummer accented every second and fourth beat, which is the standard rock-and-roll accent. He kicked the bass drum like the pit man in a burlesque house. Indeed, Avalon's performance contained echoes of burlesque. His least suggestive movements produced ear-splitting cries for more, such as when he merely kicked the toe of a shoe out toward the audience. While this may not seem erotic in cold type, the girls who saw it sighed mightily.

The sum of his performance was very young, very immature, and even tender (all said at the risk of sounding old), because Avalon had so little audible singing ability and his audience needed to believe otherwise. Moreover, though they screamed like baby banshees, the girls were making believe they were adults. They struck poses which seemed to represent their idea of *adult* poses: in a moment of sudden restraint, some would sit back, place an index finger along a cheek, tighten their eyes, and listen critically. Like opera-goers, they whispered knowingly between numbers. When Avalon's half-hour was over, they wore expressions of adultlike sophistication on their faces: cool, satisfied, almost blasé.

At the stage door, still another crowd of girls gathered to wait for Avalon, held back by a chain. They might have been the same two hundred girls who had had the choice seats in the Music Hall. They milled about the door impatiently. A uniformed guard taunted them ("He ain't never coming out, girls!") while stealing looks through a small window into the hall that led to Avalon's backstage dressing room. When Avalon appeared in the hall, the guard unhooked the chain and demanded that the girls form two lines so that the star and his entourage could pass through to a waiting auto. Instead, the girls surged forward, breathlessly. Nonchalant at first, the guard swung the chain at them, rippling it softly. Then he cracked it hard across the front rank at chest level. The girls, who had been about to crush Avalon, fell back. Avalon walked behind a phalanx made up of his guitar player, the Steel Pier press agent, and three other men. "Touch me, Frankie!" girls shouted. "Over here, man. Just look at me!" Looking neither right nor left, Avalon escaped into the back seat of the waiting car. The entourage piled in after him. Female hands, heads, and torsos surged in at the windows and jammed open the front door. Two well-aimed, shoving blows from the driver cleared the front door, the windows were rolled up, and the car drove off with its precious cargo. The girls waved, disappointed but not angry. They had enjoyed the melee, the mob violence of which was the other side of the group sex rites that had taken place inside.

Ten minutes later, safe in a restaurant, Frankie Avalon said: "I think it's great to be a teen-ager."

Avalon had no more to say, really, than this one line. Yet even that underlined the modern, crowd-cultured teen-ager's deep and novel sense of belonging to a special group. Avalon was as unaware of his function as a hero of that special group as he had once been of his own potentialities. (He had started in show business as a trumpet player.) He was their outlet for vicarious sex and real violence, those primitive means of self-expression to which one turns when prouder means—ambition, creativity, ability, the sheer desire to change the world—have been denied, devalued, or have failed. Avalon did not know it and, not knowing, felt no sense of responsibility for it.

While Avalon was in New Jersey, six teen-age heroes were in Hollywood pursuing their various commitments to television, movies, and night clubs. Ricky Nelson was taping "The Adventures of Ozzie and Harriet" with his mother and father. Edd "Kookie" Byrnes was acting in "77 Sunset Strip," a filmed weekly TV show. Pat Boone and Dick Clark (the non-singer of the group) were making movies and, simultaneously, Clark was producing some of his TV programs for tape. Fabian was working in a movie called *Hound Dog Man* and Bobby Darin had an adult-world night-club date. One could see them individually in the surroundings of their trade.

Ricky Nelson was rather well protected by his father and the family press agent in a barren office across from the "Ozzie and Harriet" TV-show sound stage. When they let him in edgewise, it was apparent that he was at least partially conscious of the nuances of his appeal to teen-agers. His commodity is sincere sex. He was most aware of the need for sincerity. It seemed crucial to him that no one should get the idea that he was different—"I'm just another teen-ager," he said—or that he was anything but sincere. Like most teen-agers, his sentences were larded with the phrase "you know," partially from habit, but also, it seemed, to impress one with his complete frankness and desire to be understood.

In 1957, when he was sixteen, Ricky studied guitar for a while, then walked on the stage of Hamilton High School in Los Angeles for his first public appearance as a prospective solo performer. He did not swing his hips or otherwise attempt to excite the audience. Yet, the screaming began before he sang a note, the girls got out of hand, and the members of the football team had to help him escape. Thus the hero was born, as all teen-age heroes are born, in the presence and at the pleasure of screaming young women. Six of his records have since sold over one million copies each, representing a cool net of $40,000 each. His personal appearances have been smashing, thanks in some degree to the careful organization of 10,000 fan clubs all over the country. His income last year was estimated to be $400,000. To earn it, Ricky selected each hit song by himself from hundreds of demonstration records submitted by publishers and song writers. He knew exactly what he wanted:

"The record should not be too complicated," Ricky said. "If it's not, you know, sincere, it's not too good. In a song, you know, I hate to hear lingo, you know, about hop and bop. I like a song that tells a story without meaningless words, you know, like 'dig that crazy chick.' Now you listen to *Lonesome Town*. It should be a simple song like that, you know? *Lonesome Town* is about this fictitious town called Lonesome Town, you know, where you can forget this girl. I mean lots of times you get jilted and feel like the end of the world's come. So, it's from what I feel sincerely, I decide to do a song. Now, you asked me about teen-age values. I feel my values are pretty good. I mean, I like anything I feel is sincere."

Edd "Kookie" Byrnes touches a different chord out of necessity. He is perhaps the only teen-age hero who achieved his exalted position by playing a role—that of "Kookie," the jive-talking parking-lot attendant of "77 Sunset Strip"—and maintains it by continuing to be what he isn't. In public, his speech sounds like a tape-recording made at the bar in Birdland. The rest of the time he talks like a conventional twenty-six-year-old. Seen at lunch and between scenes at Warner's, there was nothing about him that suggested the character of "Kookie" except the long brown hair and routine good looks. To teen-agers, however, he is "Kookie" whose long suit is a devilish narcissism. His trade-mark is a comb which he is endlessly passing through his locks. Teen-agers might be expected to frown on such self-conceit, but "Kookie" manages to convey the impression that he is just kidding. If teen-agers were really in revolt against the adult world instead of merely huddled together in their own adultified colony, Byrnes's "Kookie" probably would not be a strong-enough character to appeal to them. As it is, he is a symbol of a small rebellion. He says that the "77 Sunset Strip" adventure that won the teen-agers for "Kookie" involved an incident in which he was falsely blamed for an auto accident. "They think I did it," "Kookie" said, "because I'm young." The line could have been the title of a rock-and-roll golden record. Inevitably, as his fame grew, Byrnes turned to the teen-age record market. After a dozen or more attempts to record his first tune on key, the A & R man sent him home and pasted together a master out of pieces from each of the tapes. The result was *Kookie, Lend Me Your Comb,* which sold 2,000,000 single records, a monument to the taste and perception of our teens.

Fabian, like "Kookie," became a teen-age hero in spite of the fact that he was no bundle of singing talent. "Maybe I would have never made it if I could sing," Fabian has said. His appeal is similar to Ricky Nelson's, but also he elicits motherly sympathy from the girls because he is so obviously awkward and inept. It is now one of the hoary legends of Teen-Land that Fabian was discovered sitting on a doorstep in South Philadelphia by Bob Marcucci, a former waiter who is himself not yet thirty. With his partner, Peter De Angelis, Marcucci had discovered and then promoted Frankie Avalon to stardom. Having developed the magic touch, he searched for and found Fabian two years ago. Fabian was fourteen, had never sung a note in anger, and thought that the $6 a week he was earning in a drugstore was fair money. When last seen, he was getting $35,000 for acting (not badly, by Hollywood standards) in Fox's *Hound Dog Man*.

Sitting just behind the camera in one of those canvas chairs, Marcucci was watching every move his gold mine made. Marcucci is a short, swarthy man who reminds one of a nervous assistant director at a boy's camp. He has the ability to analyze precisely the demands of the teen-age public and to know what to do about it. He has found a career in exporting talent to Teen-Land. First, he selects promising raw material. Then he molds it. He indoctrinates it for three months. Then he takes it to live TV shows so that it can see what the business is like. Then he lets it make a few test records. Since it cannot sing too well without an orchestra and the electronic facilities (echo chambers, bass and treble modulators, tape splicers and the works) of a recording studio, he teaches it to pantomime while its records play over the loud-speaker during its first public appearance before an audience of two hundred. He dresses it, first in sweaters and white bucks, then in open-Belafonte shirts and big belt buckles. He coifs it by modifying the duck-tail and getting more of the Ricky Nelson bob. He postures it, taking advantage of good shoulders, which should bunch forward, and narrow hips, which should always be off-keel. He takes it on the road, shows it to disc jockeys, and advertises it in trade papers. He decides (brilliantly) to use only its first name instead of its last. He interests Dick Clark in it, and after one shot on TV, it breaks up an audience of 24,000 in Albany, New York. It sells 300,000 copies of a record called *I'm a Man*, then 750,000 of *Turn Me Loose*. It records *Tiger*:

> . . . You kept my heart jumping like a kan-ga-roo
> I'm float-ing like an on-ion in a bowl of stew . . .
> Come right now, 'cause I'm on the prowl
> Like a ti-ger oo-oo-oo, like a ti-ger.*

After these lyrics (tiger is the word you *hear*), it is known not only as Fabian, but as Tiger, too. It is a hero.

In Fabian, Marcucci consciously or unconsciously produced a caricature that combined the sure-fire qualities of Ricky with those of his own Frankie Avalon. The mood in Teen-Land permits even such an obvious construction to become a hero. What Marcucci could not have planned, however, was the fact that Fabian's inability to sing would really be an asset. Marcucci tried to teach him; he went through four singing teachers trying. Fortunately, all efforts failed. Here was the ultimate in humbleness

* *Tiger*, by Ollie Jones. © 1959 by Roosevelt Music Co., Inc.

and teen-audience identification. Nobody in the audience could sing either, so that made the inept sex-pot, Fabian, seem all the more accessible. Mediocrity fell in love with its own image.

Bobby Darin has what Fabian doesn't have and vice versa. Instead of half-closed eyes, a build and a hairdresser, Darin has the most low-down, mature, masculine voice of all the teen-age heroes. During the past year, his records have sold more than 5,000,000 copies (*Splish Splash, Mack the Knife*, which got the Grammy award, etc.). Found at a Sunset Strip night club, Darin (without teen-agers) demonstrated that the humbleness required by them does not become him; he fairly bursts with self-confidence before an adult audience. He is about twenty-four, short, average-looking, and honest with himself. "I know I'm not a pretty boy." he said. "I feel a little out of place in front of teen-agers because even though they buy my records they don't have that fervor for me when they see me. It's a physical thing with them. I don't put them down for it, but I don't think I'm one of them." He said he would sing anything teen-agers wanted to hear—à la Avalon, the sense of responsibility was missing. "It's bad the way the papers have screwed them up. The kids have got the idea now that they all have to band together and act like teen-agers. They have phony heroes and no individuality. They don't know who's leading them. I feel for them, but I'm *not* going to lead them, Charlie. You call the roll of commercial guys, put me first."

Pat Boone would save the teen-ager from himself if he could. His book, *'Twixt Twelve and Twenty*, was a tender try in that direction and he has said, "I hope that fellows like me and Ricky and Elvis aren't distracting kids from the real things in life and from becoming people instead of just fans." Boone has been around longer as a teen-age hero than anyone except Elvis Presley. He was a married man with a baby and a second (with two more in the future) on the way before he became a popular idol. He was deeply religious. Thus, he was absolutely safe and pure, too. This combination was immensely appealing to many teen-age girls. His records sold 20,000,000 at last count, second only to Elvis. On the movie set, *Journey to the Center of the Earth*, a wholesome Jules Verne tale, Boone seemed made for Victorian costumery. He does not have conventional good looks, but rather a strong, open boy's face which suggests ball games and picnics. He does not simmer like the members of the Presley-Nelson-Fabian-Byrnes syndrome. In his time, though, he has had his share of screaming and fainting and clothes-grabbing by teen fans. "I can't believe it's bad or abnormal," he said. "It's fun and a form of recreation and a release of tension."

Dick Clark has defended the teen-agers' *status quo* even more stoutly than Pat Boone. He has become virtually a go-between in the two worlds.

To the teen-ager, he is an adult who likes them, a big brother who watches out for them, and an authority who sanctions both their idols and their folkways. For the adult world, he is an emissary from Teen-Land not many years out of the age group himself (he's thirty, looks twenty), a young man whose taste and judgment are respected (after all, indecent lyrics are banned from his programs); and a celebrity who approves of their children. With all this going for him, it's no wonder that Clark is one of the hot properties in show business. He has six TV shows a week on ABC, many magazine-writing assignments, and a fat contract with Columbia Pictures. (Until recently, when he was advised to withdraw, he had a music-publishing and record-pressing business.)

Television is Clark's first love. Both *American Bandstand* and the Saturday *Dick Clark Show* are major outlets for teen-age heroes and their music. The shows are so popular that Clark is probably the most powerful personality-and-song plugger in the teen field. Such power implies responsibility, so Clark is due his share of credit for conditions that prevail in Teen-Land. Last summer, after watching two Saturday shows from the wings (Clark tapes his summer Saturday shows mid-week), one could be sure Clark would never have one of those "There, that'll hold the little bastards!" episodes in his career. He is a careful man and, besides, he believes in teen-agers "the way they are." All of his TV programs devote many minutes to camera views of teen-agers.

Clark's magazine-writing career is based on a column in *This Week Magazine,* but his "talks to teen-agers" have also appeared in *Seventeen, Look,* and others. He is the teen-agers' Norman Vincent Peale. His position is reassuring: the way teens live is pretty much okay. Nothing downs his optimism. Typically, he sums up his advice with, "Keep at it and I know you'll be successful"; or, "I think you will be surprised at how soon there will be nothing to worry about." Once, however, in a conversation, he said:

"I don't think teen-agers are doing anything today that adults don't do also. They have all the same problems that adults have nowadays—money problems, success problems, appearance problems. They are appreciated as a group as never before and they want to be looked on as adults. They're worldly, so much more worldly than we were. They're practically adults. They're sophisticated at a very early age. Take the day Sal Mineo was leaving my studio. He got in his car and a teen-age girl threw herself under the front wheels. 'Run over me, Sal!' she cried. That was dreadful, yes; but a week later in Atlantic City, a forty-year-old woman in a mink coat threw herself in front of Frank Sinatra's car and cried, 'Run over me, Frankie!' That's what I mean. There's no difference between teen-agers and adults."

Clark apparently meant this as a justification for himself as well as the teen-agers who idolize him. In any case, it was an accurate description of juvenile adults and adultified teen-agers.

What Clark and the others suggest in symbol and sentiment is that millions of teen-agers have taken refuge in a pseudo-world that is spoiled and banal and hypererotic and in headlong flight from reality and easily fooled and commercialized and exploited and fatuous. Such a world may be satisfactory for adults, but somehow one has greater expectations from youth.

Every world has means of expressing itself—a culture. Our 18,000,000 teen-agers (exceptions duly noted) spend $10,000,000,000 to support theirs. They have publications written in their own language (Teenglish?) which keep them abreast of their times. *Dig, Ingenue, Seventeen, 16, Teen,* etc., instruct them in custom, ritual, propriety, sex mores, and proper-think; their goal is to inculcate group values. One magazine not long ago defined "What is a Square?" for its readers, who were told, among other things, that a square is one who refuses to go with a group to a movie he has already seen. Then there are motion pictures, television shows, and radio programs, which provide a kind of cultural game of ring-around-the-rosie. The teens influence the adults who provide the entertainments which in turn influence the teens and so on, and on. After sex and violence, the main theme of these entertainments is a kind of dead-pan morality which would be funny if it did not border on madness. Thus, the producer of *I Was a Teenage Frankenstein* defended himself against an attack on his very popular picture by pointing out that none of the young villains and monsters in the movie drank or smoked. And in the basic boy-meets-girl film, scripts are adjusted to make sure that a curious kind of justice, appealing to teen-agers, triumphs. In a teen picture, after the boy gets the girl pregnant, he's got to get stabbed. Watching rock-and-roll programs, citizens of Teen-Land may learn the newest folk dances while they follow the fashions of the times. Hearing disc jockeys on radio, too, teen-agers can absorb their culture. They are infused with meaningful backbeat rhythms and simultaneously absorb the philosophies of the modern jocks, which are a mixture of Beat, Babbitt and Payola. Beyond these visual and aural items of acculturation, there is the automobile. What the frontier was to our pioneers, what Miami is to our modern adult culture, the auto is to the teen—the means of getting away.

Finally, away out on the fringe of Teen-Land, heroin takes some teen-agers where they cannot get by car.

The primary focus of the teen culture, however, is the teen-age hero who, like heroes of all cultures, represents the final expression of those values by which it lives. The seven aforementioned heroes are the Apollos and Zeuses of Teen-Land. A few years ago, the movies supplied most of the heroes for adolescent Americans. Marlon Brando and James Dean were two, but the former's receding hairline and the latter's death disconnected them from the young. Chances are they would have faded anyway, because rock-and-roll was bigger than both of them. Now, except for Dick Clark, every first-class teen-age hero is a recording star. No athlete, politician, businessman, or intellectual is accorded comparable esteem, nor could he be, given the teen-agers' demand for safety. The ideal athlete is admired for courage, the politician for principles, the businessman for enterprise, and the intellectual for devotion to hard truths—all represent values that tend to separate the individual from the crowd, that expose him, and that lead him into an uncertain and dangerous future. Teen-agers make virtues of conformity, mediocrity and sincerity. It is a simple matter of survival: there's safety in the crowd. They can express themselves through their safe-sex heroes, each one of whom represents his own brand of sex—rebellious sex, sincere sex, clean sex, low-down sex, motherly sex, cool sex—at no risk. It's perfect: it's sex, but it's safe. Without leaving the warmth and security of the crowd, you can say what you want to say to the world.

You can have your cake without being eaten.

It is not easy to know precisely what the teen-agers want to say through their heroes. The means of expression is primordial; the words are often indistinguishable from straight static. In that they are designed (often willfully) to hold a mirror up to the nature of teen life, they offer perhaps our most significant clue.

Two of the most successful people in the teen-age song business are Jerry Leiber and Mike Stoller, a words-and-music team which seems to know precisely what it is that teen-agers want to say. Their rock-and-roll songs have sold over 30,000,000 records: *Hound Dog* sold more than 5,000,000 records; *Black Denim Trousers,* a supposed spoof of motorcycle bums which was taken seriously by them, sold more than 2,000,000 records; *Love Me, Loving You, Searching, Don't* and *Jailhouse Rock* also sold more than 2,000,000; *King Creole, Charley Brown, Yakety Yak, Along Came Jones* and *Poison Ivy* sold more than 1,000,000. After eight years of song-writing (each is now but twenty-six years old) Leiber and Stoller have sold four times as many records as Jerome Kern sold in his lifetime.

It did them no harm that Elvis Presley (still in the Army as this is written) performed several of their songs. Along Tin Pan Alley, it is still generally assumed that Presley, the king of the teen-age heroes, could sell one million records of himself singing Clementine Paddleford's recipe for boiled beef to the tune of *Juanita.* He is expected to resume the throne upon his discharge this spring.

Leiber and Stoller had the good fortune to begin writing songs for teen-age heroes in the early Fifties when Negro music known as "rhythm and blues" was being discovered by white teen-agers. About 1953, this music was taken over for the commercial teen market although it had been played for years on Negro radio stations and had been sung down South as a form of the blues since the Civil War. At the same time, "country music" with its strong influence from both the Baptist church and white folk music was discovered. The two themes, one earthy, the other moralistic, both plaintive, came together and were revised downward to the teen-age level; they became "rock-and-roll." The rock-and-roll fad spread like a pox, carried first by independent record companies with singing groups, and then by Elvis Presley, with his country guitar and Gypsy Rose Lee hips. In Presley's larynx, songs that had arisen out of realistic needs for a job, a woman, or a drink were replaced by teen-age needs and expressions that were only dimly related to the sources of the new music. "Cold pouring down rain blues" became "They don't understand us because we're teen-agers rock."

Presley was followed by a horde of imitators. The surprise was that they were almost as successful as he was. Always before, a segment of youth had zeroed in on a single personality—a Vallee or a Sinatra—and had disdained copies of the real thing. Elvis, however, was more than a personality; he was the leader of a movement which provided a hero for every boy and girl, and finally resulted in the identification of teen-agers as a race apart. Leiber and Stoller wrote on the head of a drum.

"Anger and protest, self-pity and adulation, these are the things the teen-age heroes sing about," Jerry Leiber says.

Repeating the same salty, nasty phrase again and again, such a song as *Hound Dog* is a pure expression of hostility while *Don't* is equally pure self-pity. What teen-agers seem to want to say is, "I'm mad at the world, at authority, at the way things are," and "I can't do anything about it, so pity poor me." Both would be perfectly legitimate statements, loaded with potentialities, if that was what teen-agers actually meant.

"Basically," Leiber says, "these songs are a means of escape from reality. We write the lyrics deliberately vague. The songs aren't addressed to anybody real, but to dream characters. The songs are egocentric and dreamy. Lots of basic blues ideas wouldn't work as rock-and-roll ideas because the blues are too real, too earthy. You have to make them dreamlike and very moral. That's why you're rarely going to hear even a plain *happy* rock-and-roll song, because happiness is a real emotion."

We have, therefore, not only rebels without causes, we have a generation with nothing to say. All that seems real about teen-age self-expression through the safe-sex heroes is their dedication to unreality, to songs of watered-down, self-pitying blues-that-aren't-blues, and to aimless hostility.

One can hope that in some area of life, teen-agers are giving as much passionate attention to the real business of youth—which is growing up as well as older—as they are giving to their heroes. But if Dick Clark is right, that there is no difference between the generations as he sees them, growing up may be as outmoded as the 78 r.p.m. phonograph record. There may be nothing to grow up to. Yet a comparison must be made. The adult world has an existence apart from its obvious responsibility for what has happened in Teen-Land. There are adults and there are teen-agers. Even on the teen-agers' terms, if a choice had to be made, one would a hell of a lot rather have his woman run over by Frank Sinatra.

COMMENT

To write a coherent description of the teen-ager as he is revealed through his heroes requires an organizational scheme capable of holding together a great mass of facts, impressions, and theories. Mr. Morgan has chosen to construct his essay upon a basic metaphor: the teen-ager is a citizen of another world. Notice how he uses constant cross-reference and parallel structure to unify his writing.

SUGGESTIONS FOR WRITING

1. Write a paper controlled by a basic metaphor, a paper in which you discuss one thing in terms of something else: "Strange Customs of Parent-Land," "Homo Sapiens, Species Coed," "The Care and Feeding of the Automobile."

2. Write an essay entitled "Square Heroes" in answer to Mr. Morgan. Decide what you think to be the outstanding characteristic of the square and organize your material around it. Follow Mr. Morgan's lead by studying the Lawrence Welk program.

3. Develop a paper in which you describe and comment upon the public image a particular political figure tries to create. Narrow your subject carefully.

Thomas O. Brandt

LANGUAGE
ADJUSTMENT

IN THIS AGE of mass organization and mass communication we are trying to design a style of language capable of reaching anyone who can read or hear. The greatest mistake in such an attempt is the display of an individual style unless it is gleaned from the "common" man, whereby we note that "common" has two distinct though somewhat interrelated meanings. In other words, we aim at a mediocre or low intelligence which we flatter to be sophisticated by endowing our communications stylistically with subjective objectivity, condescending humility, polished ruggedness, and a reverberating integrity. Words and phrases are divested of their essential meaning and rearranged to such patterns that they express something entirely different from what they actually say.

This deliberate abuse of the American language issues from an unwillingness to subscribe to any definite linguistic status or standard. The American language is pliable to an incredible degree because of its uninhibited use; it is elusive and elastic, so much so that foreigners find it the easiest language to learn and the most difficult to command.

Aspiring to a periscopic modesty and a depersonalized individuality, many Americans will exercise great care not to appear superior to their neighbors out of a mistaken notion of democracy. The result is the applied law of mass gravity. Being afraid of speaking down to their fellowmen, they will take an immediate shortcut and establish themselves linguistically at a lower level at once. And they will strive to ennoble the mistakes of the uneducated by saying "there is two sides to this matter," or "got beat," or "everybody should mind their business," etc.

Nothing gives us so perfectly away as language. It is the only known means by which we can coherently think and draw logical conclusions. The American language, in constant flux, is in a course of rapid development—considering the slow pace languages in general observe. Its formation and advancement does not proceed without trials and tribulations. It

Reprinted by permission of the author and of *The Colorado Quarterly*.

can be most beautiful as Jefferson and Lincoln, and the works of Sherwood Anderson, Thomas Wolfe, and Hemingway have shown. But more and more we avail ourselves of a technical language, apparent for example in David Riesman's *The Lonely Crowd:* "We must study not only the individual but the gear box which, with various slips and reversals, ties behavior in with institutional forms." We take a hint from business and industry and "sell an idea," "offer a resolution," "contact people," "are at service," and become "products of a college." The language of mass media, after having climbed down to the bottom of the masses to ingratiate itself and to prepare the market for mass circulation, rises again and creates an honest impression in the *Reader's Digest* or a sophisticated air in *Life* and particularly in *Time,* which—adjusting facts to the level of the consumer —behaves as if it had been in the harbor of Providence since time began.

The monotony of the average prefers the passive voice ("Your letter has been received," "It is being felt")—or a passive attitude ("I see no reason why this should not be done")—or tones everything down and considers itself the more objective the more impersonal it is. There is a great though concealed insistence by the speaker himself that he be as inconspicuous as possible so as not to offend those whose intellect is not their strongest feature. He will be careful not to avail himself of metaphors unless they are taken from the realm of business, technology, or popular science; he will usually start a speech with an anecdote or a joke whose favorite target he is himself, to refute any notion in advance that he might be endowed with greater intellectual capacity than his listeners. Out of a supposed modesty he will say "I feel" where he should say "I think" or "I believe," and he will be anxious to hide any emotion no matter how appropriate and justified it may be, for "emotional" in this country has become a synonym for "unbalanced," that is, "maladjusted." In no other country are the poets of less concern to the people than in America.

To make up for this modesty and lack of originality the well-adjusted person will, on assorted occasions, indulge in devastating superlatives and pretend to admire matters that are "different." So great is his effort to convince others that "different" things are "exciting" that these same different and exciting things will be accepted by a multitude of persons who, of course, will adjust them as rapidly as possible to a new norm. The salesman will say, "It's different. We sell lots of it."

Competing for attention the average man will trade essence and quality for frequency and intensity and use absolute superlatives abundantly whether they are built-in adjectives ("tremendous," "terrific," "brilliant") or comparisons of adjectives in the third degree. They are so much used and abused that writers and announcers slide into a barrage of double superlatives until an innocuous invitation to subscribe to a magazine contains no less than twenty to thirty superlatives. Such usage is commensurate with a preference for appealing to man's desire for sensation, not his judgment.

With our predilection for keeping everything smiling and in harmony it is no surprise that the word "fun" has attained rare prominence. Rearing children, reading, picnics, company, work, thinking, music, worshipping together—all are "fun." This word is subject to such diversified interpretation that it is essentially meaningless. The same can be said about "happy," which only in comparatively few instances signifies what it professes; most frequently it means "ready" ("happy to answer your letter"), "satisfied," "pleased," "glad." Something similar we notice with the word "love." We love God, a woman, a book, swimming, fun, and cheese. The three steps, to like, to be fond of, and to love, have been flattened into one convenient form.

At first glance it seems to be paradoxical that the use of the first person pronoun singular, so severely suppressed in personal letters, is favored in circular letters and printed communications. All of us are receiving such circular letters from finance companies whose presidents ask our indulgence for writing "personal" letters conceived in the spirit of enthusiasm for our convenience and welfare. We realize, of course, that these electrotyped or printed letters in "I" form have been deprived of any privacy, just as a round-robin letter is a meaningless convenience that states facts and feelings conforming to a general norm, applicable in any average situation. The adjusted man expresses himself in an adjusted language which has lost its identity.

A retirement into general expressions is at the same time a retirement from ourselves. It is not very admirable that we feel secure in such generalities, "secure" being a favorite word today and meaning "imperturbably poised." After all, only the gods and the dead are secure. It is this "You know what I mean" and "I am just an average citizen" attitude that makes for stereotype phrases consisting almost exclusively of formulae and easily comprehensible patterns. Now, to attain a certain position of respectability (attainable by anyone) the "educated" man will try to distinguish himself by aiming at sophistication. He is taking a matter "under advisement," he "places stress on a point," he will "give thought to an idea" (a rather charming picture), a fact "escaped his attention" (though it never may have reached his mind). He will speak of his "philosophy" where he merely means thought, view, or opinion without engaging in a "love for wisdom." "Prior" sounds more learned to him than "before," for he aspires to a scholarly language, superior and a bit flippant, and the result is a strange jargon, noted by H. L. Mencken: Custodian Engineer, Educational Engineer, Aesthetic Engineer, Odor Engineer, Sales Engineer, Touchdown Engineer.

While trimming up the ego of his listener or his reader, he will be careful to keep his addressee on the leash within easy reach. Speedily he will crash through all personal barriers and land within seconds at the first name of the man he has just been introduced to. This goes so far that he will be able to give the first names of his "good" friends quite easily but he will excuse himself for not knowing their surnames on the grounds of being intimately acquainted with them. Nowadays everybody is a "friend" so that this word has become an empty shell. The saleslady will alternate "Madam" with "Honey" and "Dear." Actually, to address a man as "Mister" and add his last name is a sign of coolness, just as "My dear Mr. Smith" is more chilly than "Dear Mr. Smith."

The fields where the decline of inner form and language are most noticeable are, of course, advertising, radio, television, and the movies. In order to arouse attention, agents and announcers will not recoil from the most blatant exaggeration which—however "hot" it may be—must be presented in a "cool" manner. Their horrifying English stems from the desire to be understood by everybody, and since the uneducated are the least critical, they are the most easily overcome. One step removed, but not higher, are speeches and announcements which start out in a jovial manner, assert that all of us are human beings striving for the better, and then, in the midst of their "message" insert sophisticated or technical terms which still can be vaguely understood by the naive. To this category belong references of conversationalists who will say "as you so aptly put it," whereas the recipient of this compliment has put nothing except perhaps his tongue into his cheek. As a rule, however, the target man will willingly identify himself with the unidentifiable. He will be reverent upon learning that a certain automobile (so excellent as to be beyond comparison) is endowed with all kinds of "appointments," "irregardless" of any other brand, and he himself will "use" occasionally pseudo-sophisticated language which—if nothing else—will bring him into logical trouble.

By dint of his incessant one-ear listening and his newspaper and magazine reading (which bathe his eyes with a soothing film of political events, distant tragedies, meaningless sensations, enraptured advertisements, and plain chatter), he acquires a hodgepodge of expressions. His partner-in-Babel pretends to understand him, which is all that matters. He would be utterly dumbfounded or annoyed if somebody told him that language has creative and magic values. He uses it like knife and fork, as something which is not directly associated with him. Rhetoric cares more for fluency than for precision, more for smoothness than for beauty, and this, in turn, is expressed in the voice of the speaker.

We are told from our childhood that one of the greatest virtues men can acquire is the ability of getting along with each other. We are not equally encouraged to get along with ourselves. In most instances language will suffer severely because it will try to adjust itself to a usage as practiced by the majority. We can see this quite clearly in our public schools where the intellectually outstanding student is suspect not only by pupils but by counselors as well. Individual traits are considered to be disturbing; a developed and beautiful way of expression taxes too much the comprehension and the comfort of the common man. Carelessness is the hallmark of the adjusted language. There are islands of childhood tradition of which radio commentators avail themselves benignly ("Remember when . . . ," "Those were the days . . ."), meaningless words like "well," "interesting," "privilege," "pleasure," "integrity" when speaking of art; these pass readily since no other language has so many acoustical illusions as the American. A word actually attains significance or meaning only in a given word environment. Such exercise is more easily spoken than written since word intonation, vocal emphasis, pauses, and gestures come into play.

The average conversation is so limited and stereotyped that by its noncommittal tenor it must remain more or less indifferent and evoke an impression of permanent satisfaction. The carelessly placed frequency of phrases, idioms, words, exclamations, etc. is striking: "supposed to," "glad to," "will check," "good to see you," "had a good time," "wonderful," "give me a ring," "nice day," "am afraid so," "awfully nice," "be good," "God bless you." They permeate our radio programs; they pervade our newspapers and magazines like the *Reader's Digest,* which in its very title indicates that it has taken upon itself the difficult task of editing man's mind. This linguistically precision-oiled periodical is a predigested dream of an ideal way of life adjusted to the vague notions of the average man who, in turn, is adjusted to this adjusted dream. It is a perfect "virtuous" circle which makes everybody "happy."

There is an almost messianic tendency to keep everybody informed about everything. This trend is a shallow reflection of the Period of Enlightenment of the eighteenth century and is aimed at the greatest possible multitude of men. The means by which its realization is envisaged is education. Such education is required to be realistic and pragmatic. Here the pursuit of truth and knowledge takes place in the realm of the concrete, not necessarily in that of thinking. The urge to render everything comprehensible and explicable imbues our language with smooth and "low brow" sentences and has in its wake more discussion than study, more consideration for the learner than for thought. Consequently, the target is always within comparatively easy reach. Once it has been attained, a new target is established. There is, of course, nothing wrong with such a method provided the target is not held too close to the face of the person subjected to this procedure. Such spacing, however, is rare and frequently considered to be undemocratic.

During the process of "enlightenment," which sees the epitome of wisdom in a perambulating encyclopedia and which recognizes facts as truth without further investigating them, language and meaning are adjusted to the beneficiary. Comic strips, for instance, have a major "educational" function, even a religious one, as illustrations of this kind pertaining to the Bible bear out. One is reminded of medieval illustrations when the general public was unable to read, and one wonders whether much has changed since that time except the acquisition of a visual skill. Reading as an art has certainly become problematic. Condensed books, excerpts, abstracts, speed reading, outlines are hardly witnesses to the contrary. Television, spellbinding and immobilizing, suggesting a variety of shortcuts to the intellectual labors of man, attempts to advance our passive reception by refuting our imagination and making contemplation superfluous. It gives the public what it wants and the public preferably wants action in pictures.

The decline of language as an art is further evidenced by our increasing inability in letter writing, by the fragmentary character of our conversation (for which the cocktail party is a telling common denominator), and by our impatience with form. In his *Democracy in America* Tocqueville speaks of men who "do not readily comprehend the utility of forms: they feel an instinctive contempt for them . . . as they commonly aspire to none but easy and present gratifications, they rush onward to the object of their desires, and the slightest delay exasperates them." Our linguistic adjustment has reached the consumer level whose norm is the idiom of the salesman.

In order to appreciate and to evaluate a thing we have to compare it with other things of the same nature. In the realm of language we do this by reading and listening. The cheaper listening has become (broadcast symphonies, operas, sermons, etc.) and the less effort we have to exert, the duller is our perception. We rarely are capable of expressing finesse anymore for we either indulge in an ironic style, as members of the learned professions like to do, or we fall into bathos as the majority of preachers demonstrate. We are always anxious to put a "message" across. Thus language is little more than a convenience, a commodity, or a means of communication. Such an attitude is not very propitious to the study of foreign languages. These, however, like nothing else, can make the student aware of his native tongue, which by the foreign tongue becomes more finely wrought, more precise and resilient. The present upsurge and stress on foreign languages is an expedient one, not one in essence; it has a practical goal which one approaches with converted mass production methods. We forget too easily that the mastery of a foreign idiom depends—as far as its interpretation and application are concerned —upon the mind of man. Language as a tool is merely a tool, and tools are auxiliary means. Their command alone guarantees nothing creative. Text-books trade willingly cultural values for everyday situations with sports events, traffic problems, and entertainment—even in Latin. This incredible adjustment is being justified by the assertion that the interest of students will be greatly aroused. What kind of interest? one feels compelled to ask.

Not so long ago I took a group of graduate students to Europe. In Oxford we were shown around by a young, tall, and athletically built chap. He led us through various colleges and the one where he himself was studying. What was he studying? the group wanted to know. Latin and Greek and the great poets. What for? was the astonished and almost compassionate question. Was he going to teach? He did not think so. He was planning to go into business, or commerce, as he put it. Into business? What did he need Latin and Greek for? Our guide looked at us pensively. "To be a man, you've got to be a man, haven't you?" he said. "It's very beautiful and quite practical, you know."

We have courses for remedial reading in colleges; we put aside anything that is not immediately comprehensible to us unless a closer and more laborious study promises us financial reward or physical comfort. The more basic our language is, the more abbreviated and dedicated to convenient grooves, the poorer our very lives are. Adjustment usually has a downward motion and comes to an end only when there is sufficient resistance. This resistance can only be in the mind of man. Unless he is willing to see that poor language necessitates poor thinking and a shallow life, he will adjust himself more and more to lower strata and be commensurately "happier" until he reaches the blissful stage of an animal. There, however, unforeseen troubles will lie in wait for him.

COMMENT

Using his key phrase "Nothing gives us so perfectly away as language," Mr. Brandt proceeds to analyze the American character as it is revealed through the language Americans use. To this end, he successively analyzes a number of different speech adjustments, each of which seems to grow out of the same general trait in the American character. He concludes with a plea that we cease to "adjust" our language (and ourselves) to lower levels.

SUGGESTIONS FOR WRITING

1. Begin an essay with a variation on Mr. Brandt's key phrase—"Nothing gives us so perfectly away as (clothes, manners, habits, etc.)."

2. The average student employs only a limited vocabulary to distinguish between his acquaintances. Make a list of the most common words of

approval and disapproval and write an essay demonstrating the lack of discrimination revealed by this language deficiency.

3. Follow Mr. Brandt's practice. Take notes on habitual phrases (greetings, farewells, expletives). What speech characteristics separate professors from other adults? Can you distinguish between seniors and freshmen? athletes and nonathletes?

Our Movie
Mythology   DORE SCHARY

IF WE AS A PEOPLE are inclined to look for happy endings, it is perhaps because we are accustomed to them. To this day, whatever its distortions, the success story is the American goal. We believe that obstacles are made to be overcome, that Americans *do* scale unscalable mountains and cross impossible rivers, and that although we don't like wars, we never lose one.

All this has been reflected in American culture in a number of ways, but surely the most dramatic representation of the American dream and its folk heroes has appeared in our motion pictures. None of us has to be reminded how integral a part of American culture the motion picture has become, for good and for ill. Spell it with a small "c," if you like, but the relevance of the movies to the American scene and the American character cannot be denied. And if we are inclined to consider the earlier movies naïve, let us be prepared to admit the same about our countrymen and about ourselves. Through the years, the American screen has acted as a mirror of the American character, a mirror not without flaws but nevertheless a mirror. Let us examine some of its reflections.

I don't think it is any accident that the most durable and best patronized type of movie is the Western. Westerns continue to be made for the simple reason that customers flock to see them, and producers know they have a steady market for them. One Western may vary infinitesimally from another; it doesn't seem to matter. I think it is because the Western stirs in all of us pride and admiration for our own heritage—a heritage we owe to the men of a new nation who carved its history with tomahawk and knife and secured it with shotgun and raw endurance. The details of an individual Western are secondary; what is irresistible, apparently, is that the old, beloved tale of a good man winning over insurmountable odds, defeating the bad man in an honorable way, is being retold. In a way, we are repeatedly honoring the heroes who were our forebears; it is a kind of ritual offering to their memory.

As Americans, we love a hero, a winner, a champion. It is not in the

Reprinted by permission of the author and of *The Reporter*.

American character to be drawn to a loser, no matter how honorably he lost. This may not be good, but it is true all the same. We are impatient of anything short of success.

Since this country was not settled except for scattered Indian tribes, conquering the wilderness was a job for strong and courageous young men. So the young, strong, courageous man has become our symbol, and the Western is perhaps the ideal method of perpetuating it. Most of the prime television time is devoted to Westerns nowadays, no matter how dreary some of them are. The great Western classics of the screen remain on many of the all-time-best lists, starting away back with *The Great Train Robbery,* on through *The Iron Horse, The Covered Wagon, Stage Coach, The Big Country, Shane, Giant, Red River,* and *High Noon.* And of course, the redoubtable *Virginian.* And the end, my friends, is nowhere in sight.

Not surprisingly, the most durable stars in the history of the screen are male. Not only male, but strong, rugged types, starting with William S. Hart and Tom Mix right down to Gary Cooper, John Wayne, Gregory Peck, Clark Gable, Burt Lancaster, and Alan Ladd. These men represent, or at one time represented, the ideal. Audiences never seem to tire of them. The phenomenon of the Western's durability has not been lost on shrewd actors whom at first glance you would not associate with the Western type. James Stewart, for example, returned to the screen after the war in a series of Westerns, beginning with *Winchester.* Unlikely casting though it might have seemed, he became a bigger star than ever. Spencer Tracy made the switch with great success. And so did James Cagney and Tyrone Power. And Bogart, in *The Treasure of Sierra Madre.* Everybody *has* to try a Western—from Wallace Beery to Marlon Brando.

Every so often a different breed of star appears, of the type Charles Ray represented, or Wallace Reid. Today I can think of Cary Grant, or perhaps David Niven. Quiet, well-mannered fellows all, but their real appeal lies in the fact that they usually have been called upon, three-quarters of the way through the picture, to abandon those qualities and emerge, however apologetically, as "heroes." I recall Jimmy Stewart in *Destry Rides Again,* and all the old Harold Lloyd films, and Charles Ray in *The Egg Crate Wallop.* And in a fairly recent film, *The Big Country,* the entire point of the picture was the leading character's aversion to settling disputes with violence. He was played by Gregory Peck. It was a fascinating idea, but you know as well as I do exactly what Mr. Peck was doing in the last reel. He and Charlton Heston were clobbering each other, and the audience was satisfied that Peck was a handy man with his fists after all, just as it had hoped.

The American preoccupation with violence and crime was never more manifest than during the cycle of gangster pictures. The development of the public attitude toward the bootlegger can be traced, not surprisingly, in the movies of the time. At first the bootlegger was an amiable enough fellow who went amiably about his business, purveying his wares to his neighbors while the forces of law and order tolerantly looked the other way. Or he was back from the First World War, having learned nothing but how to shoot Germans, to find his girl had betrayed him, no job waiting, and so forth. But not until the Capone empire became so enormous and so deadly did Americans realize what had been bred in their midst. Some of the better gangster films attempted to be honest exposés of the gunmen and racketeers, showing the cruelty and viciousness of the system and the men who comprised it, but almost always the portraits turned out to be sympathetic. Why? I think it was because audiences secretly (or not so secretly, come to think of it) admired the gangsters' supposed manliness and ruggedness, and the easy way in which they kicked over the traces—something that all of us, sometime or other, have a hankering to do, even if we do not have the nerve or gall to go through with it. Big stars were created in that milieu: Cagney in *Public Enemy,* when he pushed a grapefruit into Mae Clarke's face; Muni in *Scarface,* Bogart in *The Petrified Forest,* Robinson in *Little Caesar.*

The real gangsters of the era met their match in the men of the FBI and the battle was joined on the screen as well. The forces of justice— the G-Men—became the new strong men of the screen. And who were the actors playing them? The same fellows who had played the gangsters: Robinson, Cagney, Bogart & Co. And never were the American ideals of law and order, fair play, strong male personalities, justice, and violence mixed into a more palatable brew.

Again, in the gangster cycle, the stars who emerged were men. All through movie history, this emergence of the powerful male figure as an idol is evident, and it is true in other walks of American life. We constantly reiterate our adoration of the virtues of courage, strength, endurance, and masculinity in our hero worship of sports figures. The tendency is sometimes carried to ridiculous length. Endurance for its own sake is so admired that we find ourselves paying respectful attention not only to Channel swimmers but also to flagpole sitters or people who can dance the longest period without dropping in their tracks or eat the tallest stack of pancakes at a sitting. Anyone who can do anything longer, faster, bigger, higher, wetter, hotter, colder, or easier than anybody else is automatically a hero. He exemplifies achievement. Even when our heroes are out-and-out fakes, as in the wrestling matches on TV, we cheer on our favorites, we identify our villains, though we see the fraud perpetrated before our eyes.

Again and again the dominance of the male shows up in any analysis of the American character. Consider the number of films that have dealt with the admiration, affection, and love between two men. Immediately we think of the two-man teams motion pictures have produced: Gable and Tracy, Burt Lancaster and Kirk Douglas, Cagney and Pat O'Brien. And away back, Jack Holt and Ralph Graves, Richard Dix and David Butler, Raymond Hatton and Wallace Beery, Karl Dane and George K. Arthur—even Laurel and Hardy. In all the pictures these teams made, a girl, of course, figured in the proceedings, but she usually ran a poor third to the two men. You certainly remember that in the Westerns of not so long ago, the hero remained respectfully distant from the girl, and at the story's end he was permitted to bestow a chaste kiss not on the girl but on his horse.

I hazard the guess that if you were to ask most Americans to name the twenty movies they found most memorable, there would be very few love stories on the list. Chances are, most lists would include such films as *From Here to Eternity, The Best Years of Our Lives, The Informer, I Am a Fugitive from a Chain Gang, All Quiet on the Western Front,* and perhaps the current *Ben-Hur,* whose main emotional stories involve men —Ben-Hur and Messala in one instance, and Ben-Hur and Quintus in the other.

You may be struck by the fact, as I am, that five of the six pictures I just referred to are in some sense war pictures. Inadvertently I have underlined another illustration of the American appetite for violence. It has been my experience, too, that although American audiences go to see good and often bad war movies, they resist documentary films on the same subject, in spite of the fact that several extraordinary ones have been made. I can only account for this by suggesting that while we do not exactly shrink from hard, cold facts, we prefer them dished up as fiction, letting ourselves become involved emotionally rather than intellectually. The very best movies succeed in involving audiences both ways.

It is an accurate assessment of the American character to say that it is suspicious of anything smacking of the "intellectual." The brainy man is considered effete, somehow lacking in character; there's something almost un-American about him. This belief has gained currency as a corollary to our worship of brawn, muscle, stamina—what we consider the masculine traits. Why the egghead should be ridiculed and the cowpoke revered is one of the mysteries that perhaps can be solved by looking at our heritage. The feeling seems to be that all the quiet, brainy man can do is sit around and talk a subject to death. The man of action (our hero) is a man of few words, and he Gets Things Done—with his fists, probably, or with his trusty six-shooter. Back in the old days, the frontiersmen didn't *debate* the fine points of rustling cattle. When they caught a rustler or a horse thief, they strung him up from the nearest tree and that was that. Extreme offenses called for extreme measures in a time when

men lived constantly on the brink of extinction. The concept of the vigi-
lantes arose out of sheer necessity in a West without law, but it still survives today, even when there are laws with teeth in them. Occasional
lynchings furnish deplorable proof of this.

I do not mean to suggest only unattractive elements in the American
character. One of the strongest instincts we have is the sense of fair play.
We hate a bully. We champion the underdog. We protect the defense-
less. We believe in the "fair shake"—a peculiarly American phrase.
Sometimes our feelings about these things are demonstrated in odd ways.
One incident comes to mind about the time we were making *Crossfire.*
The central character had little to recommend him; he was a triple mur-
derer, brutal and menacing. In the original script, this man got his come-
uppance when he was machine-gunned by a group of MPs. From a story
point of view, he was only getting his just deserts, and we shot the scene
as it was written. I learned that it is a mistake to overstate retribution.
The first audience that saw this version didn't like it. And they didn't
like it because the character, terrible as he was, was trapped like a rat,
and the audience thought it was reprehensible for *anybody* to be made to
die that way. We redid the ending and dispatched the man with a single
shot under "fair" circumstances.

Americans normally have an aversion to informers, to stool pigeons.
Also in *Crossfire,* it was vital to the capture of the villain that one of his
Army buddies provide information about him. Quite in the American
character, he balked. Still, he had to be persuaded, and we had to rewrite
the scene carefully so that he could, in good conscience, give the information. "You're not informing," the boy is told by an Army major;
"you're serving justice." It is very difficult to sympathize with a man
who has betrayed a friend, or thinks he has, and no matter how you try
to justify it, you never quite succeed. This was even true of the gangster
pictures. I remember *Scarface* vividly, and particularly the sequence in
which Paul Muni was battling a lot of policemen. The audience, believe
it or not, was rooting for the gangster, not because they admired or respected this despicable character but because the odds were against him.
It's a cockeyed kind of sportsmanship, maybe, but it's sportsmanship.

There is a strain of healthy cynicism in Americans, along with their
somewhat romantic view of themselves. It is detectable especially in the
realm of politics and public figures. We tend to think of most politicians
as corrupt or at least corruptible. We accept this belief in the spirit of
amusement, and we resign ourselves to our political leaders and our states-
men with the offhand philosophy that after all they are the best of a bad
lot. I suppose this view stems directly from the frontier attitude—a good-
natured acceptance of the checked-vest, self-seeking politicos of that disorganized period in our history. The lavish promises, the baby kissing,

and the funny hats appealed to isolated, uninformed people who loved nothing better than a good show. And in those days, shows were few and far between. If the show was good, it was enough; you didn't have to believe it. And all it cost you was your vote. That opinion of politicians remains to this day, right or wrong, good or bad. Some excellent men have remained in political obscurity because of the low esteem in which we hold politicians. It is the price we've paid for our cynicism.

Americans also have a strange but sneaking admiration for con men and resourceful hucksters who live by their wits, getting something for nothing and operating (correctly) on the Barnum theory that there's one born every minute. The admiration goes back, I think, to our esteem for the loner, the man on his own who makes up his own rules, plays the long shots, and sees them pay off. Even the victim can only gasp in admiring outrage at how he has been taken. He chalks it up to experience and does little else, because by now the hoaxer is well on his way out of town. The victim concedes, ruefully and with a kind of respect, that he has been outsmarted. Americans do go by this curious rule, and it is another facet of our highly competitive natures. The hustler has always been a folk character, colorful, breezy, friendly, and larcenous, and we are usually pleased to see him get away with it. We are pleased and amused to read that the Brooklyn Bridge is still changing ownership regularly, that iceboxes are being sold to Eskimos, and that there's still a brisk business in the gold-brick trade. The great W. C. Fields became a major star by portraying this typically American character in a number of memorable film variations on the same theme. We immediately warm to the character because he's a go-getter, enterprising and indomitable. And it's fun to be fooled. Let him not get caught, though. Once that happens, he's no smarter than the rest of us and we have no use for him, and no more affection. Because he's a cheat and a liar? No! Because he isn't very good at it.

The honest go-getter still wins the affection of Americans today, just as surely as he did in the days of Horatio Alger. Today, the American Dream has been taken over by the Madison Avenue contingent, which has sure-fire ways of educating all of us in what we must like, what we must want, and even what we are. The Dream gets a little nightmarish now and then, because it has come to seem that the ideal state is for all of us Americans to be exactly alike and to want exactly the same things— always *things*—in endless quantity.

What other purely American characteristics can we find reflected in our culture? Let's look again at our champions, our hero figures. We are very jealous of them, and will not permit them to deviate for very long from our carefully circumscribed portrait of them. We can be fickle if they disappoint us. When he was champion, Dempsey was not popular, for reasons relating to the time; he did things, or failed to do things, which as champion we expected of him. But Dempsey was defeated by Gene Tunney, who also was not very popular as champion because he was so unlike the American idea of one. He read Shakespeare and was otherwise an educated man; Americans didn't quite know what to make of him. He was a gentleman, which in our book just didn't square with his being heavyweight champion of the world. As a result, Dempsey became more popular after he lost the championship, mainly because we didn't approve of the new champion. On the other hand, Babe Ruth, a real immortal, had all the stuff. He still holds the all-time home-run record, and in addition he was everything we demanded of a champion. He was a hard drinker, battled with his bosses, had a weakness for the ladies, and ingratiated himself with kids. He was a natural, and nobody in baseball has ever replaced him.

Such is our regard for the dominant male, the recurring motif in our cultural pattern. It's interesting that we have few legendary women in our folklore. Beyond Barbara Frietchie and Molly Pitcher, it is hard to enumerate many women whom we venerate as heroines. And these two, curiously enough, are remembered for doing things that were decidedly unfeminine; they were brave and they were defiant, both masculine qualities.

If I have suggested that man's appetite for woman has been neglected during the history of the motion picture, let me hasten to correct the impression. In fact, the very first motion picture to attract any kind of attention was a short, curious little item called *The Kiss*. The film was simple to the point of imbecility, but it did show a man kissing a woman. And to this day, men are kissing women in movies with as much enthusiasm as ever—more, judging from certain films that don't worry too much about the Production Code. Our biggest female stars over the years reached their peak as sex symbols: from Theda Bara and Nita Naldi, through Clara Bow, on to Joan Crawford, Lana Turner, Ava Gardner, Elizabeth Taylor, and Marilyn Monroe. The healthy animalism of these women is still one of the major foundations on which the American film industry rests. How long we can hold the movies in bounds against the flood of sex detail, bosoms, and bordellos that has inundated our books and magazines is a question that interests critics and audiences. Nothing could be more explicit than a movie—and what business it could mean!

However, there is an even longer list of women who represent other qualities. When women in movies have not been caricatures of the red-hot momma, they have tended to be unapproachable symbols of matronly purity. The refined, almost unattainable symbol of woman on a pedestal has been personified by such people as Mary Pickford, the Gish sisters,

Janet Gaynor, Irene Dunne, Greer Garson, Loretta Young, Katharine Hepburn, and Grace Kelly. This "pure" woman figure was more natural to the American character as it developed. The lone frontiersman of the American past saw so little of women as a rule that they became a sort of unrealized ideal and an overworked stereotype. Mother was always there cooking a hot meal and ready to forgive us even if we robbed, murdered, and raped. A picture years ago that showed a mother turning her boy over to the FBI failed to make the grade because Mom couldn't do that.

It is only fair to point out here that even in the early movie days, a slim, golden thread of genuine artistry ran through the homespun fabric of the average motion-picture output—with films such as *The Crowd* and *Hallelujah!* through the years to *East of Eden* and *The Nun's Story*, demonstrating a genuine awareness of the more elusive facets of life. It is equally fair to point out that these films were highly appreciated in their time by American audiences—the same audiences, incidentally, whose movie habit had grown so strong that to satisfy it, hundreds of films of no cultural value except to historians filled the movie screens. Here, the movies were no worse offenders than the run-of-the-mill potboilers turned out by book publishers—books that contributed little to America's understanding of itself. But the point is that both fields reflected America's taste and its lack of interest in its position in the world scene.

As America has grown, it has become more and more complex. The movies are growing complex too, reflecting the shifting colors of the country, its growing subtleties, its changing patterns. The current and upcoming crop of motion pictures offers a number of provocative and unfettered comments on the world about us. Audiences demand it now. America is growing up, and is able at last to take a grown-up look at itself, based less on past accomplishments and more on the awareness that we are part of a bigger world.

Our culture, including the motion picture, which has accurately portrayed American character in the past, will continue to keep pace. Let us hope that it will reflect an America that has come of age creatively, politically, and emotionally.

COMMENT

This essay is a useful example of the way in which specific evidence can lead to generalizations. The author begins with his assumption that the movies, for better or worse, reflect American culture; he then proceeds to examine this reflection. The immense popularity of Western, gangster, and war movies demonstrates the kind of heroes we want and testifies to our love of violence and of fair play, and to our peculiar form of cynicism. Mr. Schary then discusses the corollary attributes of our female stars and concludes with general remarks about the future of the American culture.

SUGGESTIONS FOR WRITING

1. Mr. Schary tells us how the public's wishes shape the content of the movies. Write an essay in which you explain the ways in which the movies and television have altered the taste, ideas, or behavior of the public. Because generalizing is so dangerous and so often boring in a short paper, concentrate on the way in which a particular movie or television program has affected a particular person.

2. Movie audiences composed primarily of college students often react differently from others. Try to describe and account for these differences. Use concrete examples wherever possible.

3. Write an essay on a particular aspect of college mythology. What does the college student want to be? to seem to be? Who are his heroes? his villains? How can the behavior of the college student be better understood through knowing his mythology?

WAR
OF
THE
GENERATIONS

Louis E. Reik

BY THE TIME a student reaches college age, he should be well launched on a good, brisk war of independence. His object is to express to his satisfaction the ferment of energy with which sometimes he is all but bursting. He no longer endows his elders with the godlike authority they had for him in the days of his helpless childhood. In fact, now that he has learned that even his parents are not so wealthy, wise and infallible as he had previously imagined them to be, he enters a phase when he exaggerates their shortcomings. Not infrequently, he feels constrained to apologize for them to his friends, or to express a blend of rebellious attitudes ranging from condescension to open hostility. At the point where cold war threatens to give way to a hot one in the home, he packs up and goes off to college, often to the immense relief of all concerned.

In its physical aspect, a college campus seems one of the most peaceful and beautiful places in the world. But behind this idyllic façade, the student continues to wage his war for independence. He has achieved a truce, if not a victory, in his struggle to free himself from those powerful despots in the home who had only to assert their wishes to establish them as family law. But at the university he is confronted with some of the same demands for unquestioning obedience to the seemingly arbitrary dictates of his elders and presumably his betters. It is true that at first he is ready to have more tolerance for these elders than for his parents, but the role of submissive neophyte in which he is cast, with its demands for subordinating private inclinations to an unrelenting succession of assignments, requirements and examinations inevitably stirs up the urge to revolt to a more or less intense degree. But while this urge is probably common to students everywhere, it remains for the most part covert and unnoticed, except in occasional times of riot. Students, obviously, have too much to lose to run the risk of open rebellion during their college days. Actually, there seems to be a clear and startling analogy between the educational customs of civilized people and the primitive initiation rites

Reprinted by permission of the publisher, *The Nation*.

for adolescents practiced the world over from ancient times. The modern student, like his primitive brother, is faced with the necessity of submitting to an ordeal at the hands of his elders as the price he must pay for the privileges of adulthood. It is debatable which ordeal is worse— the student's with its prolonged psychological torments, or the primitive boy's with its relatively fleeting physical hardships. In any event, the student's initiation into the world of civilized men cannot be assumed, even under the most auspicious circumstances, to be an entirely painless affair, or to proceed without provoking conflict, hidden or expressed.

Both at home and in the university, there are confusing elements that prevent the average student from achieving independence, or even from recognizing clearly that this may be desirable. After all, it is undeniable that parents and teachers ostensibly have his own best interests at heart, so that filial duty and gratitude demand that he give up his own inclinations when they clash with theirs. Moreover, he is confronted with the additional difficulty of discriminating between what his elders in their wisdom unselfishly advocate for him and what they mistakenly imagine is best because it would be best for themselves. Henry Fielding observed long ago of this tendency of the older generation to confuse their children's identity with their own, thus making both parties completely miserable in the process: "Though it is almost universal in parents, [it] hath always appeared to me to be the most unaccountable of all the absurdities which ever entered into the brain of that strange prodigious creature man." Bernard Shaw, in one of his prefaces, went even further, presuming not only to find the cause of the absurdity but also to prescribe for its cure: "If adults will frankly give up their claim to know better than children what the purposes of the Life Force are, and treat the child as an experiment like themselves, and possibly a more successful one, and at the same time relinquish their monstrous parental claims to personal private property in children, the rest may be left to common sense." Just recently, the veteran child psychoanalyst, Gerald H. J. Pearson, in his monograph *Adolescence and the Conflict of Generations,* after convincingly tracing some of the hidden psychological origins of the conflict, concluded that since its main roots on both sides are so deeply anchored in a tangle of emotional attitudes, of which self-love is by no means the least important, he had small hope that either parents or adolescents could profit much from a generalized intellectual explanation of the affairs of the heart—which nevertheless he proceeded to give in his book.

These emotional affairs of the heart have such a distinct and primitive logic of their own that psychiatrists long before Freud have steadfastly and repeatedly observed that a man may be brilliantly endowed from the intellectual viewpoint and simultaneously an irresponsible child where his emotions are concerned. Or he may be the reverse: a genius when it comes to the affairs of the heart, but an intellectual moron as measured by his I.Q. In this connection, it is worth remembering that following the introduction of Binet's intelligence test in the early years of this century, situations in ordinary school and social life that before seemed baffling because someone was involved whose feeble-mindedness remained unrecognized, became clear and susceptible to control when approached with the new knowledge. Undoubtedly, some day we shall also have better indices of emotional development, a kind of E.Q., which will enable teachers and parents to take a more calm and realistic attitude towards problems posed by students that now seem inexplicable or of deliberate malevolent intent.

Meanwhile, we have outgrown old superstitions in the ruling power of witches, devils, planets and charms, but have still to discard the notions that emotional attitudes and motives are readily controlled by the intelligence, or that they depend only on external circumstances, or that they are utterly mysterious beyond comprehension. On the contrary, medical psychology, particularly during the last half-century, has been accumulating an impressive mass of clinical data, drawn from normal as well as abnormal subjects, that demonstrates something of the peculiar evolution and logic of the emotional life.

In college practice, for example, the psychiatrist has many opportunities for observing that a student's attitude towards his father seems to determine his attitude towards college authorities. A student who has been strongly attached to, and simultaneously overwhelmed by, the father is apt to view the college teacher as the embodiment of the wisdom of the ages. His war for intellectual independence does not go well because the more he admires his mentors the more he is inclined to be uncritically influenced by them and to belittle himself. Educators are familiar with students of this type, who are variously called "perfectionists," "over-achievers" or "over-conscientious." The more they belittle themselves, the less capable they become of achieving self-assurance and spontaneous, original work. Their energies, instead, are used up in curbing natural impulse and in preoccupation with superficial detail.

One such student, for example, felt compelled to memorize the dates of withdrawal and return on the librarian's card in a book of assigned reading, to say nothing of a staggering mass of excerpts he had copied down. The psychiatrist sees this as a kind of self-defeating compromise, in which there has been no wholehearted acceptance of either the self or the father. Its object, essentially, is to keep the peace and to win rewards and esteem from parents and teachers for a kind of mechanical compliance characteristic of the rote-learning of childhood days, rather than to achieve satisfying growth and true self-expression. Deficient self-esteem and an exaggerated estimate of authority make such students slaves to duty and routine, a slavery which the world too frequently applauds, but which nevertheless defeats the aims of liberal education and provides fertile soil for private misery and neurotic symptoms, such as fatigue, insomnia, incapacitating tension, and sometimes despair.

Likewise, it is frequently observed that students who have been inclined to defy and underestimate the father are similarly inclined to belittle authority in general. In extreme form, their behavior is variously regarded as immature, abnormal, delinquent or even criminal, depending on how badly the community feels its interests have been violated and how it assesses the responsibility of the offender. As long ago as 1910, the psychiatrist Stewart Paton (who incidentally was the first to advocate a mental-health program for college students) is said to have been astonished when he first began his work at Princeton University to discover "students who had pronounced suicidal, homicidal impulses, sex perverts, those who stole, cheated, were exceedingly egotistical, aggressive and showed other signs of serious maladjustment." He saw no point in making "every attempt . . . to induce all, the unfit as well as the fit, to pass through the educational mill" which, he noted, is in sharp contrast to the more realistic policy in schools and colleges of preventing those with weak hearts or lungs from taking part in strenuous athletic pursuits. Since then, colleges have gradually been paying more attention to the need for earlier recognition and more intelligent treatment of students with serious emotional disturbances.

When it comes to the less serious problems posed by rebellious but essentially healthy students, any good educator knows that the rebel is only confirmed in his defiance when he sees himself vindictively or scornfully treated with little, if any, concern as an individual, in spite of the professed brotherly love for him of the Christian community. The late psychoanalyst Fritz Wittels rightly pointed out the enormous difference in the effect on the culprit when punishment is administered by those who care for him, as by a father in childhood who wants to continue to love the naughty child, or by those in institutions or state who neither care for him nor are interested in his welfare. The wise father and the good teacher intuitively know that lasting repentance and ultimate self-discipline are not products of terror and force alone.

The student's war for independence does not, however, always display the more obvious forms of submission and rebellion described above. The majority of students seem to oscillate somewhere between these extremes, being on the whole perhaps more rebellious than submissive. Those who read standard histories of university life, where, as Rashdall observed, "the life of the virtuous student has no annals," are not surprised to find that they have been a rebellious lot from the beginning. Haskins in his informative *The Rise of the Universities* records that in 1317 the students at Bologna not only brought the townsmen to terms by threatening to go elsewhere, but also laid down strict regulations governing the teaching of their professors, who were subject to fines for absences and other controlling maneuvers. We also learn that in medieval Paris students went about armed with swords and knives, attacking citizens, abusing women and slashing off one another's fingers. Elsewhere, it is said that prior to the present century, outbreaks of violence against college officials and property were more extensive and frequent than they are today in American colleges, and were seemingly worst at the most puritanical colleges. On the other hand, it is well known that there have been periods when students submitted to a much more rigorous academic discipline than at present, at least in a physical sense. From the standpoint of the psychological relationship today between the older and younger generations, it would be an anomaly if in these more democratic times either generation were to revert to the attempts at physical domination of the feudal past. But he who looks will find that the conflict goes on in other less obvious ways. It has, so to speak, been driven underground.

For instance, a student complains of a perplexing inability to concentrate on academic material, yet emphasizes that he would like ultimately to follow his father's career in teaching; meanwhile, he feels tense and miserable *except* when engaged in extracurricular activities. Another has had extensive medical investigations, with entirely negative results, of his complaint of recurring digestive upset, which, on inquiry, is found to be associated particularly with times of stress and examination. A third, while professing to want to remain in the university from which his father graduated, is in danger of dismissal because he cuts classes from oversleeping, which he says he can neither correct nor understand.

Examples like these could be multiplied. But a recital of their bare outlines does not adequately convey the rich and subtle interplay of defensive and offensive maneuver that goes on. Often conflict is not ostensibly with authority at all, but with what we now recognize as its inner representative and ally, the conscience. The college psychiatrist encounters many instances where such inner warfare leads to apparently senseless dilemmas or pointless activities. These can only be understood when viewed in terms of the struggle within, reflecting in part a desire to yield to temptation and in part the scruples about it. Students can, of course, justify themselves with compelling logic and eloquence, recalling Shaw's observation that excellent reasons can be found "for every conceivable course of conduct, from dynamiting and vivisection to martyrdom." I share the feeling with colleagues that a university would be a dead and dusty place if all students were models of conformity. But I can also sympathize with the professor who once said that a university would be a wonderful place if there were no undergraduates in it.

When we turn to the strategies that the older generation employs to meet these offensive forays of students during the years of their rebellion, we find on the college campus that they gravitate toward two opposite extremes, neither of which seems sensible or practicable from a psychiatric or pedagogical point of view. At one extreme, there are those who rely heavily on impersonal disciplinary retaliation when students exhibit unusual behavior or become troublesome. These are the upholders of traditions and rules at all costs, the sensitive spirits who beneath an impersonal mask react to the offending student as though they had been personally affronted themselves. At the other extreme, there are those among the older generation so easily influenced by the student's point of view that if their attitude prevailed there would inevitably be chaos and ineffective leadership and education.

Both extremists view the psychiatrist's approach according to their own predilections. The disciplinarians assume that the psychiatrist is indubitably against any punishment whatsoever and thus favors anarchy on the campus. The opposite group tends to be so convinced of the basic stability and intellectual capacity of any student who has been admitted to college that it suspects the psychiatrist of magnifying mental pathology where none exists, or of wanting to substitute some dreary form of adjustment for all the excitement and color that rebellious youth brings to the campus. Both views miss the mark.

Concerning the disciplinarian viewpoint, it is now becoming well known that punishment must take into account the individual as well as his offense. In other words, we are beginning to realize that there are abnormal states which no amount of punishment can cure, but in fact may aggravate instead. Until the comparatively recent pioneer work of the psychiatrist William Healy, begun in 1908, the law, for example, was still operating under the assumption that the vast majority of juvenile delinquents are of essentially sound mind, can control perverse impulses and will respond favorably to punishment. Since then, through the work of juvenile courts and the psychological appraisal of offenders, society has been discovering, sometimes to its chagrin, that unwittingly it has been actively persecuting individuals who are so powerfully driven to antisocial behavior that they appear genuinely unable to restrain themselves as normal individuals can do, and so must be judged to be in some respects irresponsible and provided for in some other way than the law traditionally decrees.

On the campus, the very word "irresponsible" applied to a student is apt to evoke the itch to punish rather than the urge to investigate. The college psychiatrist, for his part, has to distinguish between students whose perversities come against a background of reasonable stability, and those who are rendered "irresponsible" by some deeply ingrained intrapsychic disturbance. Take, for example, the phenomenon of examination anxiety. Because it is present in almost everyone to some degree, it is often assumed of little importance. Yet in a large university hardly a year goes by without several more or less serious psychiatric casualties during the final examination period. The large majority of students can meet and surmount this type of pressure without serious strain. But the problem, as the psychiatrist sees it, is to recognize that there are occasional students so vulnerable already that this added strain of examinations can cause a degree of incapacity well beyond the student's ability to control. Fortunately, these exaggerated reactions to examinations are not frequent nor are they always of serious import. But occasionally they are symptomatic of deeply entrenched and extensive emotional disturbances that should be recognized as early as possible.

In the past, the first reaction of disciplinarians everywhere to the student who complains of being rattled on an examination is to turn a deaf ear, or if, as occasionally happens, a blank examination paper has been turned in, to feel incensed and to think of maximum penalties. The student may at once be assumed to be disrespectful, dishonest or flagrantly lazy, the choice of diagnosis being more in line with the disciplinarian's pet preconception than with the facts, and the treatment being dictated more by fear that other students will become delinquent on examinations than by considerations of the educational development of the individual. The disciplinarian has often, therefore, been strangely reluctant to give the offending student careful and thoughtful scrutiny. Yet from both the psychiatric and educational points of view, an inquiry aimed at some understanding of whether the student is in good mental health has a more far-reaching significance than the specific offensive itself, or the question of whether to punish or not to punish. The student who says that during an important examination his mind becomes blank or behaves like a drunken man's is confessing to inner disorganization that may have important implications regarding not only his mental health but his future educational development as well. Besides, an attitude of inquiry that seeks to establish the facts of a student's inner life will do more to alleviate cold war on the campus than one that presupposes, or is intent on, arbitrary domination.

Those lenient souls who, on the other hand, regard student aberrations and rebellions with an overly benevolent eye—perhaps finding in them a source of vicarious excitement and secret pleasure—run the same risk as the disciplinarians of overlooking the educational value of having some understanding of the student's inner problems. I agree with Chancellor Lawrence A. Kimpton of the University of Chicago, who is recently reported to have said that a great university must also have the "excitement of rebellion, the maladjustment of youth," and "occasionally it should discipline itself in freedom by embracing and supporting a weird one just for his weirdness." But I have too much respect for the force and vitality of rebellious youth to share his fear that the university "would lose all its greatness if it were tortured into adjustment through analysis" by the psychiatrist or by anyone else. The student has something to say about whether he will submit to such analysis, and regardless of how desirable others may think such a course to be, he nevertheless holds a veto power. The psychiatrist would be a megalomaniac indeed if he believed he had the magic power sometimes attributed to him for making unwilling rebels lay down their arms. In fact, he would be inclined to wonder whether those who overlook this veto power of youth are not themselves overestimating the power of the older generation to influence, guide, and to create in its own image. In short, he would caution educators and parents, as he must constantly caution himself, against the illusions of omnipotence and omniscience.

Tension and conflict between the old and the young will presumably always exist. But the problem of whether the individual's aggressive energies will be expressed in useful or destructive ways has never before cast such a deep and terrible shadow over human life. The student today, for example, must learn that atomic energy is merely the concentrated projection of these inner energies, made possible by the unified efforts of many, and thus not rightfully subject to arbitrary individual control or caprice. That the days of unbridled individualism are gone is a lesson that, at bottom, no high-spirited young man wants to learn.

Faced with the mounting urgency of this difficult problem, college teachers and psychiatrists need to pool their efforts to promote a healthy understanding of the forces in the inner world. Up until the present century, man could enjoy the luxury of dismissing this inner problem and concentrating his energies on achieving mastery over the external world. He did so partly to avoid confronting himself with unpleasant aspects of his inner life, and partly because healthy and disciplined introspection is extraordinarily difficult in the face of conflicting feeling and impulse and the demands of the outside world. Thus the very word *introspection* continues to have unfavorable overtones, suggesting to many extreme subjectivism and even disease. The psychiatrist, however, recommends a kind of introspection that is based on more than the superficial data of inner thought. It must take into account not only what a student tells us in apparent sincerity about his motives, but must also square with what can be observed about his present behavior and his past tendencies. The author-physician Oliver Wendell Holmes perceived with remarkable intuitive clarity why accurate introspection is so elusive, as the following passage published when Sigmund Freud was a mere boy of fifteen illustrates:

There are thoughts that never emerge into consciousness, which yet make their influence felt among the perceptible mental currents, just as the unseen planets sway the movements of those which are watched and mapped by the astronomer. Old prejudices, that are ashamed to confess themselves, nudge our talking thought to utter magisterial veto. . . . The more we examine the mechanism of thought, the more we shall see that the automatic, unconscious action of the mind enters largely into all its processes.

Unusual students, and students who sometimes behave in unusual fashion, raise serious questions pertaining to the philosophy of education in a democratic society. They are complex questions that have long been discussed, such as the effect of coercion on students, the optimum conditions for teaching and learning, the fate of non-conforming students in a system of mass education, and many others. The psychiatrist cannot pretend to answer them. But he would feel that the solution of such thorny questions depends not so much on generalizations, or even on technical psychological knowledge, as on an attitude towards students similar to that of the physician towards his patients. This attitude derives from the great clinicians in medicine who over the centuries discovered that if physician and patients have learned from each other it has only been because they were able to unite their energies against a common enemy— disease. Moreover, it is an attitude that permits acceptance of the individual in spite of dislike or even loathing for his sickness. Ben Jonson remarked: "I know no disease of the soul but ignorance."

Against this common enemy, ignorance, the old and the young have long sought to join forces. But only in this revolutionary twentieth century have we begun to have glimmerings of the hidden source of much of the enemy's power. Once we recognize that it resides in ignorance of the deeper and more primitive emotional self, which can bring to naught the proudest intelligence, the campus cold war will take on a healthier and more worthwhile objective.

COMMENT

This essay falls into easily observed sections: (1) a discussion of the obvious difficulties between youth and their elders, (2) a suggestion that students' attitudes toward college reflect their attitudes toward their parents, (3) a citation of the less obvious symptoms of the war between the generations, (4) a discussion of the various methods of aiding or controlling difficult student attitudes.

Considering these four sections as four separate units (as four freshman papers) illustrates a truth that the beginning writer does not always understand: you do not have to suggest a solution for every problem you discuss. You may simply describe symptoms; you may just try to discover the causes of certain phenomena; you may restrict your writing to advancing certain remedies for recognized ailments.

SUGGESTIONS FOR WRITING

1. List the differences you have noticed in your relationship with your parents now that you are in college. Arrange them into a pattern which will serve to support a generalization about parents and their growing children.
2. Contrast your attitude toward college with your former attitude toward high school. You might organize your paper with respect to your different attitudes toward studying, dating, or athletics.
3. One of the underlying assumptions of this article is that many of our attitudes are controlled by factors over which we have little control. Discuss one of these attitudes to see whether you can uncover its cause.

Aubrey Menen

THE AGING AVANT–GARDE

I HAVE JUST been reading a distinguished dramatic critic. He was complaining that although a certain play he had seen was well written, the playwright had no strikingly original and new things to say. He complained, further, that it was much the same with the books he read. Nobody had any revolutionary notions any more. In the end, he grew petulant, as though he felt cheated.

I looked him up in a reference book. He is fifty, if the book does not lie. I do him reverence. I am forty-eight. I find that at my age I am capable of taking in a new idea about once every two years, and then only by doing considerable violence to my nervous system.

For instance, I do not like the ancient Greeks. I have not liked them for a long time, because I think they have done Western civilization a great deal of harm. A year ago, I thought I ought to learn their language. I bought a grammar, and, dead against my doctor's advice, I began. Now Greek is a very difficult language because it is highly irregular and a great deal must be learned by rote. To my surprise, I found my memory was excellent. I memorized three pages of the grammar, and the information stuck in my mind.

It became my habit, after a day or so, to recite some difficult verbs while in the shower. I live in Rome, and my plumbing, being Italian, is individual. Both the hot and cold taps are marked *freddo* (cold). Usually this does not worry me. I know which is which. But now I found that while I could remember my verbs, I could never remember whether the hot tap was on the right or the left. After three days in which I alternately scalded myself and froze to the marrow, I gave up Greek.

My doctor gave me a nerve tonic and a lecture. He warned me that if I continued to strain my intellect, it would play even worse tricks. Middle-aged men, he said, learn nothing and forget everything. It was something to do with the structure of the brain, but just what I cannot—let me admit it—remember.

Yet here is this critic two years older than I, going to the theater and reading books, insisting that he is eager for new ideas as a college freshman. His mind is as wide open as the beak of a baby bird. So he would have us believe.

There are tens, perhaps hundreds of thousands of people like him in every civilized society.

They are the aging avant-garde, gray-haired but still ready to be first in the fray. I find them as touching as the sight of a bemedaled veteran of many wars stiffening to attention at the sound of a passing drum.

I know them well. In fact, what I shall have to say about them now is nothing but base ingratitude. When I was a young man they gave me a start in life. It was a farcical start. But then, as I look back over my life, perhaps it struck the right keynote. At any rate, this is what happened.

When I was twenty-two I wrote a play about the future of civilization. The predictions were all wrong, but that wasn't my fault. The play was a dramatization of H. G. Wells' *The Shape of Things to Come.* He was supposed to know what that was. He thought that after World War II we would all be very poor. We are, in fact, richer than we've ever been. Still, his false prediction meant that I could do without expensive scenery, which was all to the good since I had to mount my play with precisely $100. The wardrobe mistress spent ninety-eight dollars of this, leaving me two dollars for the scenery. I spent this on drinks for the stage staff and borrowed their ladders. Then I set the ladders artistically about the stage, lit them, and hoped for the best.

Since I was young the avant-garde flocked to the opening, hoping to be first to welcome a New Force in the theater. They thought the ladders were wonderful. I thought they looked silly. So did my mother. But my mother never had any ambitions to be thought one of the intelligentsia. I have to confess that, at twenty-two, I had. Well, we are all young once.

Only once, thank heaven. Looking back, I marvel how my head was turned. The avant-garde, mostly graying, flocked backstage at every performance. They admired the ladders. They admired me. They told me that ladders had been used by an advanced foreign producer to mount a play. When I said that I had never heard of him, they hailed me as a genius. In my boyhood I had been a candid child. Enough of my candor remained for me to say that ladders were all I could get for the cash in hand. This was brushed aside as modesty. My candor faded. I agreed that, well, what I had really thought was that the stage should be stripped of inessentials in order to emphasize the flow of the dramatic action. From that moment I was hooked—or as the avant-garde would say today, I was committed.

My admirers among the avant-garde gave me the Experimental Theatre. This was the name of the institution, or folly, or caprice—I do not know what to call it, for it certainly was anything but a theater—for which they put up the money, that is, the rent. It had no proper stage, no curtains, no scenery and no orchestra. The actors also were paid no money, and in the end we had no audience. But we got off to a flying start. Once more the avant-garde flocked, thirsty for new ideas.

I was silly enough to give them some. It was a great mistake, but I have some excuse.

My theater seated less than 200 people, but my audience was select. They were, so to speak, the officers of the avant-garde. They were professors, writers, literary critics, distinguished economists, sociologists, politicians, Freudian psychologists, and above all that kindly class of people with private incomes who, having decided that they had no need to better themselves, spent their time and money in bettering everybody else.

All of them were forward-looking. Some looked forward to a Marxist Britain; others looked forward to three-minute divorces, or Esperanto, or vegetarianism, or Beethoven for the workers; still others looked forward to the time when there would be a lovely atmosphere of culture everywhere, and not just in their own beautiful homes. There were those, too, who impatiently awaited the abolition of morals, shaving, marriage and other bourgeois values—forerunners of the beatniks who were as yet in the primordial stage of still washing. So I wrote them all a play. We had other plays on our list of productions—plays from China and Tibet were among them. But it was my theater, so I put on my own play first.

It was set on a Pacific island and it was about miscegenation. I have noticed since that certain people have made a lot of money out of the same idea, but I made nothing. The play was a disaster. It was well written, though I say it myself, and I knew all about half-castes, because I *am* one myself. It was well acted because I had a fine cast of forward-looking professional actors. But the whole thing was received with polite dismay.

The trouble was that miscegenation was not on the list of accepted New Ideas. As some readers may remember, the Thirties were the age of Social Significance. To me, miscegenation was of considerable social significance, whenever, that is, I could get into any society. But the socially significant themes in fashion were unemployment, coal mining, armament manufacturers and international finance. Had I wanted to write about a Pacific island, I ought to have dealt with the oppression of the natives by missionaries, or with the plight of pearl divers. I heard a good deal about pearl divers from my disappointed theater-club membership. They were, I was given to understand, a downtrodden lot and just the stuff for avant-garde drama. Or there was the clash of cultures—the natives taking to the white man's drink, the white man taking to the native wives. I tried to defend myself by saying this clash of cultures had all taken place before the curtain went up. But I was not convincing. Anyway, there was no curtain.

We struggled on for a few nights with a dwindling audience. We started to give tickets away, but that is not as easy as it sounds. For a few nights we had a row or two of nurses from local hospitals. But one evening the matron of one of the biggest rang us up. She said, most apologetically, that she was afraid she couldn't persuade another nurse to set foot in our theater. Nurses, she said, were not very intellectual as a rule, and anyway, she couldn't exactly say that coming to our theater was in the line of duty, could she? I sympathized with her. That night, nobody came to the theater at all.

The forward-looking actors clubbed together and bought beer and sausages. They did risqué variety acts on my austerely bare stage. There was, at least, no need of scenery in those particular sketches. We had a wonderful time, but we feared the theater would have to close.

However, among our supporters were members of what was known as the Bloomsbury set, a group of writers and artists that included such people as Virginia Woolf and Lytton Strachey, together with a number of people of a very different caliber. Presiding over the inner circle of this was J. Maynard (later Lord) Keynes, with whom I had some acquaintance.

Keynes had won world fame (and the ear of Franklin D. Roosevelt) with his theory that when things, financially, were going bad, the solution was to pump money into the economy until it revived.

Things were going classically bad with my theater, so I asked him if he would mind doing some modest pumping. Like the man of principle he was, he sent a check.

But for once his principles did not work. I had offended my audience. They had come to my theater in the hope of finding new ideas and I had insulted them by giving them ideas they had never so much as heard of, not even at their own cocktail parties. When I had spent Mr. Keynes' money, the Experimental Theatre closed.

It was all my fault, I knew. I was still of the age when one wants to be admired by one's elders and betters, so like a good boy I went to see the plays that the avant-garde liked. I queued for the cheap seats (a great stimulus to critical thought) and when I could not afford to do even this, I ransacked libraries to get the texts.

Very soon I made a discovery. The plays that the forward-looking people liked so much were almost without exception slicked-over copies of dramas that had been revolutionary a quarter of a century before. Hauptmann, Ibsen, Shaw and Strindberg had done the whole thing, and done it well. Now, to the applause of the avant-garde, it was all being done over again, with less scenery and more swearwords.

I could not explain it at the time. I can now. To do so I must refer you back to my bathroom. You will recall that I could not remember which tap in the shower was which because I was trying to learn Greek. This, in its turn, was because I was in my forties. Now so were the aging avant-garde. So are most of the influential avant-garde today.

Half an hour's study of a work of reference will show that the plays of the social realists whom I have mentioned were just about the latest thing in England when the avant-garde of my Experimental Theatre were leaving school, going to the university or just starting out in life after completing their studies. We all know how impressionable we are at those ages. We all know how receptive we are to new ideas. We can all remember how exciting those ideas were, especially if hardly anybody else knew about them. We remember; so does the aging avant-garde.

Most of us find it easy, after a lesson or so, to admit that we are no longer young. Some do not. Actresses, for instance, find it difficult. So do people of fine intellectual sensibilities who dazzled, when they were in their twenties, with the freshness of their ideas. An actress has her first wrinkle: the intellectual his first platitude. The actress looks in the mirror and sees her first gray hair; the intellectual looks in the faces of his listeners and sees the first stifled yawn. The actress goes to the beauty shop; the intellectual to the theater, the art exhibitions or the bookshop. Both are determined that they are as young as ever. After all, as they tell themselves, they *feel* young.

The actress emerges from her beauty treatment triumphantly rejuvenated.

It is not so easy for the intellectual. There are no cosmetics for the aging mind. He searches desperately for more of those stimulating new discoveries in the arts like the ones that used to make him so brilliant over coffee at his college or university. He finds them, but alas, they are the same ideas, a little disguised. They are the only ones that will go into his tired old head.

But it works, in a way. When the aging avant-garde can no longer shine over coffee, they can still browbeat over a whisky and soda. So they do find their new ideas, their new geniuses.

The plays of Samuel Beckett remind them of the days when they defended James Joyce. The pictures of the Abstract Impressionists remind them of the time when they defiantly stuck reproductions of the Fauves on their walls. The latest piece of Stravinsky reminds them of when Stravinsky *was* Stravinsky and they explained to a circle of awed young ladies why *The Rite of Spring* was music and not a joke. For artists like Stravinsky, or Picasso, are a godsend to them. Nobody can deny that they are always excitingly breaking new ground, but one can be comfortably certain that one has seen it all before.

The aging avant-garde do little harm: and to the aspiring young I would point out that there is money in them, provided, unlike myself, you handle them the right way. They are to be found on most of the committees that award grants, traveling fellowships, scholarships and prizes in competitions. My advice is to look up their age in a work of reference, find out the sort of thing that was as new as a new pin when they were in their twenties and do your best to copy that. You will not get it at all right, because you are young. But your blunders will be hailed as the revelation of a new and rebel talent. You will win the fellowship. You will carry off the prize. It will not matter if you really believe you are as good as they tell you. Your name will be forgotten in eighteen months; for, as my doctor said, the middle-aged can remember nothing new for very long.

COMMENT

"The Aging Avant-Garde" consists of an introduction, a personal narrative offered as "proof" of the author's half-serious contention, and a conclusion consisting of ironic advice to the young. Notice how Mr. Menen makes the point of his story clear before he begins to relate it so that the reader knows what to look for. The personal narrative often attracts the beginning writer because he is familiar with the form and because it seems to organize itself, but narration is not so simple as it seems. Study Mr. Menen's technique so that you can avoid the obvious pitfalls.

SUGGESTIONS FOR WRITING

1. Write an essay on "What I Learned about Athletes (Beats, Sorority Girls)." Follow Mr. Menen's scheme by opening your essay with a statement of the discovery which your narrative is to illustrate.

2. Jot down a list of attitudes which alumni, uncles, or parents seem to have toward some subject. Show how their theory does not always govern their practice. Such titles as these may suggest others to you: "The Liberal (The Life of the Party, The Boss) at Home," "Don't Do as I Do, Do as I Say," "Now, When I Was Your Age. . . ."

3. Contrast the atmosphere of your college with the aims it professes. Give this subject serious thought. Don't just contrast the college's professed desire to build character with its restrictive regulations about student parking or hours for girls.

Come Back, DETROIT, *All Is Forgiven*

Janet Agle

I CAN'T REMEMBER when I first realized I had begun to loathe my sports car. Like most high-octane romances, mine was all-consuming and, I dare say, somewhat embarrassing to my friends. Certainly they tended to drop away from me during the height of my passion, but—as is typical in such affairs—I failed to notice their defection. I had a small but steadily growing group of new friends, ones who spoke my language: other sports-car owners. If our world was hemmed in by smugness and limited in scope, none of us was aware of it—not then, at least.

How I enjoyed those days when love was fresh—and innocent! In the first gleeful hours after taking possession of my treasure, I drove to the house of my most conservative friend, taking the right-angle curve into her driveway with only the slightest slackening of speed and shifting down smartly until I came to a stop beside her terrace with the merest application of the brakes. I shall never forget the shocked incredulity on her face. Long accustomed to seeing me in the stately family sedan, my appearance in a small convertible was perhaps too dazzling. Within hours she had spread the word that I was driving a red sports car. I called her up at once.

"It's white," I told her, reproachfully.

"Are you sure?" she asked, her voice full of doubt.

"You saw it! Of course it's white."

"Maybe you're right," she admitted. "It *seemed* red."

I soon discovered that she represented a segment of the population that mentally draws up its skirts and recoils from the sports car and all its implications. In these quarters, I could scarcely have been accorded greater disdain had I started running around with a married man.

One can rise above this, however, when driving a car that automatically attracts a crowd wherever it comes to rest. Sports-car owners—in those days, at least—were treated to the sort of camaraderie hitherto known only among dog owners in New York City.

Reprinted from *Harper's Magazine* by permission of Constance Smith Associates.

"What is it?" was the first question we heard on turning off the motor, and inevitably we found ourselves surrounded by eager, admiring new friends.

"You should have seen it whistling down the Turnpike last week!" I found myself telling an interested knot of spectators once. "I held it at eighty all the way to Valley Forge . . . passed everything in sight."

Among the group I then noticed one of the local cops, thoughtfully twirling his stick.

"What mileage do you get?" he asked, wistfully. Those were the days!

With all the enthusiasm of a new bride trying to persuade her husband's friends to marry and settle down, I made my way through several social seasons hammering away on a single theme.

"You can have it," someone would remark, after hearing me on my favorite topic. "I don't want to be bothered with all that shifting."

"Bothered!" I would cry. "It's *fun!* You're not really driving when all you do is sit there and steer. In a sports car you're living, every moment. You're always on the *qui vive,* getting the most out of your car, feeling the thrill of its quick response. . . ."

Here and there an eye would kindle, but for the most part the faces that confronted me were dull—and often sullen.

"Of course if your idea of driving is to be wafted around on a magic carpet . . . !" I said once, scathingly, to a group of unbelievers . . . and fell back aghast as I saw the truth: it was.

We sports-car owners tended to huddle together at parties, communing with one another. We discussed the decline of the art of driving and the decadence and vulgarity of American cars, and there was a period when we took credit for the recent recession. Single-handedly, we felt, we had brought production in Detroit to a halt; too many had seen the rectitude of our ways and the day of the land yacht had passed.

The romance faded so slowly it was almost imperceptible, at first. I can remember that there came a day when I suggested to a friend that we drive to New York in her car instead of mine, because while mine was unquestionably easier to park and all that, still it was cold out and perhaps we might be just a tiny bit more comfortable in the big car. She leaped at the suggestion with an alacrity which somehow failed to wound me.

The fact was that the week before I had insisted on driving a friend to Virginia in my car and the memory was still green. We were scudding down the road (getting about thirty-five miles to the gallon) when she turned to speak to me.

"When we pass a pronthos, I'd like to blagdab," she said.

"What?" I shouted back.

"To blagdab hork," she replied, and I could see the veins standing out in her throat.

"Tell me at the next traffic light," I suggested.

Shrugging, she reached for the radio switch and before long more indistinguishable babble filled the air.

"Doesn't this thing work?" she screamed.

"Sure," I told her. "It's a wonderful radio. But you can't hear it when the motor's running."

I can also remember the first apostate in our happy little band—a man we had seduced into buying a Flimflam. For months thereafter he had been as insufferable as we, but perhaps a little more so, since there are degrees of caste among sports-car fans and *his* obsession was that the Flimflam was superior in every way to anything else on four wheels. Needless to say, this caused a certain strain in his relations with the owners of British Haymakers and custom-built Bloopers.

This fellow was driving through the Alleghenies during a snowstorm one day when his windshield wipers failed. After hours of going along with his head out the window while he negotiated hairpin turns, he gave up, left his car in a garage where the mechanic had never heard of a Flimflam, and came home by train. What with the pressure of affairs he was unable to return for the car when the weather cleared and it fell to his mutinous wife to make the trip. This was a woman whose loyalty to her own car—a native product—had never wavered; she had steadfastly refused any interest in her husband's toy. One hesitates to imagine her remarks when she finally delivered the object to the local garage.

I heard the rest from the man, himself, at a party a few weeks later.

"How's the Flimflam running?" I inquired. Looking furtively around, he seized my arm and dragged me behind a potted palm.

"Know anyone who wants to buy it?" he asked, through clenched teeth.

I'm sure my mouth fell open.

"You mean you want to sell it just because of a little trouble with *windshield wipers?*" I said.

"*Little* trouble!" he retorted, a wild look in his eyes. "Do you realize that Flimflam windshield wipers are collector's items, as hard to come by as Napoleon brandy or piston rings for a Model T Ford? Listen," he hissed, "each little Flimflam windshield wiper has its own little motor, and each little motor is turned out at the rate of one every six weeks, by Benvenuto Cellini, who works only on Sundays at time and a half. And his shop, I think, is in a remote hidden village in Irkutsk."

The whole subject of repairs brings on traumatic twinges. Sports-car owners are in a plight similar to that of a diabetic with hemophilia, who has just developed ulcers. The complications are beyond the scope of the family doctor; a staff of specialists must be called in. However, since foreign-car specialists are not subject to call, the ailing car must either limp or be dragged to the doctor's office—and there's the rub.

A man living in Scranton, Pennsylvania, say, and owning a Brow-beater Mark XII, will, by the process of trial and error, discover that the specialist for *him* practices in South Orange, New Jersey. This will be a mechanic named Wolfgang, who was born in the Browbeater district of Upper Silesia, and whose contempt for American cars is only exceeded by his contempt for Americans, themselves. Wolfgang manages to convey, during the first interview, his conviction that the owner's ineptitude is so gross that officials of the Society for the Prevention of Cruelty to Sports Cars—if there were such an organization—should intervene in the case. At the same time he makes it clear that such a man in presuming to drive a Browbeater is as guilty of social posturing as Khrushchev in Shetland tweeds. Humbled and respectful, the owner places himself in Wolfgang's hands and turns his pockets inside out in an effort to give his Browbeater the sort of care that will earn him Wolfgang's regard.

For several years I have been at the mercy of a surly practitioner named Gustave, whose loathing for me is so intense he can never bring himself to address a word to me. I send my car in for treatment and in due course I receive notice—through an intermediary—that the patient will be ready for dismissal at three o'clock on a given afternoon. Nine times out of ten I arrive (after a two-hour journey involving the use of several little known railroad and bus systems) to find my loved one suspended from the ceiling, its wheels in one corner, its motor in another, and its intestines sitting in a tub of grease. My outcries have never caused Gustave to so much as lift his head from his work. Besides being American and out of my social sphere in the automotive sense, I am something far worse, to a male European motor-worshiper: I am a woman and beneath contempt. All of my dealings with Gustave are carried on through the janitor.

The foregoing may have something to do with the fact that people who buy foreign cars tend to buy lots of them. The case of my friend, Peter, may serve as an illustration.

Pete started out with a small German car which is now mass-produced and widely marketed in this country. The novelty of it carried him along for a while, but before long he became aware that he had suffered a certain loss of prestige. Owners of American cars were more amused than impressed—but so were the owners of sports cars. He took to reading that rapidly growing section of the papers devoted to the re-sale of foreign cars, and soon he found himself tempted. "Bright blue convertible Horn-swoggle 120, white leather upholstery, 8,000 miles, driven only by middle-aged clergyman," he read—and a few days later his family was in for a shock.

When an aching tooth has stopped aching, one is conscious at first only of the absence of pain, and for a short period Pete enjoyed such a respite. In those first blissful days, he only rejoiced in the fact that the Hornswoggle's designers had omitted the two open vents under the dashboard which— in his first car—had aimed a steady blast of cold air at his feet.

All too soon it became clear that the "middle-aged clergyman" had cannily disposed of his Hornswoggle just as the potwhistle was burning out, the frumption ground down, and the hochspittle wires (made of llama hair chewed to the right consistency by the native women of Peru) had worn out. Pete learned that repair parts would be shipped from Spitzbergen after the spring thaw. One thing led to another, and now Pete is driving a Hornswoggle 320. But all is not well, I gather. While the 320 performs spiritedly on the road, Pete finds that after trips of longer duration than an hour or two he needs the services of a good osteopath. His wife says that lately he's been studying the Italian Alter-Ego.

At times even the most rabid sports-car fan begins to suspect the practicality of his plaything. Another friend of mine—a bachelor who proudly drives a Petite Vipère, with bucket seats for two—called me not long ago with a puzzling problem. His aged parents and his sister were coming for Thanksgiving dinner. How, he wondered, was he to transport them from the railroad station to his home, five miles out in the country? Offering him my car was no solution, and he was in no position to borrow a car from any of his friends—he had no friends, by then, who would not have made his life unbearable with their ridicule.

In this quandary, for a while we could see no alternative to his making three round trips to the station to bring his guests home one by one—and even this presented a problem. His seventy-five-year-old mother, once lowered into his car, would be almost impossible to dislodge; she weighed close to two hundred pounds. As for his father, *his* deportment and bearing made even the thought of jack-knifing him into a sports car seem like a form of sacrilege. Furthermore, as we talked it over, it seemed highly dubious that he could be bent into such a position, in the unlikely event that he was willing to make the effort.

We worked it out, finally. He sent a taxi for them.

Not long afterwards, I was confronted with a similar situation myself. Faced with the problem of making a thousand-mile drive with two children, one Irish setter, and all the accouterments essential to such a junket, namely ten or twelve suitcases, I saw no way of fitting them into a car designed to carry nothing bulkier than a pocketbook. It took some figuring.

This is how a sports-car owner arranges such a trip. He selects from among his friends one who is footloose, impulsive, and, if possible, a little bit gullible—and who owns an American station wagon. He suggests a joint vacation, pointing out that the arrangements are all made; all one has to do is jump in the car and go. If one has chosen wisely, the question of *which* car is never mentioned. In my case, the friend took a look at my impedimenta, bought herself a plane ticket, and left me to follow along in the wagon.

It was a disturbing experience. By nightfall, after a full day of driving, I was purring along a North Carolina highway, fresh as a daisy. Children and livestock slept soundly, stretched out full length in the ample space behind me, lulled by the motor's quiet hum and the car's gentle motion. The radio worked . . . and I could hear it. The lighter lit, the heater heated, and the car asked no more of me than a hand on the wheel and an occasional light tap on the power brakes. A feeling of euphoria stole over me. Caught off guard, I made a damaging admission to myself: driving an American car was a pleasure!

Shocked by my heresy, I stopped in the next town for dinner and deliberately chose the most awkward parking place I could find. The proof of the pudding is in the eating; the proof of the foreign car is in the parking, I reminded myself. I had not reckoned with power steering. With disconcerting ease the car folded itself into the designated space. It shook me.

Nor was this all.

The following morning, in an abandoned section of southern Georgia, the car, which had been performing smoothly, suddenly went into a series of bumps and grinds. I nursed it along for a mile until I came to a shanty with a dusty gasoline pump outside, and explained my difficulty to the only attendant in sight—an undersized twelve-year-old boy whose vacant eyes suggested only too clearly that he had not reached an equivalent mental age. My heart sank as he lifted up the hood.

"Your goofus has dinked," he said, in bored tones. "Wait a minute, I'll get you another."

In the time it takes to drink a Coca-Cola we were under way again, with everything in order . . . but I was thinking soberly.

It was after this that I began to avoid the sports-car enthusiasts at parties—or thought I did. After a while I realized we were all avoiding each other, and I suspect I know why. It is not easy to speak of a dead love while the ashes are still warm.

Perhaps in another year we'll be able to discuss it quietly together, without pain. Our love was passing fair and wove a wondrous spell— but she just wasn't the kind of girl you marry.

COMMENT

The first and last sentences of this article suggest that its basic scheme of organization is that of the love story; this suggestion is reinforced by the constant reference to marriage, courtship, and romance throughout the essay. Because the average reader has read or seen dozens of love stories which begin with passionate attachment and conclude with disenchantment, he is prepared for what follows and is conscious of the mock-serious nature of this piece.

SUGGESTIONS FOR WRITING

1. Write an account of your love affair with your first car, your first party dress, or your favorite sport. Watch your pacing so that your theme has movement.

2. Describe some fad that you and your friends have taken up (a movie hero, popular singer, club, or fashion) and trace the gradual decline of your affection.

Our Basic Problems and
Our Educational Program

ROBERT M. HUTCHINS

WALTER P. METZGER, of Columbia University, has said that American colleges and universities are "folk institutions": they reflect the immediate needs, real or fancied, of the people. They mirror the chaos of the world. They are "motley and mongrelized." He goes on:

> In asking "What should a university be?" every need has clamored for recognition, every craft has hoped to belong—and the result has been the unhappy association of piddling vocational and unimportant intellectual interests, the nestling together—under one faculty—of searchers, observers, and craftsmen, the crowding together of institutes, departments, hospitals, dormitories, restaurants, apartment houses, and football stadiums all under the canopy of a single administration. The university in America is not a community of scholars, but an enormous agglomerate service station, where one can be born, go to kindergarten, lower school, and high school, meet the girl friend and get married; where one can get religious solace or psychiatric help; where one learns to turn out a newspaper, to do bookkeeping, to cook. No wonder the universities have been hiring generals to run this domain.

Take this from the catalogue of a college in California:

> For Freshmen and Sophomores, *Hope Chest* 61-A and 61-B: three units each. The courses are planned to prepare students in the specialized homemaking field. The College has on its campus a modern practice home. Sophomore girls can experience various phases of home living and learning. Included in the course is instruction about buying silverware, appliances, linens, etc.

There is a Department of Mortuary Science at Wayne University in Detroit. When I mentioned this to a great industrialist there, he said, "We need morticians, don't we?" So firmly is it engrained in our minds that whatever the public thinks it needs may properly be supplied by the colleges and universities.

Reprinted by permission of the author and of *McCall's*.

The usual explanation for the bizarre courses of study found in American higher education is pressure. These things were forced on our colleges and universities by interested groups, seeking to obtain some special advantage for themselves or their children. My observation is that educational institutions are willing victims of pressure, and my belief is that if there had been no pressure at all, our colleges and universities would be about what they are today.

The proof is the conduct of the private, endowed institutions, which are free to resist pressure. They can do what they will. But they are not distinguishable in their aims, standards, and activities from public colleges and universities that are tax-supported and legislatively controlled. The triviality, frivolity, and irrelevance of American education must be blamed on those responsible for the management of it. They have decided that it is in the interest of their institutions to be trivial, frivolous, and irrelevant.

Why? They want to be attractive to students and donors. Educators believe, with some reason, that nothing is so dangerous as to be different. In the first place, you get into arguments. If you are different, you have to explain why. This means that you have to have a defensible reason for what you are doing. This means that you have to think. It is far easier and more agreeable to do what everybody else does. If you do, you will never have to answer any questions.

In the second place, "different" in our culture comes to mean "odd," or "intellectual," and may soon come to carry the implication that your students are radical, or even subversive, and probably do not bathe very often. The picture is unattractive. If you can conscientiously claim that your campus is crowded with gay young things who never had a thought in their lives and who behave and always will behave as red-blooded, well-tubbed, unthinking, rich Americans believe they should, then you have something you can sell. The package you sell is one everybody understands and most people approve.

Why sell? Well, everybody likes to be popular, and educators and university trustees are no exception to this rule. But the principal reason, of course, is money. Almost every college and university in the United States is seeking to raise enormous sums. This is no time to be different. A salesman trying to sell an automobile cannot shoulder the burden of reforming his prospect's views of the transportation he needs. He has to take these views as given and prove to the prospect that the car before him meets them exactly. The education of the American people about the aims and function of education is a very long job indeed and one that will have to be postponed until after the sales campaign.

But if tremendous quantities of money are being wasted on courses, programs, teachers, equipment, and buildings that should not exist, why not obtain the money that is needed by reducing the waste? Aside from the obvious fact that the college or university that did this would run the risk of being different, such a plan would go counter to one of the strongest forces in our culture, the American infatuation with figures.

The words of Santayana on this point are worth recalling:

> The most striking expression of this materialism is supposed to be his [the American's] love of the almighty dollar; but that is a foreign and unintelligent view. The American talks about money, because that is the symbol and measure he has at hand for success, intelligence, and power; but as to money itself, he makes, loses, spends, and gives it away with a light heart. To my mind the most striking expression of his materialism is his singular preoccupation with quantity. . . . Nor is this insistence on quantity confined to men of business. The President of Harvard College, seeing me once by chance after the beginning of a term, inquired how my classes were getting on; and when I replied that I thought they were getting on well, that my men seemed to be keen and intelligent, he stopped me as if I was about to waste his time. "I meant," said he, *"what is the number* of students in your classes?"

I am an expert on the obituaries of college and university presidents. They are all the same. When Dr. A. came to the University of X., it had an enrollment of so many students, an endowment of so many dollars, and so many cubic feet of buildings on so many acres of land. Now, thanks to his forward-looking educational program, it has so many more students, dollars, cubic feet, acres.

Every college and university president knows that this is the standard by which he will be judged. I asked a distinguished professor at a Midwestern college the other day how his president was doing. "Oh," he replied, "he's getting on fine. The money is rolling in."

Any other standard is now unimaginable. At the bottom of the Depression, when I was President of the University of Chicago, the Chicago School Board met secretly and cut the heart out of the city's educational system. I wrote several articles, which were published on the front page of a local paper, entitled, "Throw the School Board Out," a suggestion that was ultimately adopted. A trustee of the university told me that he and his friends could not understand what I was trying to do. "We thought," he said, "that you might be trying to get the support of the teachers, but we know that couldn't be so, because they haven't any money."

If the primary aim of a college or university has to be to gain the support of people who have money, and if the prevailing view is that people who have money will support only the most conventional and undisturbing institutions (plus research designed to lengthen our lives and shorten those of our enemies), then it is not surprising that American colleges and universities have become places in which the young can be accommodated until they can go to work—with medical schools and institutes of nuclear physics attached.

I have little doubt that our colleges and universities need more money, though it is difficult to be positive about this until we have developed some standard for judging what they need the money for. Certainly the maximum salaries of university professors, now about $15,000 a year, ought to be doubled if we are to attract able men into teaching and research. But if they are to teach frivolous, trivial, irrelevant subjects, what good is it to attract them?

I have the highest opinion of money and do not like to see it wasted. The only way to prevent waste is to have a program that is educationally sound and then try to raise the money to support it. The way to guarantee waste is to let the presumed possibility of raising money determine the program, rather than the other way round. An educational plan's attractiveness to men of wealth or to large numbers of paying customers has no bearing on its educational value. Money spent on a plan without educational value is wasted.

Grayson Kirk, President of Columbia University, summed up the matter when he said some years ago:

> I think that far too many of our institutions contribute unconsciously to popular confusion by trying too zealously to be all things to all men. They are too prone to yield to external pressures, too willing to accept offers of funds which have embarrassing strings attached to them, too eager to have a bewildering profusion of course offerings which make their catalogues resemble in variety the offerings of a mail-order house. An impressive array of courses is no substitute for intellectual leadership.

Mr. Kirk, condemning the standard of getting money from donors and paying customers, sets up the standard of intellectual leadership. With that I agree. This ought to be the purpose of institutions of higher learning. They should be centers of independent thought. If the quest for money becomes their main preoccupation, these institutions, instead of enlightening our society, must flatter it, and in so doing, they will flatter and perpetuate our illusions. Independent thought, on the other hand, implies criticism and, in particular, criticism of the conventional wisdom, which is another name for the prevailing illusions. The higher learning, if it does its job, will be disturbing.

How, then, can it be sold? Obviously, it can be sold only if the American people understand the value of the disturbance that centers of independent thought would create. This they can never understand as long as the universities themselves, in President Kirk's phrase, "contribute to

128 PROSE CURRENT

popular confusion." The aspects of colleges and universities that are the most highly advertised—football, fraternities, and fun—have the least visible connection with intellectual leadership. When a university president makes a speech calling for intellectual leadership, he cannot be heard over the din his publicity man is making about the newest campus queen. The colleges and universities must themselves act as though they believed their task is intellectual leadership, if they expect anybody else to believe it.

Well, suppose a college or university did decide to devote itself to true education and nothing else. True education is the improvement of men through helping them learn to think for themselves. All the work of the institution would be examined, to determine whether or not it required thinking. The faculty and students would be surveyed, with a view to eliminating those who had demonstrated they could not or would not think. Whole departments would be wiped out. The tremendous apparatus of extracurricular activities would be reduced to the size required for the students' health and recreation. The students would be limited to those who were interested in learning to think for themselves and who gave some promise of being able to do it. Approximately fifty per cent of our college and university students would disappear. The limitation of departments, professional schools, and courses to those with some intellectual content, and the retirement of professors who were incapable of, or uninterested in, taking part in such work would make possible a splendid salary level for those who remain.

Could a college or university that showed, in this way, that it took seriously the obligation of intellectual leadership survive in the United States? To say it could not is to say that the American people cannot ever achieve the view of higher education that has been a commonplace in Europe for seven hundred years and still prevails there. I have not so low an opinion of my fellow countrymen. After all, the problem of understanding is not difficult; it is perfectly obvious that intercollegiate football, for example, has nothing to do with intellectual leadership and that dedication to athletics will divert a university from its high calling and confuse the people about what its calling is. But doing something about football, as any college president will testify, is something else again.

The road to understanding is through asking what the special function of institutions of higher learning ought to be. In view of the burden they have to carry, they should not attempt to do what other institutions can do or ought to do. As Sir Edward Boyle, Britain's Parliamentary Secretary to the Minister of Education, remarked the other day, "Girls *can* learn to make coffee at home." The educational system cannot take on the responsibilities of the family and the church. If it tries, it will fail; also, it will weaken the family and the church. It cannot accept the duty of building physiques, inculcating social graces, training job holders and consumers, teaching people how to play games, and at the same time exert intellectual leadership. The reason is that an institution is held together by a vision of the end. If it has no clear vision of a definite end, it must fall apart; it must fail.

I suppose that the reason higher education in the United States has taken on aspects of a country club, housing project, and vocational high school is that there has been, till lately, no pressing reason it shouldn't. Why should we have worried about intellectual leadership when we were rich and impregnable, when we could do anything we wanted, and when we could feel that if we were not pre-eminent in a field, it was only because we did not care to be? In these terms, we did not really need an educational system; but we did need a place in which to accommodate our young people. We were committed to education for all, and this demand was satisfied by providing schools for all. Having equated education and schooling, we did not have to be much concerned about what the pupils did in school. Thus we were relieved of the obligation of thinking about the nature and purpose of education. It is hard to tell what education is and how much or little of it an individual has obtained. Schooling raises no such questions; anybody can tell what a school is, how many people are in it, and how long they have been there. The notion that schooling equals education imperceptibly leads to the substitution of accommodation for education; for schooling does not necessarily imply anything beyond mere presence in school.

The standards of a place of accommodation are well known. One asks about a resort hotel: What is the price? Are the rooms neat, clean, and well furnished? What are the opportunities for recreation? Will I meet nice people? Is the food good? What is the view? As might be expected, these are the questions the advertisements of American colleges and universities set out first of all to answer.

I suggest that the triviality, frivolity, and irrelevance of these questions should now be clear to any newspaper reader in the United States. I am not thinking of our semihysterical desire to "get ahead of Russia." If the Russians were to become our stanch allies tomorrow, this would not diminish the necessity of a drastic revision of our educational system and of our attitude toward it. A great French critic, Ernest Renan, said, "Countries which, like the United States, have set up a considerable popular instruction without any serious higher education, will long have to expiate their error by their intellectual mediocrity, the vulgarity of their manners, their superficial spirit, their failure in general intelligence."

We have been prosperous, powerful, and isolated so long that we are not concerned by waste or alarmed by ignorance and ineptitude. We have taken these things as a matter of course, for we have always been able to afford them. So we have poured billions into countless schools, colleges, and universities without bothering about what was to go on inside them. We did not take education seriously; we could see no reason to.

Now, however, we confront new problems, the solution of which is crucial to us and to all civilization. Nothing is more striking than the absence of connection between the basic problems of America and the educational program of America. Our real needs are to discover how to make democracy work, how to survive in the nuclear age, and what to do with ourselves if we do survive. A system of accommodation cannot help us meet these needs. If we are to meet them, we shall have to dedicate our colleges and universities to the production of disciplined intelligence, and to that alone.

COMMENT

The plan of this paper is announced in its title, "Our Basic Problems and Our Educational Program." Mr. Hutchins briefly summarizes the failures of the American university and college programs, explains the causes for these failures, and sketches his own remedy for them. This traditional structure for argumentation can easily be adapted to the requirements of the beginning writer because he can imagine an adversary whose objections he can anticipate and against whom he can order his arguments.

SUGGESTIONS FOR WRITING

1. Follow Mr. Hutchins' lead by quoting a paragraph of his or of someone else's (an editorial, a letter to the editor). Develop an argument for or against that contained in the paragraph you quote.

2. Study your college catalog or search your memory of your high school experience to discover what courses do not require "thinking." Defend or attack such courses.

3. Write a paragraph which summarizes the average student's (or professor's) attitude toward education. Analyze this paragraph as Mr. Hutchins does, determining the reasons behind the attitudes found in this paragraph. For a short paper you will do well to analyze one reason or attitude fully instead of expounding a complete educational theory in 500 words. Write the following familiar two sentences twenty times: "I did not come to college to become a bookworm. It is more important to learn how to get along with people than to acquire book-knowledge." Take the paper on which you have written these sentences and throw it away.

Paradox
in
Parenthesis

Edward D. Eddy, Jr.

ONE OF THE FAVORITE PASTIMES of the present age is to wring our hands in despair and cry loudly over the deep-seated decadence of today's youth. I suppose what I most rebel against is the idea that today's college youth somehow ought to be secure, purposeful, endowed with all the attributes which are so obviously missing in their adult counterparts. Too often students are criticized as if they were a breed apart, to be judged by entirely different standards than anybody else. On the one hand, they are accused of having no spark; on the other, heads shake when the spark ignites occasionally in the wrong way. Many adults now appear to have forgotten that youth is a time of ferment not cement.

Now that I have said this, let me proceed to contradict myself by indulging in some rash accusations (to be taken, however, in the spirit in which they are now expressed—a supreme, unbending confidence in the silent generation and a sneaking suspicion that it is the older generation that is really at fault). What I am going to say emerges for the most part from a study which is reported in full in *The College Influence on Student Character,* published in March by the American Council of Education. Last year I was one of a group of three who, under the sponsorship of the council, set out to take a look at the American college student and the process of gradual enlightenment which is generally called "higher learning." Two of the three—James L. Yakovakis and Mary L. Parkhurst —were recent college graduates whose job it was to become as much a part of the campus as possible. We spent time at twenty colleges and universities—of all types and sizes—in seventeen different states across the country. On each campus the staff members lived with the students in dormitories, fraternities or sororities. They ate with them, went to class and to meetings, participated in bull sessions, drank countless cups of coffee and mugs of beer. In addition, we interviewed members of the faculty and staff on each campus.

Reprinted by permission of the publisher, *The Nation.*

In our observations and conclusions we leaned heavily on the reaction of students to the collegiate experience. We did this in the belief that *how* students receive education conditions *what* they receive. Everywhere we traveled, we found the majority willing and often anxious to talk about what was happening to them. In many cases we noted a genuine sense of urgency. We emerged with no easy definition of education or of the contemporary college student. The best capsule summary I can offer is that we found the student to be a "paradox in parenthesis."

Let me explain, first, the word "parenthesis." Over and over again college students told us that, in their opinion, the content and form of higher education are *not* sufficiently related to the rest of life, nor is education genuinely relevant to their concerns. Because of this, students tend to regard the four years of college as a parenthesis setting off a time in which they can perhaps enjoy themselves for the last time before "real maturation" sets in. The parenthesis encloses something which has no particularly striking relationship to what went on before, or to what will follow. Nevertheless, it is socially necessary—both as a custom and for the sake of a better life (which usually means a better job for the boys and a happier home for the girls). This is the background for the concern of one student who told us, "They keep telling me that college is preparation for life, but I'm alive now."

The absence of relevance in collegiate education has some side effects of substantial importance. If college is regarded only as a pleasant respite, the student may well come to feel that there are two worlds in which he may live—the here and the then. Not infrequently, for instance, we came across the student who was frank enough to admit, "I really don't see any relationship between my cheating on an exam now and what I'll do later in life. Because I get my kicks today, doesn't mean that I'm always going to be living it up."

That's the parenthesis and the danger of its maintenance. Now what about the paradox?

First of all, let me pose the initial paradox: Beneath the student's studied pretense of indifference and apathy lies an unfashionable but searching desire for meaning in all that he does.

On almost every campus we visited—from California to New England —student apathy was the major topic of conversation. This apathy was often expressed by the student in the simple phrase: "I couldn't care less." The phrase was supposed to apply to academic work, to leadership positions in activities, to any number of campus events. A faculty member told us, "Apathy is another way of describing the attitude that registers *superficial* or studied indifference. The unfortunate result is satisfaction with mediocrity." The student, it appears, wants never to become excited or involved.

Yet when we probed more deeply, we found another and wholly contradictory characteristic: the student is interested, often urgently, in an honest search for meaning. To many the search is not easy, for they are just beginning to sense the dimensions of truth. As one student wrote in his campus newspaper: "I do not know what I want out of life—or what I want to contribute to it—but I am learning. First I had to learn that it was necessary to have some idea about these questions. It didn't take me long to discover that there are no simple answers." The search, it seems, is often hid under a crusty layer of non-concern—but it's there.

If beneath this crusty layer of non-concern, the students are genuinely searching for meaning, why is there among them so scant a satisfaction with higher education? I put the blame squarely on us—the faculty, the administrators. In Ordway Tead's phrase, much in college education today is "so chatty, so trivial, and so inconsequential." In a nutshell: college does not demand enough from the student.

On only a handful of the campuses which we visited did many students claim that they were really performing to their full capacity. Much time is expended on meaningless activity. College campuses may be busy places, but it's surprising how much trivia consume the important hours of growing up. Students are much too easily distracted, much too quickly dumped into a rut of self-pity and sometimes self-indulgence. It's fashionable, of course, to be busy—but the busyness is often more important than the achievement. Prestige comes from busyness. The student who can sing the loudest, "I've got more to do than you" gets the lead in the campus musical comedy.

Something rather dramatic and encouraging happened last spring on the campus of the University of Wisconsin. Over 200 student leaders sent to the university president a petition which, according to our study, reflects well the sentiments of many students throughout the country. It read in part:

> Although the university is constantly making attempts to improve its standards, we believe that it has failed to challenge its students sufficiently. In many senses, it is too easy for thousands of students to "get by" and never learn to become critical, analytical thinkers or to achieve an understanding of the world around them. Students on all levels of attainment feel that they have not worked to the limits of their ability and time.
>
> The university must raise its standards. In some cases this means simply requiring more work; in many more it means emphasizing an improved quality of work and an intelligent, analytical approach to the subject matter. Students must extend themselves to achieve a deep and meaningful understanding of material. But this is possible only if the faculty seeks to help us by challenging us more fully.

I come now to the second paradox: While wanting to know what he should know, the student protests that he should have increasing opportunity to think and act for himself. The student, like all human beings, is naturally self-centered. He views education in terms of what it will do *for* him rather than *with* him. And so, over and over again, he complains about his instructor: "If *only* he'd tell us what he wants us to know."

While desiring more independence in both thought and action, the student, nevertheless, has a strong urge to know *exactly where* he stands at any given moment—and at the same time demands the right to influence the conditions affecting the stand. On a campus threatened with more stringent restrictions, a junior girl student wrote a typical letter to her college newspaper protesting that students desire to be treated as something better than machines:

> It is time to herald the Thinking Machine. No emotion, no benefit of experience—just an enormous brain—reading, listening to scholars, writing papers, taking exams. Learning about democratic ideology, but not having the terrible conflict of acting. And if the machine lasts four years without breaking apart or running down [it will be given] a piece of paper and [made into] a man or woman, prepared to assume its role in a much less bright society.

This paradox is beautifully illustrated by the response to one of our most challenging questions. We asked a student to describe the ideal person. His initial answer reflected, for the most part, society's current admiration of the well-adjusted person who gets along with anybody. But to this was quickly added praise for the person who reasons and acts for himself. The man of character, according to the student, is one who does not accept too readily the point of view of others and yet has the knack of understanding and working with all who cross his path. Obviously, the student's desire for individual thought is gravely threatened and compounded by his equally strong desire for social acceptance.

Moving on to the third paradox: Often intensely dissatisfied with the programs and processes of education, the student, nevertheless, is reluctant to play much part in change.

The average student is not happy with the higher learning he is getting. We came across strong criticism of classroom methods: the overemphasis on marks or the heavy stress on the use of the curve in determining grades, for instance. One student told us: "We don't mind competing, but this is encouraging unhealthy competition. And then it often ends up this way—instead of competing with one another, we all gang up on the prof and compete with him!"

A frequent complaint centered on the over-use of objective-type examinations. An editorial in the Colorado student paper, discussing the question of whether or not the college graduate learns how to think, concluded:

> In too many cases the answer is no. Four years in college may simply signify that one is more adept than most at surviving the multiple-choice, true-false exams which are given in most classrooms. Colleges are turning out satisfied men with empty heads—and it is the colleges themselves which are primarily guilty.

The freshman year seems to take the brunt of the criticism. Here the courses are said to be the most tradition-bound and the teaching the least inspiring. Unless the student is challenged and becomes, to some degree, fascinated at this early stage, later efforts to interest him will meet with more resistance. As one student commented, "In the middle of my freshman year, I suddenly discovered that I'd become awfully sour. I was pretty cynical about the great things the college said it was going to do with me. I've recovered somewhat but that first experience started me off on no feet at all."

Despite this sometimes intense dissatisfaction with the educational process, students are reluctant to take part in change. Perhaps because they are campus transients, they are not eager to uproot traditional forms. Students will cite numerous activity-groups and functions which might profitably be combined; yet, as leaders, few prove willing to initiate change or to allow their own organizations to die a relatively painless death. The question *Why?* is a neglected interrogation in *both* curricular and extra-curricular life. It is buried under the weight of the system, the custom and the tradition of the academic world.

Most students have no idea of the influence at their command. They have the unquestioned opportunity to help broaden the horizon of higher education, to force the faculty member to delve more deeply and to cherish more fully. We were delighted to find one student who told us, "In our class, the students agreed the teaching was lousy. The treatment was superficial. We backed the prof into a corner and shot so many questions at the poor man that he had to go back and take a second look at his own knowledge as well as his method."

The next paradox: Keenly interested in experiencing the totality of life and knowledge, the student often reacts by preferring to compartmentalize his own life and knowledge.

The interest in totality is obvious. The inquiring student seeks the broader implications and relationships of what he studies. He frequently complains that too few of his teachers begin the encounter by discussing their concept of the over-all purpose of the course, the place it may hold in the student's educational development, its relationship to other subjects, and what it might say to the student as a living, striving person. No matter what the field of study, that field does have a relationship to fundamental issues. A faculty member put it this way:

> Do I insist that what is important is and must be important in the *immediate present*? Or shall I be willing to consider the past? Do I identify myself simply with my colleagues who are living now, or do I try to sense the whole experience of the race? Am I willing to consider the question of tradition? Do I consider, for instance, the human image simply as I happen to meet it—walking around on the street, God help me—or do I view the human image at all times and in all places and contexts?

There, in a nutshell, is the heart of liberal learning. And how does the student react? Like the instructor, he proceeds to compartmentalize, to make no attempt to relate, to live *today*. A good example of this is the student who gives lip service to integrity as a fundamental value of the human race—and then cheats on the next examination, or copies the theme of another, or does any number of things which are quite foreign to the logic which he demands of the teacher.

The last student paradox: While respecting and honoring the adult who has explicit convictions, the student prefers to hide his own in the shelter of the group.

Over and over again, students claim to value far more highly the faculty member who has convictions and is willing to make them known. They agree that often they first recognize the importance of taking a stand only after they have actually observed a person who is honestly and carefully committed. They sense immediately and are suspicious of any teacher who tries to hide under a façade of assumed objectivity. One student concluded, "We're called the silent generation, but can you really blame us? We've studied under those who often make a fetish of silence." A Harvard Student Council report commented:

> Students frequently receive the impression that this noncommitted objective stance is the only one that is scholarly and scientific. Hence they may think that they should try to maintain it all of the time, even when commitment is in order. . . . If suspended judgment is connected with a scholarly approach, students may remain suspended until they leave the academic community, and then revert to earlier social norms or unthinkingly adopt new ones offered them by the society they enter.

The student says he likes a man with convictions; but what, really, does he himself practice? As one student told us, "We prefer to hide our convictions under a blanket of superficiality because of the social pressures of the crowd." It is not popular on a campus to have a well-considered, entrenched concept. We found that while most students are idealistic individually, the group norm does not sanction expression. The setting of standards, for instance, is a group process. Relatively few students profess to maintain individually held values.

For this, they blame the world around them. Here is a beautifully phrased rendition of the current attitude, as reflected in a campus editorial:

> We are the antiseptic generation. We have grown up protected from the germs of extremisms which had given our elders a case of intellectual gout. For us history is a study only of the past; greatness today is not our necessity. Therefore, we concentrate on "life adjustment" which helps us rid ourselves of the little idiosyncrasies of which greatness is made. [Malcontentism] is as great a sin as adultery and probably more often punished. But somewhere in the back of our minds we know that this protection is but a flimsy wrap. We want to know more, hear more, do more, think more, but our society neither encourages nor rewards those who inquire.

Parenthetically, let me add that we found significant differences in overt idealism between men and women. In a word: the women want to be better and the men better off. Most students are deeply introspective. They want a frame of reference for their lives—but not necessarily a religious one. The student is not anti-religious, but he is usually uninspired by the usual pattern of religious activity. And often he confuses religious belief with mere humanitarianism. The student will not respond to empty moralizing. He will not commit himself religiously until he has found what is for him adequate grounds for commitment. This is why he prefers, at present, to intellectualize religion.

We found, too, that most students associate morality with their inability to comprehend and accept absolutism. For example, many expressed an inability to understand what they term the vestiges of a God-centered system of self-discipline to which their grandparents subscribed—and their parents less so. They contend that this system of Puritan ethics has been diluted by generations of incessant questioning. It involves more compromise and hypocrisy than they wish to embrace. So the moral standard becomes: "I'll take my chances, but I will play it safe in the future." Here again the standard of double existence. To the student, morality is strictly a personal matter—but it is, on inspection, largely group-controlled.

The final paradox involves directly the college itself: The student is ready for a more searching and strenuous educational experience, but the colleges have not fully recognized, nor are they fully prepared to meet, this potential challenge. The colleges are often the purveyors of security-worship. The failure of the student to respond is basically the failure of the college to challenge. As one student told us, "We all do our best when

138 PROSE CURRENT

we really believe that somebody has faith in us. It's the indifference that
makes rationalization so much easier."

The notion that the chief role of higher education is to preserve tradition must be overcome. Wherever we traveled, we found that the
student, beneath his façade of cynicism in strange combination with buoy-
ant optimism, is ready to be challenged.

The current generation of college students may be silent at times, and
most loquacious at other times, "beat" one moment and out to beat the
world the next, self-satisfied and frightened; but it is, by and large, well
aware of its growing pains and not particularly reticent about discussing
them. If the stimulus is right, the student will respond. Without the
right stimulus, however, he will drift and finally moor in any haven
which appears most immediately attractive.

For the intelligent student as well as the perceptive college, this represents both an obligation and a magnificent challenge.

COMMENT

In the opening section of this article the author describes the problem
he faces in trying to organize his material: he and his colleagues have
just completed a long and detailed survey of American college life; he
wants now to generalize on his findings. He solves his organizational
problem by phrasing his conclusions in parallel statements and discussing
them one after the other. This method often proves useful to writers confronted with unwieldy material. Hence such titles as "Questions Deans
Should Answer," "Three Answers to an Old Question," or "Principles
Which Need Stating."

SUGGESTIONS FOR WRITING

1. Write a letter to your high school principal in which you evaluate your
   high school education with specific reference to your experiences in
   college.
2. Take one of Mr. Eddy's paradoxes and support or attack it with theories drawn from your own experience. If you were to take the first
   paradox, you might want to demonstrate that the student's apathy
   toward current events, toward education, toward moral problems is
   more apparent than real. Here, as always, be specific. Instead of
   "current events" discuss integration—integration in your dormitory
   rather than in the South.
3. Begin a paper with the author's statement "The women want to be
   better and the men better off." Take great care to avoid the obvious
   oversimplifications such a subject invites. Defend this statement to
   your friends; the ensuing discussion will sharpen your perceptions.

EDWIN L. DALE, JR.

Confessions of a Word-Eater

I HAVE BEEN READING again today. Like an alcoholic. I've tried—honestly I have—but I cannot stop. And of course now, at midnight, it has come over me again. The sense of depression, yes. But more than that. Mostly it's the awful feeling of being unable to decide which of all the terrible things that threaten us should be attacked first. I know it will happen again. I'll go to bed and, lying awake, will resolve never to read again. But then I'll go to sleep—guiltily—and tomorrow I'll start all over again.

Today was about the same as usual. It began with some of the testimony before the Jackson Committee. It turns out that We—I simply cannot help including myself in that term—are unrealistic; are too much in love with Our affluence; are confused by too much conflicting talk about our military strength *vis-à-vis* the Russians; have too many committees; are not trying hard enough; and are faced with a Total Challenge to Our Way of Life. It's terrible.

Then there were all those things about Our society. I couldn't help reading some fiction, then some criticism of fiction, then some criticism of recent work in the social sciences. Honestly, this is even worse. We are alienated. We suffer as individuals because individualism is disappearing. The loss of the Big Idea, or of God, has left Us drifting. The society is becoming more cynical than ever before (though I do not know tonight whether it is because of advertising, or Payola, or Hoffa, or the Loss of God, or nihilism, or affluence, or John Steinbeck). Urban strains—and it is time We woke up to the fact—are creating more and more misery. Love still exists, of course, but because it is more free it is more painful.

I look around me at the faces in the crowd. Many are smiling, but I know from my reading that this is deceptive. This is a lonely crowd. The people are seeking status, probably unsuccessfully. The men, I know, are enveloped by the pressures of the organization. They are politically apathetic, conformist, nervous, badly educated. Where they are not victims

Reprinted by permission of *The New Republic*.

of sprawling suburbia, they are living on the edge of the inexorably creeping slums. They are affluent and misusing their leisure, but they cannot
find decent housing that they can afford. How brave of them to smile,
I think to myself.

My throat tightens. How can We confront the Russians and try harder
when We are torn by such a deep inner struggle? Just think! While I
was puzzling out the economics of defense, juvenile delinquents were
roving the streets. I watched a sensitive play on television (everyone has
missed the *real* evil of television: It is so good at its best that it diverts
us from entertainment) about a Southern lady who suffered so much that
she probably never heard of the Russians.

Yesterday it was a Small Businessman that I read about. He had terrible trouble. Only his trouble was not either alienation or the Russians.
And you know what I did. I went back and read some more last night.
I found out why it is practically impossible for the Underdeveloped Countries to advance from poverty because of the population explosion. True,
I came away with the conviction that We should help with more economic aid. But unfortunately a friend came over after a deep quarrel with
his wife and I got nowhere at all in convincing him of the Urgency of
the problem. The worst of it was that I had read about the Roots of his
trouble, and I didn't know which problem was worse.

There was a time when I was happy. I was young, of course, but that
was not the main thing. I hadn't got the habit yet. I wasn't hitting the
books. Except those boring schoolbooks about history and things that went
in one examination and out the other. Those were the days when I thought
a Conservative was a manager who used the sacrifice bunt in the late
innings when he was one run behind.

I have learned about trouble now. Nothing that afflicts me personally,
of course. Not bored wives or Big Business or Russians or unemployment
or loneliness or Negroes, but books and magazines and newspapers. I
met a guy once who said he never reads at all. Happiest guy I ever saw.
Maybe out in Peoria or someplace most people are like that. Suffering,
of course, because that is obviously the way Our society is. But suffering
only in moderation because they don't read. Me, I can't help it. There's
no use trying psychiatric treatment, because I've already discovered from
my reading that it will never work. Anyway there is a terrible shortage of
psychiatrists. I hate my weakness, but I know I cannot cure it. And the
worst of it is, there is more and more irresistible stuff being turned out all
the time. Why, do you know that Congressional Committees alone produced five volumes of upsetting expert testimony last week. How can I
stop when I am tempted with more and more? My fellow readers are
sadistic; they keep writing.

So do I. *Mea culpa.*

COMMENT

The rapid recital of one scolding, viewing-with-alarm warning after another causes the wry humor of this piece. But even so short an essay (actually longer than most freshman compositions) must have pegs on which to hang its details. The author achieves a loose but effective structure here in the first few words in each paragraph. Read the first sentence in each paragraph rapidly in succession.

SUGGESTIONS FOR WRITING

1. Write a paper similar to Mr. Dale's on college regulations, scolding deans, and nagging professors.
2. Make a list of the remarks which have begun to exasperate you when you go home for the holidays. (Uncle Fred: "These are the happiest days of your life." Aunt Mildred: "I wish *I* had had the chance to go to college." Little sister: "Boy, are you getting stuck up!") Organize them into the basis for a paper.
3. Study all the dangers you are warned against in advertising (from tattle-tale gray washings to five o'clock shadow). Work these into a series leading to a climax and write your paper around them.

Emmet John Hughes

The Notion of an
American Gentleman

A GENTLEMAN, according to so keen and authentically American a wit as Fred Allen, is any man who would not hit a woman with his hat on. And thereby hangs a tale—part historical and part moral, quite whimsical and a little serious. The tale does not concern the mythical man whose menace is as nicely mannered as Mr. Allen suggested. It concerns the question, so sharply insinuated by Mr. Allen's humor, whether *the gentleman* is a species that can survive—if indeed it ever existed except as an object of vaudevillian scorn—in a climate so mockingly inhospitable as American society. Can the creature exist? *Does* he? What does he look like?

Now a serious definition—social or semantic—poses a problem that must immediately be (a) acknowledged and (b) ignored. The problem is a most elemental proposition: by any understanding of the term "gentleman" (American or alien), he is one not given to discussing other gentlemen in public, much less writing of them, much less still propounding presumptuous definitions of their nature. Accordingly any commentary on the matter is *ipso facto* profoundly lacking in any authority whatsoever. Hence it must be arbitrary, captious, opinionated, and a little insolent. And only in this recklessly lighthearted spirit may the inquiry be pursued. Thus. . . .

All that follows is dedicated, definitely, to proving, deviously, three quite unprovable propositions. *First:* a gentleman is a quite specific, and specifically useful, member of any society. *Second:* the requisite qualities are considerably more profound than the commandment to tip one's hat before slapping a lady. And *third:* there exists an American species of gentleman rather distinct from other types in history and the world at large, and quite estimable too. As for the tenuous evidence. . . .

The easiest aspect of any process of definition is the negative, so we may begin with the quickly demonstrable: the kinds of gentleman that the American is *not*. History seems generously populated with *these* gen-

Reprinted from *Esquire*, May 1960. © 1960 by Esquire, Inc.

tlemen, and we need note a few such types so essentially alien to the American temper. There was, for example, the scholar-gentleman of the Renaissance, elaborately defined and exalted by Castiglione in his *Book of the Courtier,* thus: "Besyde goodnesse, the true and principall ornament of the mynde in everye manne (I beleave) are letters." Whatever else may be said of this noble sentiment, it can hardly be said to have an American ring to it. If Fred Allen were alive to look back upon the decade of the 1950's, with its emphatic disdain for "eggheads," he quite possibly would observe: a gentleman is a man who always murmurs some apology to his hearer before crudely alluding to the experience, pretentious and bizarre, of having lately read a serious book.

Nor does the elaborate elegance of the Chesterfieldian gentleman of the eighteenth century seem any less foreign. "Manner is all, in everything," the English Earl wrote. "It is by manner only that you can please, and consequently rise. . . . Your sole business now is to shine, not to weigh. Weight without luster is lead. You had better talk trifles elegantly to the most trifling woman, than coarse inelegant sense to the most solid man." It is true that an *American* book on manners a century ago commended highly the gentleman who, when his servant dropped a platter of boiled tongue on the floor, remarked, calmly, eruditely, and idiotically: " 'Tis a mere *lapsus linguae,* gentlemen." But the passion for gleam and polish in manners broadly strikes the American mind as not lustrous but just ludicrous.

What, then, of the nineteenth century's stern kind of retort to the shiny vulgarity of the Chesterfieldian gentleman—the stern evangelical gentleman sentimentalized by Samuel Richardson and loosely associated with the remembrance of things Victorian? Somehow, this, too, seems to stand equally far from an American notion of gentlemanliness. The obsessive Richardsonian concern for technical chastity ("A man who offers freedoms to his female servant, deserves not, however rich and powerful, to be called a gentleman") catches the cold flavor of American Puritanism, but that is about all. For as the fluent and facile American idiom would tend to dismiss the Castiglione ideal as a "grind" and the Chesterfieldian version as a fop, so it would largely frown upon this pietistic fellow as a prig.

What history seems to suggest, nationality strives to confirm: the American notion (still assuming its existence) seems to contrast rather explicitly with favored views in lands more old and courtly. There is the ancient but suggestive aphorism about the distinct ways in which gentlemen of different nationalities are given to enter any handsomely appointed living room: the Frenchman quickly asks who owns it all; the Englishman acts as if he owned it; and the American acts as if he gave not a damn who owned it. To most American eyes and ears, the

symbols and sounds of the gentleman of England seem strange indeed:
the titles and trappings of aristocracy, the stiff poise disciplining and
disguising emotion, the subdued conversation with its stress upon the
barely audible monosyllable, the severe social accent upon accent. As
for the flourishing manners of Latin men with respect to (not necessarily
toward) the opposite sex, the American is likely to observe glumly that
it seems, to him, sensible to kiss a lady almost anywhere except on the
finger tips. In manners as in politics, the American seems likely to feel
himself rather alone in the world.

In the doubt-shedding light of all this, from the historic to the trivial,
the obvious question arises, again, whether the *genus Americanus* is not
simply and plainly a contradiction in terms. There are, roughly speaking, two arrays of witnesses who rarely tire of assuring the American
gentleman that he does not exist. They are: foreign gentlemen (largely
self-appointed) and American women (largely self-appreciative). Their
testimony can scarcely claim to be disinterested and dispassionate, but
they demand hearing, if only because it is quite impossible, in any event,
to silence the condescension of the one or the complaint of the other.

The truth is that there is probably a stronger case to be made for
the deep doubts of these critics than is achieved by their own invective.
The very vocabulary of American speech suggests a certain abiding distrust of the social sheen commonly confused with gentlemanliness. The
word "genteel" itself long ago acquired a pejorative quality. Nor has any
decently mannered American boy survived his school years without being
flayed by his classmates for being a "sissy." Grown to burly manhood,
he is likely to find himself often enough using the peculiarly American
abbreviation, "gents," as if the very word, fully syllabized, would insult
all within hearing. The incongruity of this is suggested by trying to
imagine any such shy slurring of *señor* or *monsieur*. And it is perhaps
not irrelevant that American law is heavy with provisions, notably in the
anti-trust field, condemning things called "gentlemen's agreements" (quite
valid, for example, in England).

The speech of the people reflects something, of course, of the history
of the nation. Once the Revolutionary generation presiding over the
nation's birth had disappeared, American society tended to give relatively
little living space to anything smacking of aristocracy or gentry. The
towering landmarks of the American historical scene—from the ragged
frontier of the past to the bustling metropolis of the present—have been
almost equally uncongenial to the cultivation of social conventions or
graces, there being little practical occasion for them either in wagon
train or in subway. And the time of the maturing of American society—
the Golden Age of the late nineteenth century, so crudely conspicuous
in its waste and consumption and pomp and acquisitiveness—was hardly

characterized by a matching maturing in manners or tastes. This was the time when the Modern Conquerors—the generals and geniuses of American business enterprise—ransacked the castles and churches and palaces of Europe to adorn themselves and their abodes with the trappings, but not the discrimination, of a new aristocracy. Renaissance master-pieces smiled from the walls, strains of uncomprehended Mozart and Beethoven echoed through the rooms, the full armor of medieval knights attended the doorways—of the homes of men unsurpassed in apprecia-tion of the ways to buttress fortunes by producing iron girders and tin cans, glue, cement and nails. The climate, in short, was most encourag-ing to the general notion, later popularized by aphorism, that it takes three generations, or one good guess in the stock market, to make a gentleman. It was that simple—and shallow.

The heritage, thus unkindly construed, has hardly been one to culti-vate the idea of serious self-cultivation (which has something to do with being a gentleman). This helps explain why the species (still assuming its existence) has not seemed a fabulously common one. It was a heri-tage, in fact, sure to breed that most unattractive man of manners acidly etched by O. Henry: "In dress, habits, manners, provincialism, routine and narrowness, he acquired that charming insolence, that irritating completeness, that sophisticated crassness, that overbalanced poise that makes the Manhattan gentleman so delightfully small in his greatness."

And this pseudo-gentleman, of course, is precisely the chilling carica-ture who most exasperates the most severe of all critics of the American man, the Manhattan woman. In her eyes—cold with contempt or glazed with boredom—the man in question (in question in every sense) falls pitiably and infuriatingly short of any concept of a serious gentleman. His manners are respectable but meaningless: they speak for a pose, but not for a person. His attitudes toward women range from unpleasant extreme to unpleasant extreme: either elaborately deferential but with-out true respect, or masculinely brusque without true firmness. In the serious statistics of human size, he is fatefully younger than his years and smaller than his fortune. His image and profile seem forever to blur and mingle with those of all surrounding pseudo-gentlemen. All, indeed, seem essentially faceless—their assumed manners, their acquired artifices, even their gaucheries, all seem interchangeable, undistinguishing and un-distinguished. And when on rare occasions, with a flourish of some man-ner of individual initiative, one aspires to being provocative, he generally succeeds only in being provoking.

History, O. Henry and the American woman, then, might tend to agree: the American gentleman really is nobody but that comic fellow whom Fred Allen had in mind, the man who really is not there at all.

Who says the contrary?

To begin with—and most impressively—the contrary *is* suggested by history, the muse so notoriously given to talking out of both sides of her mouth. For it is time, herewith, to get closer to the point: what *is* a gentleman anyway? And, instantly upon looking at the question, we learn that the idea of a gentleman, far from being utterly alien to American tradition, is, first, an idea essentially modern, and, secondly, an idea whose European and American versions are by no means so dissimilar as one might first suspect.

The word, and the idea, first came upon the Western scene to distinguish a man of "gentle" birth from *both* a serf and a noble: a new type of man, of a certain distinction, notably the bearing of arms. This makes him a relatively modern species, and Sir George Sitwell once remarked, for example, that no one "ever described himself or was described by others as a gentleman before the year 1413." What is more interesting is the fact that the abundant literature on the subject after the fifteenth century makes clear that views and reactions rather casually called "American" have, indeed, been voiced about gentlemen for centuries by indisputably European sources and commentators. *Thus:* no lament upon the crassness of the American gentleman in the Golden Age, and his inelegant materialism, is significantly different from the grief expressed as long ago as Chaucer's time in *Piers Plowman:* "Soap-sellers and their sons for silver are made knights." *Thus:* no American scorn for the vulgar fatuities of Chesterfieldian etiquette could surpass Dr. Johnson's snarling that the *Letters* of the fastidious Earl "teach the morals of a whore and the manners of a dancing master."

The Chesterfieldian notion of gentility, however, itself suggests something rather curious. Upon first scanning, the *Letters,* with their fierce concern for all the minutiae of personal presence, form, behavior and hygiene, seem inanely fastidious—as when the father writes his son such exquisitely refined prescriptions as: "I hope you take infinite care of your teeth; the consequences of neglecting the mouth are serious, not only to one's self but to others." But a moment's reflection suggests that, while this is hardly a common subject for paternal correspondence in America, no society has probably ever matched contemporary American society in persistent public preoccupation with cavities, falling hair, shaven legs, body odors, unsightly pimples, lip shades and hair tints. It is an incongruous suggestion, but it seems barely possible that the verbose Earl's letters may, historically speaking, have been mailed special delivery to the modern huckster, so full of commercial, if not paternal, concern for the grooming and the manicuring of his society's sons and daughters.

But—the frivolous aside—there is a certain serious substance to the oldest European idea of a gentleman that appeals, directly and forcefully, to the most modern American idea of what a man should be, in himself and to others. Consider, for example, from the early years of the seventeenth century, the observation of Thomas Gainsford: "Generositie doth not account him a gentleman which is only descended of noble bloud, in power great, in jewels rich, in furniture fine, in attendants brave. . . . But to be a perfect Gentleman is to be measured in his words, liberall in giving, sober in diet, honest in living, tender in pardoning, and valiant in fighting." The definition is good and explicit. And it is one that almost any American would both recognize and admire.

A few truths, then, slowly shape themselves from the haphazard evidence. For one thing, it seems a deceptive distinction which insists that any European idea of a gentleman must be largely a gleaming matter of surface and manner and poise—and the American idea, by contrast, a thing of baser but tougher metal, a concern with elemental character or acclaimed accomplishment, a disdain for grace or form. There are grains of truth, but no more, in such oversimplification.

And a still more serious truth would appear to be this: the *gentleman* —the word and the idea—suggests substance as well as style, meaning as well as manner. Once this is discerned, it becomes clear that the role of serious gentlemen in American history has been quite a significant one. If the Founding Fathers were not largely "gentlemen" (with a few boisterous exceptions), the word has little meaning and no nation has ever been profoundly affected, in its destiny, by gentlemen. A Jefferson stands out as example, in style as well as in serious quality, even in the weakness as well as the strength often associated with the gentleman: while writing eloquently upon the wisdom of frugality, he could speed toward bankruptcy with the full life at Monticello. And a Lincoln—so different in heritage and in bearing and in manner from a Jefferson—could hardly be denied possession of some of the profounder qualities that endow the idea of a gentleman with meaning.

Nor does the proof of the American species come only from the dusty tomes so wont to overlook the lack of grace, the gaucheries or the vulgarities of their subjects. There is plain enough proof in living examples on the contemporary American scene and precisely on that part of the scene *least* widely respected for its good manners: the arena of politics. Thus a Rockefeller and a Harriman, successive occupiers of, and contenders for, the office of Governor of the most populous State of the Union: by any standard—education, presence, sense of service, dignity of manner, awareness of propriety—surely gentlemen by any reasonable definition. Or one may consider the evident, widely appreciated qualities of the two men who have most recently, and twice, contested for the Presidency. In the popular image, the essential qualities of the person of each seem slightly different. In an Eisenhower, all see certain manifest marks of the man: integrity, honor, responsibility, graciousness, manliness. In a

Stevenson, the qualities of the man seem no less clear: dedication, sobriety, intelligence, education, charm. In politics, in personalities, in capacities, the men may differ. But in *one* thing at least, they are the same: they are gentlemen.

Nor can it possibly be contended that they stand for some remarkable and obscure minority, for all serious American professions immediately suggest obvious, and impressive, figures of gentlemen. The judiciary, of course, has been abundant with them—from a Holmes or a Brandeis to a Learned Hand: men of principle to match their presence, depth to give meaning to their manner. In the arts, one may arbitrarily note such figures as those of an Oscar Hammerstein or a Paul Muni—men of plain weight and force, in countenance as much as manner, unneedful of pretense or bluster. Criticism and letters can immediately suggest such men as John Mason Brown or Brooks Atkinson or J. P. Marquand—gentle and correct and courteous, wearing their learning or distinction with the ease and lightness of great familiarity and little self-esteem. In the sphere of higher education and the great foundations, men as different in age and in interests as a Robert Hutchins, or Notre Dame's Father Theodore Hesburgh, or Princeton's Robert Goheen, are all as one in the vigor and poise of a gentleman. And far from least conspicuous, of course, are those publicly recognized products of the American military production—men of the fiber, the innate capacity for command, of a Lucius Clay or a Walter Bedell Smith. Significantly, at the death of George Marshall last year, George Kennan wrote to the New York *Times* a moving, discerning tribute to the man, ending with this salute.

> The judgment of history may, of course, modify this estimate of General Marshall's record as Secretary of State. It cannot alter the image that remains in the memory of those who were close to him in that office. It was the image of *the American gentleman at his best*—honorable, courteous, devoid of arrogance, exacting of others but even more of himself, intolerant only of cowardice, deviousness, and cynicism.

So a conclusion comes: the *genus Americanus* does indeed exist—in some ways, but far from all ways, different from that known to other societies. Quite probably, it is to be found least commonly in those spheres of society where many most commonly seek it. If so, that is the error of the seeker. It might even be that the American woman, so skeptical of the existence of the American gentleman, should first concern herself with the question of the existence of the American gentlewoman. And the commonly lamented failure—that the man neglects to make her "feel" like a woman—is *whose* failure?

And, finally, the question no longer to be evaded: if *he* does exist, *what* is he? What *makes* the man a gentleman?

So pretentious an inquiry must be pursued, thus, to its logical conclusion—the full and boundless presumption. Accordingly, let it be categorically insisted: the American Gentleman (all lingering uncertainty of his true existence banished by the use of capital letters) must respect five marks. Specifically. . . .

HE IS A MAN. The proposition, let it be quickly affirmed, is not self-evident. Not only are transvestites excluded; so are a multitude of variations and mutations, down to (or up to) fop, dandy, gigolo, or simply the socially avid escort with an unappeasable appetite to see, to be seen, but never to be seen through. To the pseudo-gentleman's misfortune, the last is inevitable, especially in the coldly discerning vision of the one whose attentive respect he most covets—a woman. In short, the essential proposition is the obvious: to be a gentle man, a man must first be a man. For, as in all human relations, gentleness is a function and a form of strength, not of weakness.

HE IS A USEFUL MAN. The adjective may seem redundant, but it is clarifying. The gentleman does not exist simply as a piece of animated decoration or ornament. He partakes of his environment, and he gives to it. He occupies *space,* serious space—something more than the night club's choice table, the theatre's house-seats, the opera's costliest circle, or the delicately cha-cha'ed edge of the most crowded dance floor. He takes up more serious *room* in his society than these pleasurable but scarcely significant spaces. The Earl of Chesterfield notwithstanding, he has *weight* —before he worries about luster.

The matter is as profound as it is old, for the need for the substance to sustain the style has been sensed by every society's understanding of the gentleman—even back to, and including, the fabulously decorous age of chivalry. Only a shallow view of the chivalric idea could dismiss its code as "a picturesque mimicry of high sentiment." For, as one English historian has observed: "Above all, it inculcated an ideal of social service . . . service, however humble its nature, free from degradation or disparagement; service of the weak by the strong; service of the poor by the wealthy; service of the lowly by the high."

In short: the gentleman *then,* and the gentleman *now,* had to be of some use—to some one and to some thing—other than himself.

HE RESPECTS WOMEN. The respect he gives is, of course, neither unctuous nor fawning. In the best sense, it is a respect that issues from a healthy and proper self-respect, for here again, as elsewhere in human relations, the person with no responsible sense of self can only be insensible to others as well. Accordingly, the gentleman dismisses as trivial feminine fancy all notion of equality between the sexes. He conducts himself with the simple awareness that nothing so infuriates a woman dedicated to the proposition of such equality as having to contend with a man who takes the proposition seriously. For almost invariably, of course, the American woman most covetous of the status of man is the same woman who complains, with appropriate sobs, that she knows no man who makes her "feel" like a woman. And from the elemental distinction between man and woman, the gentleman proceeds to make the further discrimination—*among* women. And those deserving of his respect receive the further courtesy of his withholding it from those who do not.

HE RESPECTS MEN. He respects them as individuals. He does not see or appraise them in categories—of status or race or religion or wealth or renown. He discriminates among them not in terms of how much each has accomplished, but in terms of how much has been fulfilled of what each *can* accomplish. He does and says the things that are uncontingent and unreciprocal—the deed done, the gesture extended, the word uttered, essentially always for *its own* sake, free of ulterior motive, unhopeful of any return. Accordingly, he is particularly thoughtful to those who can be of no possible service to him. For it is still exceedingly difficult to improve upon the axiom of John Henry, Cardinal Newman: "It is almost a definition of a gentleman to say he is one who never inflicts pain."

HE IS HIMSELF—AND DOES NOT TRY TO BE A GENTLEMAN. No requisite is more basic—nor more commonly ignored. The effortful striving is the sure exercise in self-frustration, not to mention the embarrassment, or distaste, of others. For the poseur gives mockery, not respect, to what he pretends to be. The acquired but alien manner, the anxiety to impress, the earnestly assumed and studiously rehearsed role, the sustained seeking to elicit response or recognition—all are marks of the cheap replica, the pathetic parody. For, while a gentleman should obviously display good manners, their proper role is not to conceal, but to reveal the true person. And this perhaps is the rule of rules: the gentleman is never trying to *prove* something—least of all himself.

These, then, are some pertinent qualities and considerations, all stated with blithe arbitrariness. They are serious qualities, in some respects, suggesting something, perhaps, of the nature of man himself. But the line between morals and manners becomes, at points, a thin one. And so one wonders: may not some signs on the simple surface of manners suggest the presence, or the lack, of the deeper qualities of a gentleman, beneath and behind the personal presence?

Since the fashion of the day places exaggerated premium on convenient check-lists in such matters, let fashion have its way—and five of the simple surface *manners* of a gentleman be briskly noted:

HE DISPLAYS SPECIAL CONCERN FOR THOSE AT HIS MERCY OR WHIM. There is, in the modern American metropolis, no more devastatingly authoritative witness to the truth or the falsity of a man's claim to be a gentleman than the secretary in his office, the waiter in his restaurant, or the servant in his home. Fortunately for many aspirants, these are rarely garrulous witnesses. But the test stands. For it takes only *politeness* for a man to be civil to his worldly equals. It takes *courtesy* for him to be respectful to all.

HE LISTENS AS WELL AS HE TALKS. In the deepest sense, the mature gentleman heeds the maxim of childhood and speaks when, and as, spoken to—addressing himself to the sense, and the sensibility, of another. His speech does not issue from a lofty summit of self. If it were as a hand, it would never be clenched or thrusting like a fist, never thumping backs and shoulders, but would find contentment and companionship in the easy and gentle touching or joining of fingers. So voices, too, can and should meet one another.

HE SHUNS DISPLAY, AS WELL AS DISCUSSION, OF SELF. The three subjects least common in his conversation are: his fortune, his possessions, and his achievements. And the discretion of his simplest actions follows the discretion of his ordinary speech. In public places, his tips are full but not lavish, his complaints fair and firm but not querulous. In his home, he does not introduce his latest guest first (and passionately) to his Impressionist paintings, then (and casually) to his waiting friends. He is remarkable for his lack of zeal in relating his prowess at skeet-shooting last Sunday, his astute manipulation of longs and shorts last week, his shrewd tacking in last summer's yacht race, his breath-taking spill last winter on the slopes of St. Moritz. The one person, in short, for whom he shows no concern and little interest is the first person singular.

HE RESPECTS CONVENTIONS. He feels no need to display what might be called conspicuous independence or license—no gnawing urge to prove his individuality, to proclaim his personal identity, by disdain for the commonplace or the accepted, especially the inherited. He has the wit to know that conventions, even conventions of mere manners, usually have had their origin in rather sensible attempts to make one person's conduct more helpful or respectful to another. And even the observance of the trivial and the obsolete convention (such as the gentleman walking on the outside of the lady), while lacking any practical purpose, does suggest the basis of all courtesy: awareness of the presence of the other person.

HE RESPECTS PRACTICALITIES. Without this regard to balance his concern for convention, he would be not a respecter, but a prisoner, of form and fashion. It remains forever possible to be a painstaking practitioner of politeness but, at the same time, a total stranger to courtesy. And this happens when the outward form or manner is allowed to distort one's self or to disregard another. Thus the gentleman refrains from trying to impress another with extravagance beyond his means. Thus—on a trivial but practical level—he may meet the modern challenge of the low-slung taxi by entering it ahead of the lady in evening dress, if only to spare her back or gown.

Simple things, silly things, serious things; things most mundane and things most moral . . . somehow they all contrive to make a man a bit more, or a bit less, a gentleman.

While most of the matters noted are universally known, there are a few special American accents to all this, bespeaking an American Gentleman (he does exist, doesn't he?) a little distinct from all others. Indeed, the American has one notable advantage over all others, for he emphatically possesses, in his national temper, one of the most elemental, as well as the most rare, requisites for being a gentleman: he does not fret and strive too much over being one.

Least of all is he disposed to worry about anybody's definition of one. And this is probably the brightest sign that he may be one.

COMMENT

The three main divisions of this article are controlled by three questions: What evidence suggests that the American gentleman doesn't exist? What evidence that he does? What actually is the American gentleman? Many times a writer finds that he can best organize his writing by posing a series of related questions. Sometimes he finds it helpful to imagine a specific interrogator against whose objections and prejudices he can array his arguments. Such a method calls into play techniques we have used before, predisposes us to care about our subject, and enforces an awareness of our audience.

SUGGESTIONS FOR WRITING

1. Take one of the characteristics Mr. Hughes suggests and elaborate upon it through discussion of specific situations. You might, for instance, explore how well "The gentleman respects conventions" holds up under analysis.

2. Develop a series of questions leading to a definition of a "lady." Generally speaking, the more detailed your questions, the more interesting your paper will be. "What is a lady?" is clearly too broad for a short paper. "How does a lady behave toward men?" is better. "How does a lady behave on a date?" is better still, but "How does a lady behave at a dance?" probably has a better chance of success.

3. Distinguish between *politeness* and *courtesy* as the author does, or write an essay on his belief that gentleness is a function and a form of strength, not of weakness. Such topics as these require considerable thought. Do not write on them if you have to fall back on tired generalities or platitudes.

JOSEPH WOOD KRUTCH

If You Don't Mind My Saying So

SOME YEARS AGO a distinguished playwright told me how he had taken his East Side mother-in-law to see Maurice Evans in *Richard II*. The old lady—whose experience with both literature and the theater was extremely limited—listened intently in silence for half an hour, then waved a derisive thumb in the direction of the mellifluously complaining Richard and announced firmly: "I don't sympathize."

Now this was, of course, a fine tribute to the purely dramatic skill of Shakespeare. He had provoked the reaction he aimed at without any direct indication of what his own attitude was. I remember the anecdote at the moment for a simple reason. "I don't sympathize" vigorously sums up my own response to certain modern Richards, namely those who enlarge with too much self-pity upon their "alienation" from modern society, modern man and, indeed, from the universe as a whole. On the one hand I find myself ready to agree with a good deal of their criticism; on the other I am irritated by their chronic reaction to the things we both abhor.

To take the most obvious and least significant case, consider the beatniks. I dislike—almost if not quite as much as they do—the dominant middle-class and organization-man concept of the Good Life. Although we can't all be philosophers, scholars, artists or monks, I agree that too many moderns aspire to nothing more than the "status symbols" that money can buy, and far too few to what George N. Shuster recently defined as the ultimate aim of education: "sharing the life of the scholar, poet and saint." But to respond to this situation by taking a shot of heroin and driving a car at ninety miles an hour seems unlikely either to improve society or, what is more relevant, lead to a Good Life.

Sympathetic interpreters of the beatniks have described them as "taking a revenge on society." For example, the hero of a recent novel is described by a reviewer thus: "Seeing too well in a world dazed by the bomb, Re-

Reprinted from *The American Scholar*, Vol. 29, No. 3, Summer 1960. © 1960 by the United Chapters of Phi Beta Kappa. By permission of the publisher and the author.

naud undertakes an alcoholic strike against humanity." But the phrase "an alcoholic strike," like "a revenge on society," seems to me merely comic. It suggests the popular saying about "biting off your nose to spite your face," that being precisely what some intellectuals (including many somewhat above the beatnik level) are doing—as though turning into a dope addict does not hurt oneself even more than it hurts anyone else. It seems only slightly less obvious that the more respectable intellectuals who devote themselves exclusively to exploring and exploiting their "alienation" are doing much the same thing. Surely it is more productive of personal happiness and even "more useful to society" to be a candle throwing its beams into a naughty world than a beatnik crying "Revenge, revenge" from the gutter. We hear a great deal about the responsibility of society toward the individual. The individual also has a responsibility toward society. And if things are as bad as the alienated say, the only way one can discharge that responsibility is by being an honorable man.

I presume that this thesis hardly needs elaboration and is not likely to be contested outside beatnik circles. But a considerable number of the most talented novelists, poets, painters and composers of the present day reveal, even if they do not proclaim, their alienation; and it seems to me that their most frequent response is only less grotesque, not more fruitful, than that of the beatniks. Even granted, as most of them proclaim in some version of Yeats's often quoted words that "Things fall apart; the center cannot hold," is there still nothing for a wise man to do except take heroin with the beatniks or, as is usual among the alienated squares, elaborate in more and more complicated phrases their dark convictions?

To this question the hearty do-gooder will of course reply: "Why, obviously the thing to do is to work for social improvement. Join the party of your choice and the church of your choice; be sure to register for all elections and attend the meetings of your local P.T.A." Without entering into any question concerning the ultimate effectiveness of such a method of employing one's time, it must be admitted that your alienated artist or philosopher is no more likely than a beatnik to undertake it. Let us suppose, therefore, that he has, like Thoreau, both "signed off" from the church and wished that he could as easily sign off from society as a whole. Of course he will be thoroughly disapproved of almost everywhere outside the circle of the completely alienated; but he might, like a few others besides Thoreau, find in this determination to stand alone the possibility of making for himself a private world from which he was *not* alienated, instead of devoting himself exclusively to the task of saying just how alienated he is. He could even find a few justifications formulated in the past for doing just what he has done.

I seem to remember somewhere in Plato the opinion that when times are thoroughly bad a wise man will merely stand by the wall. Similarly, it would appear from the *Meditations* of Marcus Aurelius that although the Emperor was no less aware than Yeats of a world in which "things fall apart," he spent relatively little time in either elaborating or bemoaning the lack of wisdom or virtue in society. He determined instead to cultivate them in himself. Then there is even a wholehearted defense of the mere slacker, which is quoted by Montaigne from one Theodorus who held that "It is not just that a wise man should risk his life for the good of his country and imperil wisdom for fools."

As I see it, the question is not so much whether the alienated would do better to imitate Marcus Aurelius rather than Baudelaire and Apollinaire, for it is a larger and, so many will think, an outrageous question. Is it possible that present-day civilization would be in some important respects better than it is if more people had thought less about how to improve society and more about how to improve themselves?

No doubt the medieval monk was too exclusively concerned with his private salvation. But we have gone to the other extreme and are so obsessed with the idea of society as a whole that it no longer seems quite respectable to seek even intellectual or spiritual self-improvement. I am not saying that we are, in actual fact, excessively unselfish. But the cant of the time requires that we should always be asking of any proposed good, "Can everybody have it?" or "Is it an answer to the general problem?" With astonishing regularity I get letters from people who comment on something I have written with a "Well that's the answer so far as you are concerned; I guess it could be the answer so far as I am concerned. But only the privileged, or the lucky, or the well educated, or the intelligent, or the whatnot, can do what you and I can. So what is the answer for society as a whole?"

No doubt it would be fine if we could find a universal formula for salvation. I would welcome a convincing one if I ever heard it. But I never have, and I see no reason why, this being true, the individual should not save himself so long as he is not doing so at somebody else's expense. After all, society is composed of individuals. It cannot be "saved" except insofar as the individuals who compose it are.

I am not preaching universal indifference to society and social action as the highest wisdom. I am saying simply that if and when one individual feels (as so many articulate people do seem to feel) that the world is hopeless, then it is wiser to see what one can do about oneself than to give up all hope of that also. "I came into this world," said Thoreau, "not primarily to make it better but to live in it be it good or bad." If you insist, you may soften that a little by substituting "exclusively" for "primarily," but the meaning will still point in the same direction. Or as the same argument was recently discussed in that excellent "little magazine" called *Manas*:

If an artist can find nothing but bad brushes to paint with, he will not dissipate all his energies leading a revolution against bad brushes—but will develop techniques which make it possible for him to paint with bad brushes. He may even discover things that bad brushes do better than good brushes. It is one thing to fight the good fight for good brushes, and another to start to paint.

During the thirties, when most intellectuals moved leftward, quite a number of those who confessed (at least to their friends) that they had embraced communism were nevertheless engaged in writing movies for Hollywood or advertisements for Madison Avenue, while at the same time professing to regard both the movies and advertising as poisonous exhalations from a deliquescent society. Often (and I report from my own experience) they justified themselves by saying that there was no use trying to be anything but rotten in a rotten society. Comes the revolution and we will all be decent. Meanwhile, since we live in an evil society, we submit to it without any bourgeois nonsense about merely personal decency.

Such an attitude is only a logical extreme of the one taken by those who may not completely renounce either personal integrity or personal happiness, but insist upon our duty to think primarily in terms of what can be done for "society," and who sink into despair if we do not know an answer. I will even go so far as to suggest the possibility that society may be in a bad way partly because we have laid so much stress on public education—to take one example—and so little upon self-education. (Perhaps it also has something to do with the fact that I have met "educators" who were not and made no effort to be educated themselves.)

"Philanthropy," so Thoreau wrote,

is almost the only virtue which is sufficiently appreciated by mankind. . . . The kind uncles and aunts of the race are more esteemed than its true spiritual fathers and mothers. I once heard a reverend lecturer on England, a man of learning and intelligence, after enumerating her scientific, literary and political worthies, Shakespeare, Bacon, Cromwell, Milton, Newton and others, speak next of her Christian heroes, whom, as if his profession required it of him, he elevated to a place far above all the rest, as the greatest of the great. They were Penn, Howard and Mrs. Fry. Everyone must feel the falsehood and cant of this. The last were not England's best men and women; only, perhaps, her best philanthropists.

This is a tough-minded opinion. It is stated with characteristic exaggeration. But at least there is something to be said for those who do their best even though they do not see at the moment just what practical good it is going to do "for the common man."

After all, the medieval monk did perform a service. Neither the God he served nor the learning he preserved counted for much in the world from which he had retired. But he did exemplify in himself virtues that might otherwise have ceased to exist entirely, and he did preserve learning that without him would have been lost.

What it all comes down to in practice is simply this: if you despair of the world, don't despair of yourself. And it is because so many of the alienated critics of our society with whose criticisms I agree seem unable to do anything of the sort that I find myself alienated from them also.

Thirty years ago when I published a book much more pessimistic than I could possibly write now, I received a good many letters that might have been boiled down to a sentence in one of them: "If these are your convictions why don't you go hang yourself?" The answer was, and has continued to be through all such changes of opinion as I have undergone, that there is a private world of thought and endeavor which society has never been able to take away from me.

Perhaps the most curious and shocking result of the exclusive stress upon social rather than upon private ethics is the disappearance of the concept of honor as distinct from that of morality. One of the differences between the two is simply that honor is relevant to the individual only. True, society may be more affected than some social scientists seem to think by the prevalence or scarcity of honor in the code of the individuals who make it up. But the man of honor always asks first whether or not an action would dishonor him personally, and he is not influenced by an argument that his dishonorable act would have no bad (perhaps even some good) effect upon society and is therefore "moral" even if dishonorable.

The world would not now be as profoundly shocked as it was a generation ago by the phrase "a scrap of paper." We are used to having promises so treated. But the Junkers were merely a little ahead of us in their willingness to believe that since the triumph of Germany would promote the advent of the superman, there was nothing immoral in a broken oath.

Many college students, so the pollsters tell us, see nothing wrong about cheating on examinations. "Everybody does it and it doesn't really *hurt* anyone."

In such statements it is easy to see a reasonable application of the two leading principles of ethics-without-absolutes-and-without-honor, which is sometimes called "socialized morality." These two leading principles are: (1) What everybody does must be permissible since the *mores* determine morality; and (2) "Wrong" can mean only "socially harmful."

If you believe all this and also that the only difference between, let us say, an honest man and a thief is the difference between a man who has been "conditioned" to act honestly and one who has not, then there isn't much basis for argument with the student opinion.

When some scandal breaks in government or journalism or business or broadcasting, the usual reaction of even that part of the public which is shocked by it is to say that it could not have happened if there had been adequate laws supervising this or that activity. But, usually, is it not equally true that it could not have happened if a whole group of men, often including the supposed guardians of public morality, had not been devoid of any sense of the meaning and importance of individual integrity? May one not go further and ask whether any amount of "social consciousness" and government control can make decent a society composed of people who have no conception of personal dignity and honor? It was a favorite and no doubt sound argument among early twentieth-century reformers that "playing the game" as the gentleman was supposed to play it was not enough. But has the time not come to add that it is, nevertheless, indispensable?

COMMENT

Formal exposition usually begins with a statement of the thesis to be defended, proceeds through professorial firstlies and secondlies, and ends with a summary conclusion. The popular version of this scheme runs as follows: Tell them what you're going to tell them; tell them; and tell them what you've told them. The informal pattern used in this essay is quite different. Here the writer seems to be taking the reader with him through the process of his thinking. He begins his essay with a problem, moves through a series of comments, qualifications, or partial solutions, and concludes with his thesis statement. Had Mr. Krutch chosen to employ the formal structure, he might well have opened his essay with his last paragraph. Generally speaking, the informally organized essay is harder to write but more exciting to read.

SUGGESTIONS FOR WRITING

1. Draw together a group of titles from a jukebox listing. Arrange them by the kind of separation they deplore (from lover, from the gang, from the adult world) or by the attitude they reflect toward alienation (bitter, defiant, sentimental). Conclude your paper by evaluating the appeal of these songs.

2. Demonstrate by specific reference to campus politics, dating practices, college regulations, or political life the advantages of following the group, working to change the group, or constructing a private world.

3. Take some immoral or dishonest practice commonly defended with "It doesn't *hurt* anyone" and analyze it for its real dangers.

HOBBLING WITH HORATIO,

OR

THE USES OF LITERATURE

Norman N. Holland

THE ACHIEVEMENT OF HORATIO ALGER must be measured, like those of his heroes, not in excellence but in numbers. When he died in 1899, he had written with incredible speed—once he finished a novel in two weeks —over one hundred books. Though, as the *Dictionary of American Biography* somewhat belatedly says, "With the new generation of sophisticated boys such as he never knew, his popularity is dwindling," estimates of Alger's total sales range between 50 and 200 million. He is probably the most popular author America has ever had, and one of the most popular the world has ever known. And one can only wonder why. Lamely written, shabby mixtures of the most rank distrust of human nature and the most fatuous idealism, what could thirty years of American children have seen in such gelded *gestes* as *From Canal Boy to President, or the Boyhood and Manhood of James A. Garfield, Walter Sherwood's Probation, or Cool Head and Warm Heart, Frank and Fearless, Risen from the Ranks, Hobart the Hired Boy,* and the rest? What made Alger so popular?

Alger's forte was hardly style. His lame sentences seem sired by *Roget's Thesaurus* out of a tourists' phrase-book. For example, "His eyes flashed, and his youthful form dilated with righteous indignation." " 'I believe you will,' said the officer, with a revulsion of sentiment in Tom's favor." Each novel seems one long freshman composition:

> Stretched out stiff and stark were two figures, cold in death. They were men of middle age, apparently. From each the scalp had been removed, thus betraying that the murderers were Indians.

Alger's real strength lies in good old-fashioned moral instruction, and his most helpful counsel for the budding Rockefeller seems to be, People are no damn good. In Alger's books, Our Hero must run a gauntlet of sneakthieves, pickpockets, armed robbers, and confidence men. He begins to be wise when he acquires a properly Calvinistic view of man:

Reprinted, by permission, from *The Hudson Review*, Vol. XII, No. 4, Winter 1959–60. Copyright 1960 by the Hudson Review, Inc.

The young are by nature trustful. They are disposed to put confidence in those whom they meet, even for the first time. Unhappily, in a world where there is so much evil as there is in ours, such confidence is not justified. There are too many who make it a business to prey on their fellows, and select in preference the young and inexperienced.

This sludge of moral admonition through which the Alger plot limps seems hardly the sort of thing that would make boys rush out to read Alger's novels. Why then were they so popular?

The answer lies in the fact that Alger's own mind was so happily matched to the minds of his young readers. He himself remained a child all his life, an emotional cripple whose growth was twisted by the steady application of moral pressures in childhood.

He was born, his biographer Herbert R. Mayes reports, on Friday the thirteenth of January, 1832, the son of the stentorian Horatio Alger, Sr., Unitarian minister of Chelsea, Massachusetts, and a mild and browbeaten Mrs. Alger. Young Horatio wrote his first story at thirteen, but he—or his father—decided his career was to be the ministry, so he went to Harvard. When a senior, he fell in love with a girl called Patience Stires, but his father told his son that it would not do at all for a minister to marry so young, so Alger, Jr. gave her up—and never forgot her. Just as he graduated from divinity school, Horatio inherited some money from a landlord he had befriended and slipped away to Europe.

A year later, his diary carrying agonized self-appraisals after an affair with a French café singer, he returned. The Civil War broke out, and Horatio took to drilling an army of boys on Cambridge Common, Alger's Army of Up-and-Comings, laughing neighbors called them. Alger himself, though he sincerely wanted to enter the army, seems to have been accident-prone. A series of mishaps invariably occurred just as he was about to join the troops. At one point he got as far South as New York, where he was a horrified witness of the draft riots and saw Negroes hanged from Manhattan lampposts. These illnesses and accidents continued until, in 1864, he graduated from divinity school and was ordained pastor of the Unitarian Church in Brewster on Cape Cod. Though a good minister, he achieved his real success as an author of boys' stories; he resigned in 1866, and moved to New York.

The city at this time had been invaded by an army of drummer boys discharged from the G.A.R., the "street Arabs" that crop up in all of Alger's descriptions of New York. They shined shoes, delivered telegrams, sold papers, carried bags, and guided strangers about the city, taking to petty crime and tuberculosis about equally. The old Newsboys' Lodging House on Fulton Street was expanded to meet this new need and it was there that Alger found his home. He became a fixture, helping out as a teacher and minister, but mostly picking up material for his stories. The boys treated him with a mixture of admiration (for the stories) and scorn (because he was so easily fooled).

In an attempt to become more "literary" he bought a wig and cape and roamed the streets at night disguised as a lime-kiln man. He rumpled his hair, wore smocks, and kept a bust of Shakespeare over his desk. When a literary celebrity like Melville or Bret Harte visited the city, he would hang around the lobby of the Astor House for hours hoping to meet him. Dumpy, bald, and dull, Alger tried to crash New York's journalistic Bohemia, but when he found that this entailed smoking and drinking, he beat an embarrassed retreat to the world of philanthropists and moralists.

In 1878 he met a Mrs. Una Garth and fell in love. Persuaded for a time that he was a sensitive and talented soul, Mrs. Garth used to spend clandestine weekends with him at a farmhouse he had bought for the purpose, until her angry husband took her away to Paris. Alger followed, pouring his heart out to her. He was going to write the Great American Novel. It was to be called "Tomorrow." It was going to teach the common people world history and its culmination—the great destiny of America. It was going to show the world the real genius of the man who wrote boys' stories. "I spent the afternoon with Horatio and saw the opening paragraphs of his 'Tomorrow,' " wrote Mrs. Garth. "May the Lord spare the man from a knowledge of his own incapacity." Alarmed at Alger's indiscretions, she finally told him she did not wish to see him again. He had a nervous breakdown, and after a siege in a Paris hospital finally dragged himself back to the Newsboys' Lodging House in a state of near-insanity. The great "Tomorrow" was shelved, he lived on at the Lodging House, and he grew more and more famous as a writer of books for boys. In 1899 he died.

Hardly a Horatio Alger story—or is it? We use that phrase to describe the career of a young man who works hard, lives cleanly, and makes a lot of money, but in so doing, we repress, as it were, the real content of the phrase. A true Alger hero works hard and lives cleanly for 150 pages, and then inherits $50,000. Like most popular literature from *True Romances* to Norman Vincent Peale, the Horatio Alger story is a simple wish-fulfilling fantasy. In this respect, his works do not differ from other boys' books, the Frank Merriwell or Tom Swift stories, for example. Alger's novels, however, sold many times the number of copies these others did, and his popularity suggests that Alger must somehow have tapped an especially rich psychological lode.

Certainly one wish Alger gratifies is the boy's desire to become a man. Alger's young readers identify with Our Hero and vicariously through him win "grit," "pluck," and other symbols of manliness and potency.

"What sort of a fellow are you?" [the hero is asked in *Strive and Succeed, or The Fortunes of Walter Conrad*] "Have you got grit? Do you generally succeed in what you undertake?"

"I think I do," said Walter, smiling. "I wouldn't give it up, unless I was obliged to."

"I asked the question," said the young man, "because grit weighs heavily in this world. I have noticed that successful men are generally plucky, which is about the same thing."

Money is another symbol for potency, as is the watch which some older man almost inevitably buys Our Hero.

Alger, however, does more than simply gratify a boy's wish to become a man. He provides a foil, the Other Boy. Half of an average Alger novel deals with Our Hero's opposite, for example, Mark Manning in *Making his Way, or Frank Courtney's Struggle Upward*:

Mark Manning was slender and dark, with a soft voice and rather effeminate ways. He didn't care for the rough sports in which most boys delight; never played baseball or took part in athletic exercises, but liked to walk about, sprucely dressed, and had even been seen on the campus on a Saturday afternoon with his hands encased in kid gloves.

For this, however, he was so ridiculed and laughed at that he had to draw them off and replace them in his pocket.

It is needless to say that he was not a favorite among his school-fellows.

At a large school, manliness commands respect and favor, and an effeminate boy, unless caused by ill-health, is ridiculed and despised.

In Algerese, the Other Boy always looks "as though he has just stepped out of a bandbox." He takes trips to Europe and indulges expensive vices and sicknesses. He has, in short, all the things Our Hero seeks, but he gets them without effort. The Other Boy represents the infantile wish to get the symbols of adulthood without sacrificing the privileges of child-hood. When Our Hero is rewarded at the end, when he inherits his fortune (thus, in a way, achieving adulthood without effort), it is the Other Boy who is punished, who atones for the guilt of success. Typically, in the simple pattern of the Alger novel, he is reduced to the boyish state Our Hero was in at the beginning, as Halbert Davis is in *Brave and Bold, or The Fortunes of Robert Rushton*:

Halbert's pride was brought low. The wealth and position upon which he had based his aristocratic pretensions vanished, and in bitter morti-fication he found himself reduced to poverty. He could no longer flaunt his cane and promenade the streets in kid gloves, but was glad to accept a position in the factory store, where he was compelled to dress accord-ing to his work. In fact, he had exchanged positions with Robert, who was now . . . possessed of a considerable inheritance.

The Alger mother also plays her part in the wish-fulfilling constellation. She is usually a weak, fretful woman, who dotes on Our Hero, even to the exclusion of the father. Thus, when in *Making his Way* Frank Courtney's mother dies, she ignores her husband, Frank's stepfather, to give Frank "one last glance of love." The Alger hero is also likely to be the Alger mother's chief economic prop. In *Brave and Bold,*

> Great was the dismay of Mrs. Rushton when she heard from Robert that he was discharged from the factory. She was a timid woman, and rather apt to take desponding views of the future.
> "Oh, Robert, what is going to become of us?" she exclaimed, nervously. "We have only ten dollars in the house, and you know how little I can earn by braiding straw."

Here again, money (potency) is critical. The hero usually leaves his mother to win success, but guides her destiny from afar by sending money home. Finally he returns unexpectedly to her adoring arms:

> There was a knock at the outer door.
> She rose to open it, but, before she could reach it, it flew open, and her boy, taller and handsomer than ever, was in her arms.
> "Oh, Herbert!"
> It was all she could say, but the tone was full of joy.
> "How I have missed you!"
> "We will be together now, mother."
> "I hope so, Herbert. Perhaps you can find something to do in Wayneboro, and even if it doesn't pay as well—"
> "Mother," interrupted Herbert, laughing, "is that the way to speak to a rich boy like me?"

By far the most satisfying figure, however, is the Alger father, or, more properly, fathers, for there are typically three: the real father, the substitute father, and the wicked father. In most of Alger's books, the real father is dead. In many others the father is a father *manqué,* a man who seems strong and full of "grit," but somehow misses. In *The Young Adventurer,* Tom Nelson's father was lucky enough to marry "the prettiest girl in the village" but after twenty years of married life, she is still "drudging in an humble home, where there was indeed enough to eat, but little money even for necessary purposes." Tom's father was never able to best his wealthy rival, but young Tom does:

> "You have shown so much pluck and coolness that you are sure to get along."
> "I hope so, I am sure, for my father's sake."

In *Do and Dare, or A Brave Boy's Fight for Fortune,* "Herbert's father, returning from the war with the loss of an arm, was fortunate enough to receive the appointment of postmaster, and thus earn a small, but, with strict economy, adequate income." Walter Conrad's father in *Strive and Succeed* had his money stolen by the Great Metropolitan Mining Company, but, needless to say, Walter was not fooled. In *Brave and Bold*, Captain Rushton had foolishly left the family savings in the hands of the unscrupulous Mr. Davis, and wandered off to Calcutta with the receipt. Young Bob has to correct his father's blunder, and when Bob finds his father in Calcutta,

> his system, from the long privation of food, had received such a shock, that his mind sympathizing with it, he fell into a kind of stupor, mental and physical, and though strength and vigor came slowly back Captain Rushton was in mind a child.

It is Our Hero who puts the Alger father back on his feet. When Bob inherits the miser's money,

> Congratulations poured in upon our hero, who received them with modest satisfaction.
>
> "It is a good thing to have a rich son," said Captain Rushton, humorously. "Robert, I hope you won't look down upon me on account of my comparative poverty."

Not only could Alger's readers emotionally supplant their fathers—they didn't even have to feel guilty about it. Our Hero usually acquired a substitute father, another older man, by saving from peril either the older man himself or some woman attached to his family; the action, I suppose, must in many cases have stood for its opposite:

> Among the passengers was a stout, good-looking man, a New York merchant. . . .
>
> "It was providential, your seeing the rock," he said to the engineer. "We owe our lives to you."
>
> "You do me more than justice," replied the engineer. "It was not I who saved the train, but that boy."
>
> All eyes were turned upon Robert.

These substitute fathers are bountiful men who lavish praise and money on the heroes, take pleasure in relying on them, and encourage their efforts to become the man in the family. "Plucky young Bob Rushton" and Frank Courtney "with courage and self-reliance rarely found in one so young" are both befriended by wealthy New York merchants. In each case they are given important and responsible posts:

> "Do you mean to tell me," said the agent, incredulously, "that Mr. Percival would send out a boy—a mere baby—to look after his affairs, and sit in judgment upon me?"
>
> "Perhaps Mr. Percival had too much confidence in me," said Frank, "but it is so."

In each case these spirited young lads protect their patrons from other employees who are taking advantage of them, thus, in a sense, compensating for the advantage they themselves are taking of the real fathers. Herbert Carr in *Do and Dare* becomes companion to the invalid Mr. Melville and saves his life. Tom Nelson in *The Young Adventurer* is adopted by the other members of the wagon train, whom, in turn, he saves from Indians. Most of the substitute fathers buy the hero a watch, a recurring symbol in Alger for adulthood and potency. Like the real fathers, these substitute fathers are likely to be sick, old, or otherwise weakened.

The wicked fathers, on the other hand, are apt to be strong, powerful men, even if they are swindlers, misers, and bullies. Moreover, like Mr. Manning in *Making his Way* and Squire Hudson in *The Young Adventurer,* the evil fathers may be rivals for the love of Our Hero's mother. All these evil fathers either get unfairly or keep unfairly Alger's chief symbol of manliness, money, but in the end, they lose it. Alger's readers could thus project in this disguised and ostensibly just form the castration of their own stern nineteenth-century fathers.

It is in this Oedipal sense, too, that Alger's own pathetic life is itself "a Horatio Alger story," one long attempt to replace his father. His first story, written at thirteen, told of a boy who raced the wind and, when he won, boasted of it. "The wind grew angry . . . and did not come back to play." "The moral of the narrative," pontificated the elder Alger, is, "Thou shalt not set thyself against the word of the Lord." The cocksure Chelsea minister tried to mold his eldest son in his own image, naming him his junior, buying him a miniature minister's suit, forcing him toward the ministry by withholding money from him. Horatio Alger, Jr., emulated, but did not dare surpass. For a long time he stuttered, and all his life he was uneasy about speaking in public—surely a handicap for a minister. In later life, almost as if to ward off punishment, he gave away much of his money in compulsive acts of charity.

Writing books enabled Alger to surpass his father, yet avoid competing directly with him. Both in the pages themselves and in the fame they brought, he outdid his father, whom, in later life, he either squabbled with or ignored. Yet he could only write boys' books; at anything else he failed. He could write successfully only if his books compensated for his own rebellion against his father, that is, only if his books seemed to him to serve the high moral purpose of teaching the young to submit to their elders.

Actually, of course, the books showed the prospective merchant-prince replacing his father to become the sole support of an adoring mother—a delightful fantasy-version of the real nineteenth-century family situation. The Alger novel mirrors its social context in another way. As the nineteenth century progressed, opportunities for "poor boys" to make their way narrowed, yet the Calvinist belief that poverty was a sin lingered on. True virtue, potency, even divine grace, were shown by success in the things of this world: virtue brought its own reward, and other rewards too. At the same time, the Benevolent Employer without whom Our Hero could not succeed suggests the readers' and Alger's growing suspicion that virtue and industry unaided were no longer enough. The Benevolent Employer becomes a necessary supplement to Our Hero's merits, but also eases his conscience. That is, Our Hero, the budding merchant-prince, transfers his filial allegiance to another, distant, more benevolent Father who recognizes true merit and who economically rewards the good and punishes the bad. Money, "pluck," "grit," pocket-watches, and other symbols of potency are outward manifestations of this inward grace, this at-one-ness with a greater Father. At the same time, if a man fails, he must be guilty, he must have sinned against that all-knowing Father, as Alger himself had.

Having paid literary lip-service to that Father, Alger thought himself entitled to escape from the father's prohibitions in real life—at least in so far as he could. That is, as a writer, Alger pretended to a Bohemianism he was too repressed to live. For him as for many men for whom the father-image was dominant, relations with women (like relations with the mother) were surrounded with taboos. Both his affairs with women (women, by the way, he could never have married), he saw as literary companionships. "Genius," he smugly confided to his diary during his affair with the French café singer, "Genius has its prerogatives." Being an actual father, however, was not one of them. Though in Alger's Up-and-Comings and the Newsboys' Home he played father to hundreds of boys, and in his books to millions, it remained only a part he played. The real Alger was the guilty, impotent failure who, as he was dying, compared himself to The Little Lame Prince.

COMMENT

To unify his article Mr. Holland employs several techniques which can be adapted to other subjects. He manages, for instance, to keep the reader constantly aware of his basic question, "What made Alger's novels so popular?" He manipulates the parallels and contrasts between Alger's life and Alger's novels unobtrusively. Notice how a judicious selection of quotations brings vitality to a book review.

SUGGESTIONS FOR WRITING

1. Write an essay in which you describe the typical heroes and villains of television and movies. Having described them, show how their appeal for us says something about our values.

2. Take some success formula you have encountered in *Reader's Digest*, "Orphan Annie," or a commencement lecture. Analyze its terms very carefully. Ask such questions as "What does this word really mean?" and "Upon what view of human nature is this formula based?"

3. Select some familiar statement like the following and analyze its terms: It [*what is the referent of this pronoun?*] is more important [*to whom? for what purpose?*]to get along with people [*what people? all people?*] than to get book-knowledge [*how is this distinguished from other kinds of knowledge?*].

Marya Mannes

PARK AVENUE

IF YOU ARE VERY RICH and want the best that New York can offer, you will be likely to live in one of several places and several ways, all of them in one rectangle of Manhattan's gridiron bounded roughly by Central Park and the East River, between the Fifties or Sixties, where commerce prevails, to Ninety-sixth Street, where slums take over.

You will have a high apartment on Fifth Avenue looking over Central Park toward a range of buildings whose outlines in no way suggest inferior status and seem, in fact, just as desirable as your own. Or you will buy a brownstone on a quiet side street lined with trees, and remodel it to your taste; or—if you can get it—one of the lovely Georgian-style houses on Sutton Place which front on dead-end streets and conceal, behind them, rolling and flowering lawns that reach to the East River. Or, loving the life of the river with its fretwork of bridges and the ever-absorbing glide of tugs and barges and freighters on its oily current, yet preferring height, you will rent or buy an apartment or penthouse in one of the new white buildings where your balcony becomes a liner's prow, with only water below; where the opalescent ribbon of the river winds south or north changing consistency and tone with every hour; and where, at night, the flow of cars on the East River Drive is another winking river of lights, mesmeric and silent.

If you are not so rich and can't afford such conspicuous beauties and privileges, you will still pay dearly for the social and business prestige which a "good" address confers, for easy access to the best doctors and psychiatrists, and to the best shops, whether they are big and sell clothes or little and sell everything from Syrian coffee to Caspian caviar, from Burmese silk to Dresden china, from collages to sporting prints.

You will pay $500 a month for a four-room apartment built like a filing cabinet on streets where cars can barely crawl and where people who live below the tenth floor can see nothing but stone and windows. But

From *The New York I Know* by Marya Mannes; copyright © 1960 by Marya Mannes; published by J. B. Lippincott Company. First printed in *The Reporter*.

you will also be paying for the fact that this is the first section of the city to be cleared of snow after a blizzard and of garbage after a strike, and that the double-parked limousines of its residents are the last to be ticketed. They are, in fact, not ticketed at all. Privilege is the password, policed and bribed.

You pay for other things too. The men and women who walk along Fifth and Madison and Park and Lexington and now even Third are more smartly dressed than the citizens of other neighborhoods, and it is possible to see the assured bearing and the kind of well-bred face, with fine bones and clear skin, now increasingly rare in any of our cities. If the women wear minks, tweeds are underneath them, and they walk in simple pumps with low heels. On these East Side streets you are not likely to find men in vicuña coats spitting on the sidewalk or women in Dior dresses chewing gum.

Even the dogs are conscious of their breeding: the big black poodles sit bolt upright in the seat next to the chauffeur, like witty French count-esses off to the races, their tufted chins tilted above their rhinestone collars, their eyes beady, their topknots fresh from the drier. Even the tiny topiary toys seem fluffier and more impertinent on the East Side; their mistresses no more infatuated but more likely to reveal, in their doting faces, the puffiness of martinis and self-pampering.

It is because you want such things, some tangible like a view, some intangible like prestige, that you pay to live in this congested rectangle. The abiding mystery of the fashionable East Side, however, is the de-liberate choice of residence on Park Avenue, the most boring street of its kind for its entire residential length.

From Sixtieth to Ninety-sixth Street, opposing cliffs of apartment houses face each other over a river of traffic and a dividing line of meager rectangles which roof the New York Central tracks. Because most of these apartments were built forty years ago when architecture was bogged down in sterile pretentious conservatism, the view from any living-room window is ranks of small windows meanly spaced in façades of gray or dun stone undistinguished either by handsome proportions or good decorative detail. Below, the yellow cabs and the black Cadillacs stream past these graceless plots of tired privet, dusty grass, and iron railing, only sometimes relieved by lighted Christmas trees or clumps of spring or autumn flowers donated by a benefactress and sturdy enough to survive a fortnight of fumes. For this, and for an address that implies position and wealth, thousands of New Yorkers pay prodigious rents, willing to starve their eyes and congest their lungs for the security of status.

It is all the more remarkable that people of taste and no thirst for status can be found on Park Avenue, and they will probably depreciate the address and say that the rooms are large and the location handy. From the back windows, too, provided they are high up, glimpses of roofs and river give some idea of the city's superior beauties. But even these escape hatches and the penthouses with their full-grown trees and shrubs cannot be reached without the subtle penance of a Park Avenue entrance: the apotheosis of a kind of stuffiness, of a social self-consciousness, that few free spirits could face every day and night without distaste.

The Park Avenue lobby would, in fact, give pause to excavators of the future, should they find one intact and furnished. For although their shape and their contents vary widely—some are Regency, some Renaissance, some French provincial or Jacobean, some contemporary (even to subdued abstractions and wire sculpture)—they share the same muffled discretion, the same soft sell: you who enter here are in the right place with the right people. Supporting this message, of course, are the doormen, a very special breed. The better ones are courteous and helpful, but like headwaiters or jewelry salesmen or art dealers, their duty is appraisal. They do not look: they size up. For strangers, their gaze is a gantlet. And to the imaginative, their flicker of acceptance is as disturbing as tacit rejection. Only the insecure find pleasure in being considered acceptable.

If the lobby is a form of insulation from the living world outside, an even greater one is the street itself. For Park Avenue is an estrangement from the realities of New York, of which two are the most valuable: the peculiar haphazard beauty of the city, and its structure of villages.

This structure is basically triangular, and consists of the relation of side street to avenue, of residence to commerce, of privacy to common experience. Every avenue on the East Side has this corner life except Park Avenue (Fifth at least has a people's park), for the tributaries are residential like the main stream, and the purpose for walking is to exercise the dog or go to church on Sundays. To live in the side streets near Lexington or Third or Second, on the other hand, is to be part of an intimate complex of people and services that form, as time goes on, a close familiar whole in the midst of the great fragmentation which is the city. At no time are you more than a half block away from butcher, grocer, stationer, liquor dealer, cleaner, or florist, with each of whom daily contact becomes friendship as well as habit. And on every block or two there is that dim little shabby Irish bar, more haven than hangout. The big new developments obliterate more of these villages every year, substituting impersonal order for intimate confusion, but where they still cling they give New York its heart.

Park Avenue has no such beat. Few women (one hesitates to call them housewives) can be bothered often with a two-block walk, nor need they be with the telephone at hand and servants dispatchable for errands. When they leave their apartments they go to those of friends or the shops in the Fifties, confining their local excursions to a fancy grocery on Madison Avenue (to pick up some Spanish artichoke hearts) or to a place where Quiche Lorraine is made for parties. And their husbands, with the Racquet Club or "21" handier, are not likely to take in a Third Avenue bar on their homeward trip.

Park Avenue, then, is an island.

But who are the islanders? What manner of people choose this isolation? Solvency is no answer, for the rich have better alternatives. Nor is success in business or profession the determinant. Park Avenue is full of successful people, but so are the side streets. In earlier days origins played a part, but now the proportion of Jews and Gentiles is roughly equal, even though some co-operatives manage a policy of exclusion without stating it. Café society and *Social Register* society are broadly represented, philanthropists abound, and few buildings fail to include at least one member of that tenacious and long-lived little company—the only refugees blessed by society—the White Russians.

But there are other people, too, on Park Avenue. Take the young Petersons, who inherited their apartment from his family. They hate the Avenue, but where else could they afford to keep their five children on his salary as an editor in a publishing house? Or take Dr. Kuhn, the famous urologist. His office is in the building, his life is his work, and think of the time he saves. Or take Miss Worthington. She has lived in the same apartment for thirty-five years, with her two Irish maids and her ten rubber plants and her sixteen ferns: what would she do in another world, where people lived? And then, of course, there are residents like the Haggertys. Clyde Haggerty makes forty thousand a year after taxes as president of his construction firm. It costs him that much to live as he thinks he must live, on Park Avenue, and he will leave nothing when he dies. He is paying for an ice floe that will melt while others are paying for an elaborate ark in a treacherous sea, for safety within danger.

There are many reasons to live on Park Avenue; as many reasons, perhaps, as residents, as many good as bad. Yet if I were asked to describe typical Park Avenue apartments or typical Park Avenue parties, I think I would concentrate on two particular kinds. One would be the home of a *Social Register* kind of family, the other would belong, say, to the president of a chain of department stores.

Let us visit George and Amy Lansing first. George is an investment banker with a Wall Street firm, Amy is the daughter of a prominent corporation lawyer, lately deceased. George's family has lived in Glens Falls for five generations, Amy's ancestors fought the Revolution in Virginia. They have a daughter at Brearley, a son at Yale, and a house at Stockbridge, used on weekends and summer vacations. George is on many boards, Amy on many charities. Their large rooms are carpeted wall-to-wall in a neutral shade, the sofas and chairs are covered either in flowered muted chintz or in beige brocade, and the curtains drawn across the windows are of matching chintz. The furniture is mostly English antique. Over the fireplace is a portrait, thinly painted, of Amy's mother—the kind of woman with the long sloping undivided bust mysteriously achieved in her day, and an expression of mild reproof. The other pictures are mostly etchings of ducks in flight or English hunting prints, and the tops of tables are crowded with family photographs in silver frames. There is nothing in the rooms that could possibly offend anyone and nothing that could possibly delight. The Lansings have comfort for their money but no fun, and the observant guest cannot help but pity such spiritual constipation. What is more, two sets of curtains and a half-lowered shade cut out in daytime the luxury of light that their fifteenth-floor apartment could provide them, and this perpetual muffling and diffusion and carpeting and covering gives these rooms the feeling of large and elaborate padded cells in which one could die of anoxia. Physically and mentally, the Lansings are sealed in their own amber.

This is never more apparent than at one of their cocktail parties. For they invite themselves: pleasant, easy, handsome people from the world of law or finance, usually Republicans, always well-groomed and always well-mannered. In vain is the search for an expressive, unguarded face, or even an ugly one. At the Lansings you will see no Jews, no artists, no musicians, no eccentrics, and only those foreigners—usually from the north of Europe—who could be taken, except for their accents, for Americans or Englishmen of the Lansings' class. No voice is raised here except in joviality, no alien note intrudes, no new thought penetrates to surprise or disturb. The smooth organization of the party is assured by Amy's own pleasant competence and the work of two efficient maids, one attached to the Lansing household, one specially hired for the evening. These maids are an East Side phenomenon, exerting a prissy gentility which even impeccable menservants fail to impose. There is something about such women, pouring drinks or handing hors d'oeuvres around, which, since it suggests prolonged virginity, acts as a vague depressant. All in all, the Lansing living room is the social equivalent of that experiment in weightlessness and the absence of sensory reflexes in which a man is suspended in tepid water: there is nothing to move against or measure against.

The Kappels, a few blocks north, are very different in certain ways. For one thing, Joseph Kappel's grandparents emigrated from Europe in the middle of the nineteenth century and Liz is a born New Yorker of

Midwestern stock. For another, Joe started fairly humbly as a small importer of fabrics and in twenty years amassed a chain of high-class department stores in New York and the suburbs. The Kappels are much richer than the Lansings and much less inhibited about showing it.

In their apartment, they show it chiefly through the taste of a much-sought-after Fifty-seventh Street decorator who changes their decor at intervals to keep pace with fashion. Fifteen years ago Robin persuaded the Kappels to go whole hog on French impressionists, and Joe acquired a rather muddy little Renoir head, a weak Bonnard, a Seurat sketch for "La Grande Jatte," a Degas etching (the laundress), and a very blurry Monet. To complement these, Robin bought them the most expensive examples of French provincial he could find in Europe, and keyed the upholstery with infinite subtlety to their tones.

But last year a revolution took place. Joe took the impressionists to his office (where they impressed), and Robin made over the Kappel home to accommodate a Baziotes, a de Kooning, a Dubuffet, a Franz Kline, and a metal construction composed of pipes and fender strips called "Bird-watcher." All these required white walls, the severest contemporary furniture (including several couches that suggested upholstered mortuary slabs), and the occasional bright jab of an orange, black, or acid-pink pillow. An extra ceiling was suspended, above which invisible fixtures cast diffused light and gave the faces of Kappels and guests the look of recent exhumation. It was quite a room. Only when Liz took women guests to her boudoir did her interior struggle (lost to Robin except in this sanctuary) become apparent. An Edzard pastel of a wistful young girl in a ribboned bonnet hung over her frilled and canopied bed, and every white shelf in this pink-lined box was crammed with bibelots: round colored paperweights, white milk glass, and porcelain hands in every position needed to hold nuts, ashes, or a single rose, although never put to these uses.

Although the Kappels have a few close friends from former days to whom they are loyal, and dinners for business associates are given from time to time, their parties are usually reserved for celebrities they know only slightly. Having backed a few Broadway hits, they have access to people of the theater, and Robin has seen to it that the Kappels keep in touch with current newsmakers in the world of art, provided they are socially housebroken. As few of the most prominent contemporary painters qualify, the guests are likely to be museum curators, collectors, critics, and fashion photographers, who give ecstatic sanction to the Kappels' taste but pose no threat to their marriage.

Few would doubt, however, that the Kappel parties were more amusing than the Lansing ones, and the presence of smiling colored barmen adds a festive note that the Lansing maidservants lack. So do contingents of *Vogue* and *Bazaar* models, whose gaunt perfections and bizarre coiffures complement the interior.

It might be said that the major difference between these two family residents of Park Avenue is that the Lansings have roots and the Kappels have none. George and Amy are secure in their past, Joe and Liz are insecure in their present. And while the Lansings accept Park Avenue as a matter of course in their way of living, the Kappels remind themselves of their position every time the doorman greets them.

What they share in common is a dead street in a living city: a street that neither partakes of the splendid conspicuous affluence symbolized by the few private mansions still left nor has a part in the city's tumultuous present and, so far as we can see it, in the radical innovations of the future. Only above Ninety-sixth Street and below Sixtieth Street does Park Avenue come alive: to the north, dangerously and dirtily, with the worst of slums and the greatest of needs; to the south, dynamically and often beautifully, with the transparent thrust of business in the great glass canyon.

Between is an address.

COMMENT

This essay is an interesting example of the way in which discussion of our physical surroundings (a street, its apartments, its furnishings, its cars, and its inhabitants) implies cultural analysis. Notice how the point of view moves from the whole street to particular families and how the similarity of the opening and the closing passages brings unity.

SUGGESTIONS FOR WRITING

1. Describe a room (a friend's room in the dormitory, an aunt's living room) by selecting and arranging details in such a way as to suggest the personality of its occupants.

2. Discuss a social event in such a way that you characterize some person or persons connected with it. You might distinguish between two dormitory teas, two fraternity open houses, two sorority parties.

3. Clarify in your mind the physical characteristics which distinguish the ten-cent-store clerk from the clerk in a fashionable shop, the used-car salesman from his colleague in the Cadillac showroom, the college senior from her friends who stayed at home, the fraternity boy from the independent. Your success will depend on how well you can avoid making judgments for your reader. For instance, do not say, "She dressed in quiet good taste." Describe her dress and manner in such a way that the reader will derive this impression for himself.

V. S. PRITCHETT

Everyone on the UP and UP

TO BE INSPIRED by a dream is splendid; to be nagged by it the morning after is an embarrassment. This, according to pretty well all American critics and sociologists, is the present state of America. The dream is that America is a model democracy in which all have the opportunity to rise from the bottom to the top, untrammelled by class systems such as the European. This the American visitor has been proclaiming to Europeans for generations—especially to European socialists. But when any of these Europeans goes to America and gets in touch with his erstwhile American visitor there, he is astonished at the change of tone. To compliment his friend on the lack of class consciousness or class system, is considered rude. One might be accusing him of being primitive. He has a class system, he will say with some pride, as self-conscious and complex as American football. Our European retires into his usual sadness; his own class system, he has always apologised, is not his own fault; he has inherited it and tried to discard or loosen it. Now in America he is confronted by one which is enthusiastically being made from new materials. Status has become the thing. The European goes off wondering if the American dream was simply another export.

All foreign societies are sticky when one gets to know them. Mr. Vance Packard has written a book [*The Status Seekers*] to show that the American is as sticky as any other; in fact he thinks that the class systems of Great Britain, of Holland and of Denmark, for example, are far more open than the system of the United States. We should take warning, he thinks, because advanced, affluent, industrialised societies with their huge interlocking organisations are likely to go along the American way. I have heard Mr. Packard's preoccupations described as a fad; in fact he has brought the most repressed of contemporary interests to the surface. It is clever of him to have substituted the words "status seeker" for "snob"; it gets under the skin. To his own researches into status-seeking as it comes out

Reprinted by permission of *The New Statesman*.

in house-building and furnishing, shopping, club life, religion—"the long road from pentecostal to episcopal"—racial groups, schools, small and large corporations, he has added material collected from other sociologists who have had their eyes opened. The result is a book diverting, occasionally nauseating and finally alarming. At first the British reader will find himself expanding with happy complacency in the thought that perhaps his own class system—which he hardly notices, especially if he is an intellectual—is a useful myth after all, protecting him from many worse evils from the advertising industry upwards; later on, he may wonder if our own social upheaval is not producing the evils Mr. Packard describes. It is one thing for class stratifications to be inherited and fixed; it is quite another, when people start thinking that a classless society is one in which everyone ought to be on the upgrade.

This is Mr. Packard's worry. He has no difficulty in showing that American class consciousness is acute and general; he has no difficulty in showing that a fantastic increase in general wealth does not lead to social equality or intermingling; he is worried by other consequences. At a time when it becomes pretty well impossible for people to rise from the bottom to the top, when in fact they are trapped in compartments from which they cannot emerge, the stress on status becomes intensified. The religion of success, like the religion of status, has its failures.

> The main reality is our tendency toward greater rigidity in our stratification while pretending that precisely the opposite is occurring. We are consigning tens of millions of our people to fixed roles in life where aspiration is futile, and yet we keep telling them that those who have the stuff will rise to the top. We don't even allow them the satisfaction of feeling secure, dignified and creative in their low status.

The result is a "frightful shattering of integrity," the "extraordinarily high psychoses rates . . . at the bottom of the social scale," and the fantastically high figures of delinquency and crime among the younger poor. The lowest class kicks back.

Mr. Packard accepts the general view that in America, as elsewhere, society can be divided into five main classes—the real upper class, the semi-upper class (Mrs. Miniver), the limited success people, the working class and the real lower class. The pattern is easily recognised in Great Britain; we have also the same conflict, in the lower groups, between the blue collars and the depressed white collars—the new poor whites. The difficulty is to get into the two upper classes. In a society which has crystallised you can have the illusion of rising by marrying your beautiful daughter to a millionaire, by sending your son to college—but this doesn't help much if you have the wrong background—or by buying things which are thought to show status, out of your large pay packet. You become a consumption-snob, and this is what American industry and advertising has gone in for heavily. It leads to disappointment. For just when you thought that buying a very large car would do the trick, the laws of status change; the right kind of house, furniture, food become the thing and large cars become "lower class."

I do not know whether Mr. Packard has a taste for the English novel of the nineteenth century—our most vulgarly and most ethically snobbish period—but if he has, he has remained a little wide-eyed about the influence of women on his subject. One is not quite so shocked when one recognises the satisfaction and amusement that Jane Austen, Mrs. Gaskell and George Eliot got out of it. Is it all disaster? Mr. Packard himself quotes the gastronomic history of a poor Italian who eventually reached the élite. As a boy he was brought up on blood sausages, pizza, spaghetti and red wine. He got to high school and saw he had better switch to beer, beef and beans and drop "Italian" food. He moved on to become an executive and adroitly changed to steak, whisky and sea-food. Once at the top he began "winning admiration in the élite social set" by serving them— with the aid of a manservant—real Italian food once more, no inverted commas this time: blood sausage, pizza, spaghetti and red wine. But this, Mr. Packard says sadly, was when a man could rise to the top; nowadays he would be stuck, in the middle of some large organisation, damned for ever, in the beef and beans.

The Status Seekers is rich in Americana. Taxation has not reduced the number of great fortunes. The number of families with a net worth of half a million dollars has doubled since 1945. Gorgeous expense accounts, beautiful capital gains, support them. Buying rich homes has replaced the prestige of the magnificent car; the richest "homes" are advertised in French:

> *Une Maison* Ranch *très originale avec*
> 8 rooms, 2½ baths . . . 2-Cadillac garage
> . . . $21,940. No cash for veterans.

Rooms are described as the "Living Forum," the "Reception Galleria," the "Sleeping Chamber." A "split-level" house on Long Island becomes "a Georgian split, with a bi-level brunch bar in a maître d'kitchen." A developer outside Chicago aims at the wives and helps them to see the $40,000 house as a "love symbol." The "master" bedroom is said to contain "a love couch." There is a good sale for old family portraits: the buyers become convinced, after a while, that the figures on the wall are really their forebears. Dallas (Texas) has its "Presidents' Row," where the houses have His and Her bathrooms, colour television in the bedroom ceiling, air-conditioned doghouses, "authentic" soda fountains and fountains in the hall; but back in more conservative Lake Forest, the rich inhabitants have a society for the prevention of improvement of the road; and in Charlotte, North Carolina, flickering gas-lamps are put outside the most expensive houses on one estate. It is estimated that every day, 25,000 Americans move house: they hope they are going up.

In most offices, there is a great deal of prestige attached to certain floors and to certain jobs. The President and the Vice-President will have his private washroom; but the President gets a w.c. and the Vice does not. Office snobberies are, of course, universal. Americans suffer considerably from high school, private school and Ivy League snobbery; they have some trouble, but less than we do, with accents, perhaps owing to regionalism. They have a good deal of word trouble:

Upper Class	Middle Class
wash	launder
sofa	davenport
long dress	formal gown
rich	wealthy

A hostess in a small town who had invited her guests to "pot luck" saw to it that the affair appeared in the local paper's society column as a "Covered Dish Party."

Such amiable pursuits of refinement can be matched in any society. They are all part of the game of trying to be the Jones's whom others have to keep up with—men playing it in their offices, women at home. From Mr. Vance Packard one gathers that the Americans have taken to the game with an efficiency, a competitiveness and an indiscretion which are startling in a society which dreams that it is open and egalitarian. There is a very serious side to this, as he shows. It is well-known that American doctors are among the élite of any American town. They occupy the big house at the top of the hill and jealously protect their standing. They begin to vie with the small feudal barons of the past in their rapacity and they have succeeded—perhaps unconsciously—in creating an artificial scarcity of doctors: there was one doctor to 578 people in 1900, in 1957 there was one doctor to 935. One of the causes of stratification is the disappearance of the small or, indeed, the large private business which started from humble beginnings. The big corporations take their executives from the upper classes with the right educational background. The sop offered to the lower, on the cultural level, is the appalling popular literature and television programmes of sex and violence. "Popular" culture is manufactured and packaged by the top people; it is not popular at all.

Yet, although class consciousness is being exploited in America, although, for example, marriages between people of different social classes are uncommon, Mr. Vance Packard confirms a personal impression, that

Americans spend much more energy on isolating themselves in racial groups. The races work together, they get on together, but not socially. In most cities, Italians, Poles, Jews, "old" Americans, Germans and so on live on socially parallel lines that never meet. Yet the dream tells them (and they tell us) that they do.

COMMENT

Writing a book review for an English audience, Mr. Pritchett draws up a summary of *The Status Seekers* and uses it as the basis for his own comment upon the American social structure. He uses Mr. Packard's evidence to demonstrate his own theory that the American status system is more rigorous than the English class system. Read this review carefully to see if you can discern where Mr. Packard's opinion ends and Mr. Pritchett's begins.

SUGGESTIONS FOR WRITING

1. Write an essay on the class system as you have observed it. You should, of course, write about some particular instance rather than about the whole system. For example, analyze an awkward social experience of your own which was caused by some unspoken class consciousness.

2. List some status symbols and discuss how their intrinsic value compares to their value in the minds of those who seek them.

3. The college degree has come to be one of the most valuable status symbols. Analyze the effect of this belief upon college life as you have experienced it.

BOSTON

Elizabeth Hardwick

WITH BOSTON and its mysteriously enduring reputation, "the reverbera-
tion is longer than the thunderclap," as Emerson observed about the tenacious fame of certain artists. Boston—wrinkled, spindly-legged, depleted
of nearly all her spiritual and cutaneous oils, provincial, self-esteeming—
has gone on spending and spending her inflated bills of pure reputation,
decade after decade. Now, one supposes it is all over at last. The old jokes
embarrass, the anecdotes are so many thrice-squeezed lemons, and no
new fruit hangs on the boughs. All the American regions are breaking up,
ground down to a standard American corn meal. And why not Boston,
which would have been the most difficult to maintain? There has never
been anything quite like Boston as a creation of the American imagination, or perhaps one should say as a creation of the American scene. Some
of the legend was once real, surely. Our utilitarian, fluid landscape has
produced a handful of regional conceptions, popular images, brief and
naked: the conservative Vermonter, the boastful Texan, the honeyed
Southerner. "Graciousness is ours," brays a coarsened South; and the
sheiks of Texas cruise around their desert.

The Boston image is more complex. The city is felt to have, in the end,
a pure and special nature, absurd no doubt but somehow valuable. Em-
piricism will not carry one far; faith and *being,* sheer being above all, are
needed. To be it, old Boston, real Boston, very Boston, and—one shrinks
before the stale claim—proper Boston; there lies knowledge. An author
can hardly fail to turn a penny or two on this magical subject. Everyone
will consent to be informed on it, to be slyly entertained by it. *Actual*
Boston is governed largely by people of Irish descent and more and more,
recently, by men of Italian descent. Not long ago, the old Yankee, Senator
Saltonstall, remarked wistfully that there were still a good many Anglo-
Saxons in Massachusetts, his own family among them. Extinction is fore-
shadowed in the defence.

Reprinted by permission of the author and of *Encounter*.

Plainness and pretension restlessly feuding and combining; wealth and respectability and firmness of character ending in the production of a number of diverting individual tics or, at the best, instances of high culture. Something of that sort is the legendary Boston soul or so one supposes without full confidence because the old citizens of Boston vehemently hold to the notion that the city and their character are ineffable, unknowable. When asked for an opinion on the admirable novel, *Boston Adventure,* or even the light social history, *The Proper Bostonians,* the answer invariably comes, "Not Boston." The descriptive intelligence, the speculative mind, the fresh or even the merely open eye are felt to discover nothing but errors here, be they errors of praise or censure. Still, wrong-headedness flourishes, the subject fascinates, and the Athenaeum's list of written productions on this topic is nearly endless.

The best book on Boston is Henry James' novel, *The Bostonians.* By the bald and bold use of the place-name, the unity of situation and person is dramatized. But poor James, of course, was roundly and importantly informed by everyone, including his brother William, that this too was "not Boston," and, stricken, he pushed aside a superb creation, and left the impregnable, unfathomable Boston to its mysteries. James' attitude towards the city's intellectual consequence and social charm is one of absolute impiety. A view of the Charles River reveals

> an horizon indented at empty intervals with wooden spires, the masts of lonely boats, the chimneys of dirty "works," over a brackish expanse of anomalous character, which is too big for a river and too small for a bay.

A certain house has

> a peculiar look of being both new and faded—a kind of modern fatigue —like certain articles of commerce which are sold at a reduction as shop-worn.

However, there is little natural landscape in James' novel. The picture is, rather, of the psychological Boston of the 1870's, a confused scene, slightly mad with neurotic repressions, provincialism, and earnestness without intellectual seriousness.

James' view of Boston is not the usual one, although his irony and dissatisfaction are shared by Henry Adams who says that "a simpler manner of life and thought could hardly exist, short of cave-dwelling," and by Santayana who spoke of Boston as a "moral and intellectual nursery, always busy applying first principles to trifles."

The great majority of the writings on Boston are in another spirit altogether—frankly unctuous—for the town has always attracted men of quiet and timid and tasteful opinion, men interested in old families and things, in the charms of times recently past, collectors of anecdote about those Boston worthies hardly anyone can still clearly identify, men who spoke and preached and whose style and fame deteriorated quickly: Rufus Choate, Dr. Channing, Edward Everett Hale, Phillips Brooks, and Theodore Parker; names that remain in one's mind, without producing an image or a fact, as the marks are left on the wall after the picture has been removed. William Dean Howells held a more usual view than Henry James or Adams or Santayana. Indeed Howells' original enthusiasm for garden and edifice, person and setting, is more than a little *exalté*. The first sight of the Chapel at Mount Auburn Cemetery moved him more than the "Acropolis, Westminster Abbey, and Santa Croce in one." The massive grey stones of "the Public Library and the Athenaeum are hardly eclipsed by the Vatican and the Pitti." And so on.

The importance of Boston was intellectual and as its intellectual donations to the country have diminished, so it has declined from its lofty symbolic meaning to become a more lowly image, a sort of farce of conservative exclusiveness and snobbish humor. Marquand's George Apley is a figure of the decline—fussy, sentimental, farcically mannered, archaic. He cannot be imaged as an Abolitionist, an author, a speaker; he is merely a "character," a very idiosyncratic and simple-minded one. The old Boston had something of the spirit of Bloomsbury: clannish, worldly, and intellectually serious. About the historian Prescott, Van Wyck Brooks could say, ". . . for at least ten years, Prescott had been hard at work, harder, perhaps, than any Boston merchant." History, indeed, with its long, leisurely, gentlemanly labors, the books arriving by post, the cards to be kept and filed, the sections to be copied, the documents to be checked, is the ideal pursuit for the New England mind. All the Adamses spent a good deal of their lives on one kind of history or another. The eccentricity, studiousness, and study-window slow pace of life of the historical gentleman lay everywhere about the Boston scene. For money, society, fashion, extravagance, one went to New York. But now, the descendants of the old intellectual aristocracy live in the respectable suburbs and lead the healthy, outdoor life that atrophies the sedentary nerves of culture. The bluestocking, the eccentric, the intransigent bring a blush of uncertainty and embarrassment to the healthy young couple's cheek.

Boston to-day can still provide a fairly stimulating atmosphere for the banker, the broker, for doctors and lawyers. "Open end" investments prosper, the fish come in at the dock, the wool market continues, and workers are employed in the shoe factories in the nearby towns. For the engineer, the physicist, the industrial designer, for all the highly-trained specialists of the electronic age, Boston and its area are of seemingly unlimited promise. Sleek, well-designed factories and research centers pop up everywhere; the companies plead, in the Sunday papers, for more

chemists, more engineers, and humbly relate the executive benefits of
salary and pension and advancement they are prepared to offer. But otherwise, for the artist, the architect, the composer, the writer, the philosopher, the historian, for those humane pursuits for which the town was
once noted and even for the delights of entertainment, for dancing, acting, cooking, Boston is a bewildering place.

There is, first of all, the question of Boston or New York. (The question is not new; indeed it was answered in the last decades of the last
century in favor of New York as the cultural center of America.) It
is, in our day, only a private and personal question: which of the two
Eastern cities should one try to live and work in? It is a one-sided problem. For the New Yorker, San Francisco or Florida, perhaps—Boston,
never. In Boston, New York tantalizes; one of the advantages of Boston
is said, wistfully, to be its nearness to New York. It is a bad sign when
a man who has come to Boston or Cambridge, Massachusetts, from another
place begins to show an undivided acceptance of his new town. Smugness
is the great vice of the two places. Between puffy self-satisfaction and the
fatiguing wonder if one wouldn't be happier, more productive, more appreciated in New York a thoughtful man makes his choice.

Boston is not a small New York, as they say a child is not a small adult
but is, rather, a specially organized small creature with its small-creature's
temperature, balance, and distribution of fat. In Boston there is an utter
absence of that wild electric beauty of New York, of the marvelous excited rush of people in taxicabs at twilight, of the Great Avenues and
Streets, the restaurants, theaters, bars, hotels, delicatessens, shops. In
Boston the night comes down with an incredibly heavy, small-town final-
ity. The cows come home; the chickens go to roost; the meadow is dark.
Nearly every Bostonian is in his own house or in someone else's house,
dining at the home board, enjoying domestic and social privacy. The
"nice little dinner party"—for this the Bostonian would sell his soul. In
the evenings, the old "accommodators" dart about the city, carrying their
black uniforms and white aprons in a paper bag. They are on call to go
anywhere, to cook and serve dinners. Many of these women are former
cooks and maids, now living on Social Security retirement pensions, sup-
plemented by the fees for these evening "accommodations" to the community. Their style and the bland respectability of their cuisine keep up the
social tone of the town. They are like those old slaves who stuck to their
places and, even in the greatest deprivation, graciously went on toting
things to the Massa.

There is a curious flimsiness and indifference in the commercial life
of Boston. The restaurants are, charitably, to be called mediocre; the famous sea food is only palatable when raw. Otherwise it usually has to endure the deep-fry method that makes everything taste like the breaded

pork chops of the Middle West, which in turn taste like the fried sole of Boston. Here, French restaurants quickly become tea-roomy, as if some sort of rapid naturalization had taken place. There is not a single attractive eating-place on the waterfront. An old downtown restaurant of considerable celebrity, Locke-Ober, has been expanded, let out, and "costumed" by one of the American restaurant decorators whose productions have a ready-made look, as if the designs had been chosen from a catalogue. But for the purest eccentricity, there is the "famous" restaurant, Durgin Park, which is run like a boarding-house in a mining town. And so it goes. Downtown Boston at night is a dreary jungle of honky-tonks for sailors, dreary department-store windows, Loew's movie-houses, hillbilly bands, strippers, parking lots, undistinguished new buildings. Midtown Boston—small, expensive shops, the inevitable Elizabeth Arden and Helena Rubinstein "salons," Brooks Brothers—is deserted at night, except for people going in and out of the Ritz Carlton Hotel, the only public place in Boston that could be called "smart." The merchandise in the Newbury Street shops is designed in a high fashion, elaborate, furred, and sequined, but it is never seen anywhere. Perhaps it is for out-of-town use, like a traveling man's mistress.

Just as there is no smart life, so there is no Soho, no Greenwich Village. Recently a man was murdered in a parking lot in the Chinatown area. His address was given as the South End, a lower-class section, and he was said to be a "free-spender," making enough money as a summer bartender on Cape Cod to lead a free-wheeling life the rest of the year. One paper referred to the unfortunate man as a "member of the Beacon Hill Bohemia set." This designation is of considerable interest because there is no "Bohemia" in Boston, neither upper nor lower; the detergent of bourgeois Boston cleans everything, effortlessly, completely. If there were a Bohemia, its members *would* live on Beacon Hill, the most beautiful part of Boston and, like the older parts of most cities, fundamentally classless, providing space for the rich in the noble mansions and for the people with little money in the run-down alleys. For both of these groups the walled gardens of Beacon Hill, the mews, the coach houses, the river views, the cobblestone streets are a necessity and the yellow brick structures of the Fenway are poison. *Espresso* bars have sprung up, or rather dug down in basements, but no summer of Bohemianism is ushered into town. This reluctance is due to the Boston legend and its endurance as a lost ideal, a romantic quest.

Something transcendental is always expected in Boston. There is, one imagines, behind the drapery on Mount Vernon Street a person of democratic curiosity and originality of expression, someone alas—and this is the tiresome Boston note—*well-born.* It is likely to be, even in imagination, a *she,* since women now and not the men provide the links with the old traditions. Of her, then, one expects a certain unprofessionalism, but it is not expected that she will be superficial; she is profoundly conventional in manner of life but capable of radical insights. To live in Boston means to seek some connection with this famous local excellence, the regional type and special creation of the city.

An angry disappointment attends the romantic soul bent upon this quest. When the archaeological diggings do turn up an authentic specimen it will be someone old, nearly gone, "whom you should have known when she was young"—and could hear. The younger Bostonians seem in revolt against the old excellence, with its indulgent, unfettered development of the self. Revolt, however, is too active a word for a passive failure to perpetuate the ideal high-mindedness and intellectual effort. With the fashionable young women of Boston, one might just as well be on Long Island. In the nervous, shy, earnest women there is a lingering hint of the peculiar local development. Terrible *faux-pas* are constantly being made by this reasonable, honorable person, followed by blushes and more false steps and explanations and the final blinking, retreating blush.

Among the men, the equivalent of the blushing, blurting, sensitive, and often "fine" woman is a person who exists everywhere perhaps but nowhere else with such elaboration of type, such purity of example. This is the well-born failure, the amateur not by choice but from some fatal reticence of temperament. They are often descendants of intellectual Boston, odd-ball grandsons, charming and sensitive, puzzlingly complicated, living on a "small income." These unhappy men carry on their conscience the weight of unpublished novels, half-finished paintings, impossible historical projects, old-fashioned poems, unproduced plays. Their inevitable "small income" is a sort of dynastic flaw, like haemophilia. Much money seems often to impose obligations of energetic management; from great fortunes the living cells receive the hints of the possibilities of genuine power, enough to make some enormously rich Americans endure the humiliations and fatigues of political office. Only the most decadent and spoiled think of living in idleness on millions; but this notion does occur to the man afflicted with ten thousand a year. He will commit himself with a dreamy courage to whatever traces of talent he may have and live to see himself punished by the New England conscience which demands accomplishments, duties performed, responsibilities noted, and energies sensibly used. The dying will accuses and the result is a queer kind of Boston incoherence. It is literally impossible much of the time to tell what some of the most attractive men in Boston are talking about. Half-uttered witticisms, grave and fascinating obfuscations, points incredibly qualified, hesitations infinitely refined—one staggers about, charmed and confused, by the twilight.

But this person, with his longings, connects with the old possibilities and, in spite of his practical failure, keeps alive the memory of the best days. He may have a brother who has retained the mercantile robustness of nature and easy capacity for action and yet has lost all belief in anything except money and class, who may practice private charities, but entertain profoundly trivial national and world views. A Roosevelt, Harriman, or Stevenson are impossible to imagine as members of the Boston aristocracy; here the vein of self-satisfaction and public indifference cuts too deeply. Indeed great vulgarity of mind is not always alien to the finest Boston stock of the present age.

Harvard (across the river in Cambridge) and Boston are two ends of one mustache. Harvard is now so large and international it has altogether avoided the whimsical stagnation of Boston. But the two places need each other, as we knowingly say of a mismatched couple. Without the faculty, the visitors, the events that Harvard brings to the life here, Boston would be intolerable to anyone except genealogists, antique dealers, and those who find repletion in a closed local society.

Unfortunately, Harvard, like Boston, has "tradition," and in America this always carries with it the risk of a special staleness of attitude, and of pride, incredibly and comically swollen like the traits of hypocrisy, selfishness, or lust in the old dramas. At Harvard some of the vices of "society" exist, of Boston society that is—arrogance and the blinding dazzle of being, *being at Harvard.* The moral and social temptations of Harvard's unique position in American academic life are great and the pathos is seen in those young faculty members who are presently at Harvard but whose appointments are not permanent and so they may be thrown down, banished from the beatific condition. The young teacher in this position lives in a dazed state of love and hatred, pride and fear; their faces have a look of desperate yearning, for they would rather serve in heaven than reign in hell. For those who are not banished, for the American at least, since the many distinguished foreigners at Harvard need not endure these piercing and fascinating complications, something of Boston seems to seep into their characters. They may come from anywhere in America and yet to be at Harvard unites them with the transcendental, legendary Boston, with New England in flower. They begin to revere the old worthies, the houses, the paths trod by so many before, and they feel a throb of romantic sympathy for the directly-gazing portraits on the walls, for the old graves and old names in the Mount Auburn Cemetery. All of this has charm and may even have a degree of social and intellectual value—and then again it may not. Devious parochialisms, irrelevant snobberies, a bemused exaggeration of one's own productions, pimple the soul of a man upholding tradition in a forest of relaxation, such as most of America is thought to be. Henry James' observation in his book on Hawthorne bears on this:

. . . it is only in a country where newness and change and brevity of tenure are the common substance of life, that the fact of one's ancestors having lived for a hundred and seventy years in a single spot would become an element of one's morality. It is only an imaginative American that would feel urged to keep reverting to this circumstance, to keep analysing and cunningly considering it.

If the old things of Boston are too heavy and plushy, the new either hasn't been born or is appallingly shabby and poor. As early as Thanksgiving, Christmas decorations unequaled for cheap ugliness go up in the Public Garden and on the Boston Common. Year after year, the city fathers bring out crèches and camels and Mother and Child so badly made and of such tasteless colors they verge on blasphemy, or would seem to do so if it were not for the further degradation of secular little men blowing horns and the canes of peppermint hanging on the lamps. The shock of the first sight is the most interesting; later the critical senses are stilled as year after year the same bits are brought forth and gradually one realizes that the whole thing is a sort of permanent exhibition.

Recently the dying downtown shopping section of Boston was to be graced with flowers, an idea perhaps in imitation of the charming potted geraniums and tulips along Fifth Avenue in New York. Commercial Boston produced a really amazing display: old, grey square bins, in which were stuck a few bits of yellowing, dying evergreen. It had the look of exhausted greenery thrown out in the garbage and soon the dust-bins were full of other bits of junk and discard—people had not realized or recognized the decorative hope and saw only the rubbishy result.

The municipal, civic backwardness of Boston does not seem to bother its more fortunate residents. For them and for the observer, Boston's beauty is serene and private, an enclosed, intense personal life, rich with domestic variation, interesting stuffs and things, showing the hearthside vitality of a Dutch genre painting. Of an evening the spirits quicken, not to public entertainment, but instead to the sights behind the draperies, the glimpses of drawing-rooms on Louisburg Square, paneled walls and French chandeliers on Commonwealth Avenue, bookshelves and flower-filled bays on Beacon Street. Boston is a winter city. Every apartment has a fireplace. In the town houses, old persons climb steps without complaint, four or five floors of them, cope with the maintenance of roof and gutter and survive the impractical kitchen and resign themselves to the useless parlors. This is life: the house, the dinner party, the charming gardens, one's high ceilings, fine windows, lacy grillings, magnolia trees, inside shutters, glassed-in studios on the top of what were once stables, outlook on the "river side." Setting is serious. When it is not serious, when a splendid old private house passes into less dedicated hands, an almost exuberant swiftness of deterioration can be noticed. A rooming-house, although privately owned, is no longer in the purest sense a private house and soon it partakes of some of the feckless, ugly, municipal neglect. The contrasts are startling. One of two houses of almost identical exterior design will have shining windows, a bright brass door-knocker, and its twin will show a *"Rooms"* sign peering out of dingy glass, curtained by those lengths of flowered plastic used in the shower bath. Garbage lies about in the alleys behind the rooming-houses, discarded furniture blocks old garden gateways. The vulnerability of Boston's way of life, the meanness of most things that fall outside the needs of the upper classes, are shown with a bleak and terrible fullness in the rooming-houses on Beacon Street. And even some of the best houses show a spirit of mere "maintenance," which, while useful for the individual with money, leads to civic dullness, architectural torpor, and stagnation. In the Back Bay area, a voluntary, casual association of property owners exists for the purpose of trying to keep the alleys clean, the streets lighted beyond their present mediaeval darkness, and to pursue worthy items of neighborhood value. And yet this same group will "protest" against the attractive Café Florian on Newbury Street (smell of coffee too strong!) and against the brilliantly exciting Boston Arts Festival held in the beautiful Public Garden for two weeks in June. The idea that Boston might be a vivacious, convenient place to live in is not uppermost in these residents' thoughts. Trying to buy groceries in the best sections of the Back Bay region is an interesting study in commercial apathy.

A great many of the young Bostonians leave town, often taking off with a sullen demand for a freer, more energetic air. And yet many of them return later, if not to the city itself, to the beautiful sea towns and old villages around it. For the city itself, who will live in it after the present human landmarks are gone? No doubt, some of the young people there at the moment will persevere, and as a reward for their fidelity and endurance will themselves later become monuments, old types interesting to students of what our colleges call American Civilization. Boston is defective, out-of-date, vain, and lazy, but if you're not in a hurry it has a deep, secret appeal. Or, more accurately, those who like it may make of its appeal a secret. The weight of the Boston legend, the tedium of its largely fraudulent posture of traditionalism, the disillusionment of the Boston present as a cultural force, make quick minds hesitate to embrace a region too deeply compromised. They are on their guard against falling for it, but meanwhile they can enjoy its very defects, its backwardness, its slowness, its position as one of the large, possible cities on the Eastern sea-coast, its private, residential charm. They speak of going to New York and yet another season finds them holding back, positively enjoying the Boston life. . . .

. . . Outside it is winter, dark. The curtains are drawn, the wood is on the fire, the table has been checked, and in the stillness one waits for the guests who come stamping in out of the snow. There are lectures in Cambridge, excellent concerts in Symphony Hall, bad plays being tried out for the hungry sheep of Boston before going to the hungry sheep of New York. Arnold Toynbee or T. S. Eliot or Robert Frost or Robert Oppenheimer or Barbara Ward is in town again. The cars are double-parked so thickly along the narrow streets that a moving vehicle can scarcely maneuver; the pedestrians stumble over the cobbles; in the back alleys a cat cries and the rats, enormously fat, run in front of the car lights creeping into the parking spots. Inside it is cozy, Victorian, and gossipy. Someone else has *not* been kept on at Harvard. The old Irish "accommodator" puffs up stairs she had never seen before a few hours previously and announces that dinner is ready. A Swedish journalist is just getting off the train at the Back Bay Station. He has been exhausted by cocktails, reality, life, taxis, telephones, bad connections in New York and Chicago, pulverized by a "good time." Sighing, he alights, seeking old Boston, a culture that hasn't been alive for a long time . . . and rest.

COMMENT

The problem of making a coherent statement about anything so complex as a modern city is not easily solved. Often, as in this essay, the writer finds that he can do better if he works by a series of comparisons and contrasts. Here the author briefly establishes the character of old Boston and proceeds to describe the new Boston by comparing it with New York. She is then able to discuss the peculiar interplay of old and new which characterizes the people and the physical appearance of Boston and Cambridge.

SUGGESTIONS FOR WRITING

1. Select a group (a club, fraternity, section of town) which enjoys a reputation for some quality. Demonstrate how this quality is reflected in the mannerisms of the members of the group.

2. Notice how Miss Hardwick concludes her essay by citing the particular details which characterize the personality of Boston. Collect a similar list of significant details about a city, a street, a person, or a school. Select the most interesting of these details, arrange them in a pattern, and write your paper.

THE RIDDLE OF INEQUALITY

PAUL TILLICH

> *"For to him who has will more be given; and from him
> who has not, even what he has will be taken away."*
> Mark 4:25

ONE DAY a learned colleague called me up and said to me with angry excitement: "There is a saying in the New Testament which I consider to be one of the most immoral and unjust statements ever made!" And then he started quoting our text: "To him who has will more be given," and his anger increased when he continued: "and from him who has not, even what he has will be taken away." We all, I think, feel offended with him. And we cannot easily ignore the offense by suggesting what *he* suggested—that the words may be due to a misunderstanding of the disciples. It appears at least four times in the gospels with great emphasis. And even more, we can clearly see that the writers of the gospels felt exactly as we do. For them it was a stumbling block, which they tried to interpret in different ways. Probably none of these explanations satisfied them fully, for with this saying of Jesus, we are confronted immediately with the greatest and perhaps most painful riddle of life, that of the inequality of all beings. We certainly cannot hope to solve it when neither the Bible nor any other of the great religions and philosophies was able to do so. But we can do two things: We can show the breadth and the depth of the riddle of inequality and we can try to find a way to live with it, even if it is unsolved.

I

If we hear the words, "to him who has will more be given," we ask ourselves: What *do* we have? And then we may find that much is given to us in terms of external goods, of friends, of intellectual gifts and even of a comparatively high moral level of action. So we can expect that more will be given to us, while we must expect that those who are lacking in all that will lose the little they already have. Even further, according to Jesus' parable, the one talent they have will be given to us who have five or ten talents. We shall be richer because they will be poorer. We may cry out

Reprinted by permission of the author and of *The Union Seminary Quarterly Review*.

against such an injustice. But we cannot deny that life confirms it abundantly. We cannot deny it, but we can ask the question, do we *really* have what we believe we have so that it cannot be taken from us? It is a question full of anxiety, confirmed by a version of our text rendered by Luke. "From him who has not, even what he *thinks* that he has will be taken away." Perhaps our having of those many things is not the kind of having which is increased. Perhaps the having of few things by the poor ones is the kind of having which makes them grow. In the parable of the talents, Jesus confirms this. Those talents which are used, even with a risk of losing them, are those which we really have; those which we try to preserve without using them for growth are those which we do not really have and which are being taken away from us. They slowly disappear, and suddenly we feel that we have lost these talents, perhaps forever.

Let us apply this to our own life, whether it is long or short. In the memory of all of us many things appear which we had without having them and which were taken away from us. Some of them became lost because of the tragic limitations of life; we had to sacrifice them in order to make other things grow. We all were given childish innocence; but innocence cannot be used and increased. The growth of our lives is possible only because we have sacrificed the original gift of innocence. Nevertheless, sometimes there arises in us a melancholy longing for a purity which has been taken from us. We all were given youthful enthusiasm for many things and aims. But this also cannot be used and increased. Most of the objects of our early enthusiasm must be sacrificed for a few, and the few must be approached with soberness. No maturity is possible without this sacrifice. Yet often a melancholy longing for the lost possibilities and enthusiasm takes hold of us. Innocence and youthful enthusiasm: we had them and had them not. Life itself demanded that they were taken from us.

But there are other things which we had and which were taken from us, because we let them go through our own guilt. Some of us had a deep sensitivity for the wonder of life as it is revealed in nature. Slowly under the pressure of work and social life and the lure of cheap pleasures, we lose the wonder of our earlier years when we felt intense joy and the presence of the mystery of life through the freshness of the young day or the glory of the dying day, the majesty of the mountains or the infinity of the sea, a flower breaking through the soil or a young animal in the perfection of its movements. Perhaps we try to produce such feelings again, but we are empty and do not succeed. We had it and had it not, and it has been taken from us.

Others had the same experience with music, poetry, the great novels and plays. One wanted to devour all of them, one lived in them and created for oneself a life above the daily life. We *had* all this and did not have it; we did not let it grow; our love towards it was not strong enough and so it was taken from us.

Many, especially in this group, remember a time in which the desire to learn to solve the riddles of the universe, to find truth has been the driving force in their lives. They came to college and university, not in order to buy their entrance ticket into the upper middle classes or in order to provide for the preconditions of social and economic success, but they came, driven by the desire for knowledge. They had something and more could have been given to them. But in reality they did not have it. They did not make it grow and so it was taken from them and they finished their academic work in terms of expediency and indifference towards truth. Their love for truth has left them and in some moments they are sick in their hearts because they realize that what they have lost they may never get back.

We all know that any deeper relation to a human being needs watchfulness and growth, otherwise it is taken away from us. And we cannot get it back. This is a form of having and not having which is the root of innumerable human tragedies. We all know about them. And there is another, the most fundamental kind of having and not having—our having and losing God. Perhaps we were rich towards God in our childhood and beyond it. We may remember the moments in which we felt his ultimate presence. We may remember prayers with an overflowing heart, the encounter with the holy in word and music and holy places. We had communication with God; but it was taken from us because we had it and had it not. We did not let it grow, and so it slowly disappeared leaving an empty space. We became unconcerned, cynical, indifferent, not because we doubted about our religious traditions—such doubt belongs to being rich towards God—but because we turned away from that which once concerned us infinitely.

Such thoughts are a first step in approaching the riddle of inequality. Those who have, receive more if they really have it, if they use it and make it grow. And those who have not, lose what they have because they never had it really.

II

But the question of inequality is not yet answered. For one now asks: Why do some receive more than others in the very beginning, before there is even the possibility of using or wasting our talents? Why does the one servant receive five talents and the other two and the third one? Why is the one born in the slums and the other in a well-to-do suburban family? It does not help to answer that of those to whom much is given much is demanded and little of those to whom little is given. For it is just this inequality of original gifts, internal and external, which arouses our question. Why is it given to one human being to gain so much more out of his being human than to another one? Why is so much given to the one that much *can* be asked of him, while to the other one little is given and little *can* be asked? If this question is asked, not only about individual men but also about classes, races and nations, the everlasting question of political inequality arises, and with it the many ways appear in which men have tried to abolish inequality. In every revolution and in every war, the will to solve the riddle of inequality is a driving force. But neither war nor revolution can remove it. Even if we imagine that in an indefinite future most social inequalities are conquered, three things remain: the inequality of talents in body and mind, the inequality created by freedom and destiny, and the fact that all generations before the time of such equality would be excluded from its blessings. This would be the greatest possible inequality! No! In face of one of the deepest and most torturing problems of life, it is unpermittably shallow and foolish to escape into a social dreamland. We have to live now; we have to live this our life, and we must face today the riddle of inequality.

Let us not confuse the riddle of inequality with the fact that each of us is a unique incomparable self. Certainly our being individuals belongs to our dignity as men. It is given to us and must be used and intensified and not drowned in the gray waters of conformity which threaten us today. One should defend every individuality and the uniqueness of every human self. But one should not believe that this is a way of solving the riddle of inequality. Unfortunately, there are social and political reactionaries who use this confusion in order to justify social injustice. They are at least as foolish as the dreamers of a future removal of inequality. Whoever has seen hospitals, prisons, sweatshops, battlefields, houses for the insane, starvation, family tragedies, moral aberrations should be cured from any confusion of the gift of individuality with the riddle of inequality. He should be cured from any feelings of easy consolation.

III

And now we must make the third step in our attempt to penetrate the riddle of inequality and ask: Why do some use and increase what was given to them, while others do not, so that it is taken from them? Why does God say to the prophet in our Old Testament lesson that the ears and eyes of a nation are made insensible for the divine message?

Is it enough to answer: Because some use their freedom responsibly and do what they ought to do while others fail through their own guilt? Is this answer, which seems so obvious, sufficient? Now let me first say that it *is* sufficient if we apply it to ourselves. Each of us must consider the increase or the loss of what is given to him as a matter of his own responsibility. Our conscience tells us that we cannot put the blame for our losses on anybody or anything else than ourselves.

But if we look at others, this answer is not sufficient. On the contrary: If we applied the judgment which we *must* apply to anyone else we would be like the Pharisee in Jesus' parable. You cannot tell somebody who comes to you in distress about himself: Use what has been given to you; for he may come to you just because he is unable to do so! And you cannot tell those who are in despair about what they are: Be something else; for this is just what despair means—the inability of getting rid of oneself. You cannot tell those who did not conquer the destructive influences of their surroundings and were driven into crime and misery that they should have been stronger; for it was just of this strength they had been deprived by heritage or environment. Certainly they all are men, and to all of them freedom is given; but they all are also subject to destiny. It is not up to us to condemn them because they were free, as it is not up to us to excuse them because they were under their destiny. We cannot judge them. And when we judge ourselves, we must be conscious that even this is not the last word, but that we like them are under an ultimate judgment. In it the riddle of inequality is eternally answered. But this answer is not ours. It is our predicament that we must ask. And we ask with an uneasy conscience. Why are they in misery, why not we? Thinking of some who are near to us, we can ask: Are we partly responsible? But even if we are, it does not solve the riddle of inequality. The uneasy conscience asks about the farthest as well as about the nearest: Why they, why not we?

Why has my child, or any of millions and millions of children, died before even having a chance to grow out of infancy? Why is my child, or any child, born feeble-minded or crippled? Why has my friend or relative, or anybody's friend or relative, disintegrated in his mind and lost both his freedom and his destiny? Why has my son or daughter, gifted as I believe with many talents, wasted them and been deprived of them? And why does this happen to any parent at all? Why have this boy's or this girl's creative powers been broken by a tyrannical father or by a possessive mother?

In all these questions it is not the question of our own misery which we ask. It is not the question: Why has this happened to *me*?

It is not the question of Job which God answers by humiliating him and then by elevating him into communion with him. It is not the old and urgent question: Where is the divine justice, where is the divine love towards me? But it is almost the opposite question: Why has this *not* happened to me, why has it happened to the other one, to the innumerable other ones to whom not even the power of Job is given to accept the divine answer? Why—and Jesus has asked the same question—are many called and few elected?

He does not answer; he only states that this is the human predicament. Shall we therefore cease to ask and humbly accept the fact of a divine judgment which condemns most human beings away from the community with him into despair and self-destruction? Can we accept the eternal victory of judgment over love? We cannot; and nobody ever could, even if he preached and threatened in these terms. As long as he could not see himself with complete certainty as eternally rejected, his preaching and threatening would be self-deceiving. And who could see himself eternally rejected?

But if this is not the solution of the riddle of inequality at its deepest level, can we trespass the boundaries of the Christian tradition and listen to those who tell us that this life does not decide about our eternal destiny? There will be occasions in other lives, as our present life is determined by previous ones and what we have achieved or wasted in them. It is a serious doctrine and not completely strange to Christianity. But if we don't know and never will know what each of us has been in the previous or future lives, then it is not really *our* destiny which develops from life to life, but in each life it is the destiny of someone else. This answer also does not solve the riddle of inequality.

There is no answer at all if we ask about the temporal and eternal destiny of the single being separated from the destiny of the whole. Only in the unity of all beings in time and eternity can a humanly possible answer to the riddle of inequality be found. *Humanly* possible does not mean an answer which removes the riddle of inequality, but an answer with which we can live.

There is an ultimate unity of all beings, rooted in the divine life from which they come and to which they go. All beings, non-human as well as human, participate in it. And therefore they all participate in each other. We participate in each other's having and we participate in each other's not-having. If we become aware of this unity of all beings, something happens. The fact that others have-not changes in every moment the character of my having: It undercuts its security, it drives me beyond myself, to understand, to give, to share, to help. The fact that others fall into sin, crime and misery changes the character of the grace which is given to me: It makes me realize my own hidden guilt, it shows to me that those who suffer for their sin and crime, suffer also for me; for I am guilty of their guilt—at least in the desire of my heart—and ought to suffer as they do. The awareness that others who *could* have become fully developed human beings and never *have,* changes my state of full humanity. Their early death, their early or late disintegration, makes my life and my health a continuous risk, a dying which is not yet death, a disintegration which is not yet destruction. In every death which we encounter, something of us dies; in every disease which we encounter, something of us tends to disintegrate.

Can we live with this answer? We can to the degree in which we are liberated from the seclusion within ourselves. But nobody can be liberated from himself unless he is grasped by the power of that which is present in everyone and everything—the eternal from which we come and to which we go, which gives us *to* ourselves and which liberates us *from* ourselves. It is the greatness and the heart of the Christian message that God—as manifest in the Cross of the Christ—participates totally in the dying child, in the condemned criminal, in the disintegrating mind, in the starving one and in him who rejects him. There is no extreme human condition into which the divine presence would not reach. This is what the Cross, the most extreme of all human conditions, tells us. The riddle of inequality cannot be solved on the level of our separation from each other. It is eternally solved in the divine participation in all of us and every being. The certainty of the divine participation gives us the courage to stand the riddle of inequality, though finite minds cannot solve it. Amen.

COMMENT

Professor Paul Tillich, probably the most influential theologian of our day, here addresses himself to one of the greatest riddles of life. His effort to answer this riddle follows the classic form of the sermon: citation of text, commentary, and conclusion. One question follows from another, each leading deeper into the subject. Perhaps the most valuable lesson for the beginning writer to learn from this piece is that every question does not have to have a final answer: honest and impassioned questioning engages the reader.

SUGGESTIONS FOR WRITING

1. Dr. Tillich contends that no maturity is possible without the sacrifice of enthusiasm and innocent belief. Take some belief of your own in which you can discern some change over the past few years (about parents, sex, religion, education). Conduct an honest appraisal of the nature of the change, its causes, and the gains and losses which have followed from it.

2. Take some popular answers to the riddle of inequality. Examine them as deeply as you can. (Some of the more obvious are: If you don't have one thing, you have something else just as good. Everyone finally gets what he deserves. Misery exists to teach the more fortunate to be grateful.)